CiTY·SMaRT™
GUIDEBOOK

Vancouver

Ray Chatelin

John Muir Publications
A Division of Avalon Travel Publishing

A Division of Avalon Travel Publishing
5855 Beaudry Street
Emeryville, CA 94608

Printed in the United States of America.
First edition. First printing May 2000.

ISBN: 1-56261-4827
ISSN: 1525-3635

Editors: Laurel Gladden Gillespie, Chris Hayhurst, Sarah Baldwin
Graphics Editor: Bunny Wong
Production: Janine Lehmann
Design: Janine Lehmann
Cover Design: Suzanne Rush
Maps: Julie Felton
Typesetter: Diane Rigoli
Printer: Publishers Press
Front cover: © John Elk III—Vancouver skyline
Back cover: © John Elk III—Queen Elizabeth Park

Distributed to the book trade by
Publishers Group West
Berkeley, California

CONTENTS

See Vancouver the City•Smart Way   v

1 Welcome to Vancouver   1
Getting to Know Vancouver 2 • A Brief History of Vancouver 7 • People of Vancouver 11 • Weather 13 • Dressing in Vancouver 14 • When to Visit 15 • Calendar of Events 16 • Business and Economy 19 • Housing 20 • Schools 21

2 Getting Around Vancouver   24
City Layout 24 • Public Transportation 25 • Driving in Vancouver 26 • Biking in Vancouver 28 • Air Travel 28 • Train Service 30 • Bus Service 31

3 Where to Stay   32
Downtown 33 • Uptown 47 • Point Grey 48 • East Vancouver 49 • North Shore 50 • Eastern Suburbs 52 • Southern Suburbs 54

4 Where to Eat   58
Downtown 60 • Uptown 73 • Point Grey 77 • East Vancouver 83 • North Shore 87 • Eastern Suburbs 89 • Southern Suburbs 89

5 Sights and Attractions   92
Downtown 93 • Uptown 105 • Point Grey 107 • East Vancouver 109 • North Shore 109 • Eastern Suburbs 113 • Southern Suburbs 114

6 Museums and Galleries   117
Art Museums 117 • Science and History Museums 121 • Other Museums 127 • Art Galleries 128

7 Kids' Stuff   135
Animals and the Great Outdoors 135 • Fun and Educational 138 • Theater and Festivals 142 • Stores Kids Love 143 • More Fun Activities 144

8 Parks, Gardens, and Recreation Areas   146

9 Shopping   157
Shopping Districts 158 • Notable Bookstores and Newsstands 172 • Markets 173 • Major Department Stores 175 • Major Shopping Malls 177 • Factory Outlet Centers 180

10 Sports and Recreation   182
Professional Sports 183 • Amateur Sports 186 • Recreation 189

11 Performing Arts   203
Theater 204 • Music and Opera 206 • Dance 212 • Concert Venues 214

12 Nightlife   219

Music Clubs 219 • Pubs and Bars 224 • Gay Clubs 230 • Comedy Clubs 231 • Gambling 232 • Pool Clubs 233 • Quiet Places 233 • Movie Houses of Note 235

13 Day Trips from Vancouver   236

Bowen Island 236 • Hell's Gate 237 • Victoria 239 • Whistler 242

Appendix: City•Smart Basics   244

Emergency Phone Numbers 244 • Hospitals and Emergency Medical Centers 244 • Other Important Numbers 244 • Airlines (Major) 245 • Airlines (Regional) 246 • Canadian Consulates in the United States 246 • Foreign Consulates 246 • Information Services for the Non–English Speaking 247 • Multicultural Resources 247 • Recorded Information 247 • Visitor Information 248 • Post Offices 248 • Car Rental 248 • Disabled Access Information 248 • Babysitting/Childcare 249 • Newspapers 249 • Magazines 249 • Bookstores 250 • Radio Stations 250 • Television Stations 250

Index   251

MAP CONTENTS

Vancouver Zones

3 Where to Stay
Downtown Vancouver
Uptown/Point Grey
East Vancouver
North Shore West
Southern Suburbs

4 Where to Eat
Downtown Vancouver
Uptown Vancouver
Point Grey
East Vancouver
North Shore West
Southern Suburbs

5 Sights and Attractions
Downtown Vancouver
Vancouver Buildings
Uptown/Point Grey
East Vancouver
North Shore
Southern Suburbs

6 Museums and Galleries
Vancouver Museums and Galleries

11 Performing Arts
Concert Venues

13 Day Trips from Vancouver
Vancouver Region

Restaurants, hotels, museums, and other facilities marked by the ♿ symbol are wheelchair accessible.

See Vancouver the CiTY·SMaRT™ Way

The Guide for Vancouver Natives, New Residents, and Visitors

In *City•Smart Guidebook: Vancouver,* local author Ray Chatelin tells it like it is. Residents will learn things they never knew about their city, new residents will get an insider's view of their new hometown, and visitors will be guided to the very best Vancouver has to offer— whether they're on a weekend getaway or staying a week or more.

Opinionated Recommendations Save You Time and Money

From shopping to nightlife to museums, the author is opinionated about what he likes and dislikes. You'll learn the great and the not-so-great things about Vancouver's sights, restaurants, and accommodations. So you can decide what's worth your time and what's not; which hotel is worth the splurge and which is the best choice for budget travelers.

Easy-to-Use Format Makes Planning Your Trip a Cinch

City•Smart Guidebook: Vancouver is user-friendly—you'll quickly find exactly what you're looking for. Chapters are organized by travelers' interests or needs, from Where to Stay and Where to Eat, to Sights and Attractions, Kids' Stuff, Sports and Recreation, and even Day Trips from Vancouver.

Includes Maps and Quick Location-Finding Features

Every listing in this book is accompanied by a geographic zone designation (see the following pages for zone details) that helps you immediately find each location. Staying on Robson Street and wondering about nearby sights and restaurants? Look for the Downtown label in the listings and you'll know that statue or café is not far away. Or maybe you're looking for an art gallery. Along with its address, you'll see a Downtown label, so you'll know just where to find it.

All That and Fun to Read, Too!

Every City•Smart chapter includes fun-to-read (and fun-to-use) tips to help you get more out of Vancouver, city trivia (did you know Chinese immigrants weren't given Canadian citizenship until 1949?), and illuminating sidebars (for the influence of artist Emily Carr, for example, see page 118). And well-known local residents provide their personal "Top Ten" lists, guiding readers to the city's best theaters, bars, movie houses, view restaurants, and more.

VANCOUVER ZONES

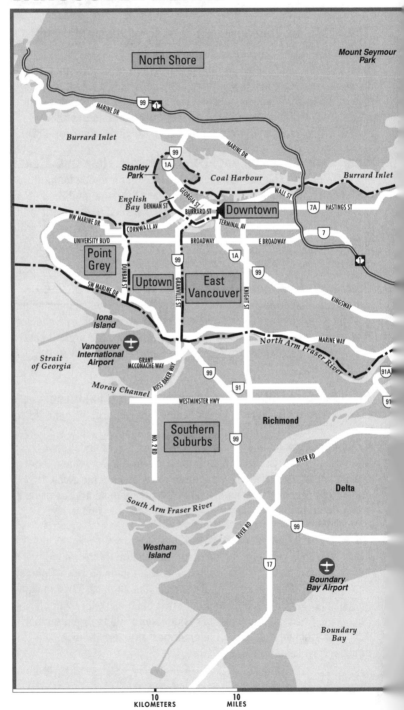

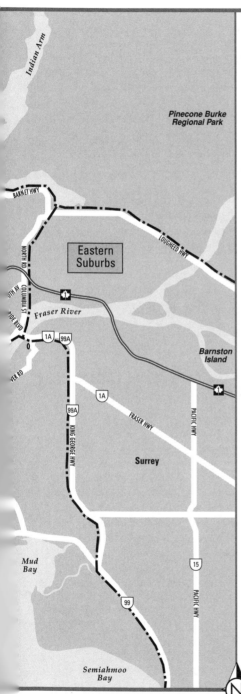

VANCOUVER ZONES

Downtown:
Bordered by Main Street to the east, Stanley Park to the west, False Creek to the south, and Coal Harbour to the north. Includes the West End, Gastown, Yaletown, and Chinatown neighborhoods.

Uptown:
Bordered by Granville Street to the east, Dunbar Street to the west, First Avenue to the north, and Fraser River to the south. Includes the Oakridge, Shaughnessy, and Granville Island areas.

East Vancouver:
Bordered by Main Street to the west, Fraser River to the south, Burrard Inlet to the north, and Boundary Road to the east. Includes the Little Italy and Little India neighborhoods.

Point Grey:
Bordered by the Strait of Georgia to the west, English Bay to the north, Fraser River to the south, and Dunbar Street to the east. Includes the Kitsilano, Kerrisdale, Southlands, and University of British Columbia neighborhoods.

North Shore:
Includes North and West Vancouver. Bordered by Burrard Inlet and Coal Harbour on the south, Indian Arm River on the east, Strait of Georgia on the west, and the North Shore Mountains on the north. Capilano Drive divides North and West Vancouver.

Eastern Suburbs:
Includes the Burnaby, New Westminster, and Coquitlam neighborhoods.

Southern Suburbs:
Bordered by Bondary Bay to the south, the Strait of Georgia to the west, King George Highway to the east, and Marine Way and Fraser River to the north.

© John Elk

1

WELCOME TO VANCOUVER

Vancouver just happens to be the most gorgeous city on the continent. Those who live here have always known this (it has, admittedly, made us a bit smug), and visitors discover it quickly.

Vancouver is a physically imposing city, and its topography dictates much of what we do within and outside its borders. Endowed with spectacular natural surroundings, it's an outdoor enthusiast's dream. Only Rio de Janeiro and Hong Kong can compete with this setting, where ocean, mountains, and city miraculously merge. Five minutes north of Downtown are the Coastal Mountains, where you can ski in the winter and hike the many trails that lace the North Shore in the summer. The well-sheltered Coal Harbour opens into English Bay, which in turn opens into the Strait of Georgia and Howe Sound to the west, beckoning visitors to explore the beauty of the region.

Because of the city's position on the edge of nature, Vancouverites are more likely to encounter wildlife than are most urban dwellers. The mountainous forests across Burrard Inlet dominate the communities of West and North Vancouver, and the residents there have been known to encounter black bears, deer, and the occasional mountain lion. Waterways in this region still carry migrating salmon to their spawning areas. Now and then an orca will take a wrong turn at the entrance to English Bay and sail into the harbor. Coyotes can be seen throughout city parks, and amused golfers often must wait for the wily critters to cross their fairways. Bald eagles are so common that when they hover overhead they're often ignored.

It's this natural environment that has allowed Vancouver to define itself. Residents embrace this environment, package it in the veneer of a casual play ethic, and enjoy it to the hilt, while at the same time acknowledging the cultural imprints left by the original native inhabitants.

But there's more to Vancouver than just a naturally pretty face. Walk the streets and you'll find a complex brew of Oriental mystery, old English traditions, Native mythology, European charm, and unique Canadiana. And despite its size—the greater Vancouver area has a population of 1.9 million—the city has a sense of community that can only be described as quintessentially West Coast. Citizens typically maintain relaxed lifestyles spiced with a rich and varied cultural scene in which large ethnic communities—among them Japanese, Chinese, Italian, Greek, and South Asian—augment Native culture and tradition. Thanks to this diverse population, Vancouver has more restaurants per capita than any other city in Canada. And, according to national statistics, Vancouverites read more, shop more, eat out more, drink more wine, spend more on sporting equipment, smoke less, and take longer coffee breaks than anyone else in Canada.

As you wander around and experience the city, you may find yourself thinking that the stunning beauty, the live-and-let-live lifestyle, and the overwhelming civility can't be real. They are.

Getting to Know Vancouver

Vancouver's outward growth is limited by mountains to the north, the ocean to the west, the U.S. border to the south, and land preserved for agriculture to the east. So the city has expanded vertically. That's why the city's downtown district hosts both office towers and high-rise condominiums. Major hotels, nightclubs, restaurants, and theaters can also be found clustered together in this central core. A city of neighborhoods, Vancouver is perfect for walking—it's safe, colorful, and vibrant. And the gridlike streets of Downtown make it difficult to get lost. If you do find yourself disoriented, locate a mountain—that's north.

Downtown
The heart of Downtown, where West Georgia Street crosses Granville Street, is Vancouver's main gathering place. Both the weird and the commonplace mingle on the Vancouver Art Gallery steps or at the Granville Mall. Shoppers congregate in the Pacific Centre—accessed through any of the

stores on the four corners of Georgia and Granville—where some 200 stores and services are hidden on three floors beneath three city blocks. A block south and to the west is Robson Street, lined with high-fashion and trendy boutiques, restaurants, and cafés.

Vancouver's new theater district begins at the intersection of Granville and Hamilton. Presiding here are the Queen Elizabeth Theatre and Playhouse complex (home of the Vancouver Opera) and the Canadian Broadcasting Corporation Building. Nearby is the new, 1,824-seat Ford Centre for the Performing Arts. The main post office and the new, $100-million Vancouver Public Library at Library Square are also in this area. The library, which holds more than 1 million books and a large collection of electronic databases, is also home to 15 stores and 15,000 square feet of retail space.

At the eastern end of Downtown is Chinatown, the third-largest Chinese district in North America. (Only San Francisco's and New York's Chinatowns are bigger.) It's impossible to simply stroll through Chinatown; rather, you have to squeeze your way through the throngs. A six-block complex of bustling outdoor vegetable stalls, crowded meat shops bordered by hanging ducks, busy restaurants, and enticing pastry shops, the area is vibrant with humanity. On the narrow sidewalks people mingle elbow to elbow in a swirl of chatter and haggling—day and night. Stop here. Quickly turn there. Feel the life. Chinatown has been declared a historic site, ensuring that the district's character will forever be preserved and enhanced.

If you go past the Canadian Pacific Railway Terminal building (around the corner from the Convention Centre/Pan Pacific), where the first CPR train steamed into town in 1887, you'll find Gastown, Vancouver's birthplace. In 1867 "Gassy" Jack Deighton came to town and built a saloon on what was then the site of the Stamps Sawmill. Deighton was Vancouver's first non-native resident, a man who came in search of striking it rich in log-

Spelling Bee

If you're from the United States, you'll notice that Canadians spell things differently, like "metre" and "labour" and "centre." You pay bills with checks, while we use "cheques." In reality, most Vancouverites (and Canadians in general) have adopted a mix of American and British spelling in daily use. Newspaper style, for example, is to use mostly American spellings, even for proper nouns. (In this book, we'll use American spellings except for proper nouns, such as the Ministry of Labour and the Pacific Centre mall.)

ging and ended up as a saloon owner. He was a boisterous man whose loud storytelling and drinking capabilities earned him his nickname. There wasn't much of a town before Deighton arrived, but one pretty much grew up around his saloon and was named Gastown in his honor. Gastown was eventually renamed Granville and 16 years later it incorporated as the City of Vancouver. Shortly thereafter, most of the city was destroyed by fire, but rebuilding began immediately. Today you can still enjoy the area's nineteenth-century architecture. Renovated warehouses, mews, courtyards, and passages now host restaurants and boutiques filled with the good, the

Cruise on up to Alaska

Want to take a cruise? Well, you've come to the right place. Ten cruise companies, operating a total of 19 vessels and making about 300 trips to Alaska each year, use Vancouver as a port. Almost 800,000 passengers set sail each year, supplying an estimated $200 million to the local economy.

The city is home to two modern cruise terminals: Canada Place, part of the Pan Pacific Hotel/Convention Centre complex, and Ballantyne Pier, close to the city center and host to the largest ships. Here's a list of Vancouver's Alaskan cruise lines (and their ships). Call a travel agent for more information or to book a cruise.

> *Carnival Cruise Lines* (Jubilee)
> *Celebrity Cruises* (Galaxy)
> *Crystal Cruises* (Crystal Harmony)
> *Holland America Lines* (Maasdam, Noordam, Ryndam, Statendam, Westerdam)
> *Mitsui OSK Line* (Nippon Maru)
> *NYK Cruises* (Asuka)
> *Norwegian Cruise Lines* (Norwegian Dynasty)
> *Princess Cruises* (Dawn Princess, Island Princess, Regal Princess, Sky Princess, Sun Princess)
> *Royal Caribbean International* (Legend of the Seas, Rhapsody of the Seas)
> *World Explorer Cruises* (Universe Explorer)

bad, and the tacky. The area attracts thousands of visitors by day and cabaret patrons by night.

West of Gastown, the West End is Vancouver's downtown residential area, made up primarily of apartments and condos. It's because of the West End that Downtown never sleeps. The businesses and entertainment spots simply merge with the apartments weaving throughout the area, so people can live, work, and hang out all in one part of town. The West End is one of Canada's most densely populated urban areas, and it has everything every city would die for. Denman Street is a mass of character and characters, of small shops, restaurants, tree-lined streets with Victorian bed-and-breakfasts, and people crushed together on sunny days when the high-rises are empty. Surprisingly, the West End is also one of Vancouver's safest and most livable areas. The neighborhood boasts western Canada's largest gay and lesbian population, as well as a mix of both young adults and seniors.

If you want to see urban change take place before your eyes, spend some time in Yaletown, at the south end of Downtown, and then come back again in a week. You'll probably find new shops, more condos, and more converted warehouses. Located just north of False Creek, site of the 1986 World's Fair, Yaletown now boasts a combination of trendy new condos and warehouse lofts. In its nineteenth- and early-twentieth-century heyday, Yaletown boasted more saloons per acre than anywhere else in the world. Now this heritage area along Pacific Avenue is home to restaurants, art galleries, and furniture and fashion boutiques, as well as the hip loft apartments of architects, designers, and filmmakers.

Uptown

Uptown begins on the south side of False Creek. The name False Creek is appropriate: many an early sailor came into this inlet and found himself at a dead end. Today, the eastern end of the creek is marked by the Science Centre, while North False Creek hugs Yaletown; to the south are Granville Island and the condos and townhouses that march up the hill above Second Avenue.

Surprisingly, Granville Island was quite an eyesore in the 1960s—a cesspool of industrial pollution that infected the entire downtown core. It's

TRIVIA

Try to avoid parking at the cruise-ship terminal—it's the most expensive place in town. The closer you park to the waterfront, the more you'll pay per hour. Try The Bay parking lot (opposite the bay on Seymour St.), which is secure and relatively inexpensive. The cheapest downtown lot is beneath the main library (two blocks east of the bay's parking lot, across the street from the post office), but it's often full.

since been transformed into something quite different. The initial idea behind Granville Island's revitalization was to convert run-down waterfront property into public markets and avant-garde retail space. But while such changes did take place, the area also developed stylish restaurants, art galleries, artists' studios, craft shops, and theaters. The former industrial site under the south end of Granville Street Bridge is now 37 acres of parks, walkways, renovated warehouses, and a successful combination of 200 commercial, cultural, and boating enterprises.

When the Canadian Pacific Railway chugged into Vancouver, the company's corporate elite built their homes in Shaughnessy. Today this area remains the city's wealthiest residential neighborhood. Actually, Shaughnessy now has three different developments. The first and most exclusive—south of 16th and north of 28th—is the original, where heritage landscapes blend into houses set on perfectly manicured lots along winding streets. The other two Shaughnessy developments are relatively new and lie to the east and south of the original.

Point Grey

If you're in Stanley Park looking south across the water, the strip of land you see is Point Grey. It sprawls from Burrard Street on the east to Pacific Spirit Park and the University of British Columbia to the west, and it encompasses some of Vancouver's most livable areas, including Kitsilano, the Southlands, the beaches along English Bay, and Kerrisdale. Prepare for big homes, plenty of trees, and high rent.

Kitsilano is where Vancouver's hippies went yuppie. The city's answer to San Francisco's Haight-Ashbury neighborhood, this former gathering place for the long-haired set of the 1960s has, like its former residents, matured. It nonetheless remains one of Vancouver's liveliest neighborhoods. The Southlands, on the other hand, are unlike any other urban neighborhood in North America. In this neighborhood, which lies within the city limits and is a mere 25 minutes from Downtown, multimillion-dollar mansions and horse ranches sit alongside rickety houses held together only by moss and prayers. The English Bay beaches are a connected string of sand that runs from Kitsilano to the tip of Point Grey and the University of British Columbia (UBC). During the summer, bodies beautiful and bizarre grace the beaches that expand and contract with the tides. Above them are the University

Endowment Lands and the northern edges of Pacific Spirit, edging onto the campus of UBC.

East Vancouver

East Vancouver sits roughly to the east of Main Street and includes some of the most colorful areas of the city. Because land and housing values are considerably lower than those to the west, you'll find younger and more distinctly ethnic neighborhoods.

While thousands of Indo-Canadians live throughout the city, their cultural focal point is in Little India, particularly between 49th and 51st on Main Street. Here you'll find the 18 jewelry stores and 25 fabric shops that make up the Punjabi Market. Here also are a variety of food stores, as well as a gorgeous Sikh Temple designed by architect Arthur Erickson.

A couple of decades ago, Little Italy, along Commercial Drive, was entirely Italian. If you wanted to experience the district to its fullest, you were advised to know some phrases that would gain you access to special dishes at restaurants and the top lines of clothing. Now the cultural center of East Vancouver, this neighborhood is a mix of ethnic minorities, giving it a truly international flavor, though the area has retained much of its Italian character.

A Brief History of Vancouver

Vancouver today bears little resemblance to the grimy, rough, and raw logging town it was at its birth in 1886. In fact, the city's most exciting history is taking place right now. For unlike many of Canada's major cities, until re-

The Public Market and Arts Club on Granville Island

Granville Island Public Market

VANCOUVER TIMELINE

1778 Captain James Cook arrives and trades with the Indians while he overhauls his ship.

1791 Spanish explorer Lieutenant José Maria Narváez anchors west of present-day Point Grey and explores and charts the region.

1792 Captain George Vancouver, once apprentice to Captain James Cook, explores and charts Burrard Inlet.

1827 The first Hudson Bay Company building is constructed at Fort Langley.

1856 Gold is discovered in British Columbia.

1864 The first legislative assembly of the new British Columbia colony is held in New Westminster.

1867 "Gassy" Jack Deighton builds a saloon; the area around his bar will eventually become Gastown.

1871 British Columbia joins the Canadian confederation after being promised a railway link to the rest of the country.

1886 The town of Granville (previously known as Gastown) is incorporated as the City of Vancouver. Soon thereafter, fire destroys most of the new city. Rebuilding begins at once.

1887 The first Canadian Pacific Railway passenger train arrives. Population growth begins to accelerate.

1908 The University of British Columbia is founded.

1915 The Vancouver Millionaires hockey team wins the Stanley Cup.

1929 Vancouver's population jumps to 250,000 after the adjacent townships of South Vancouver and Point Grey become part of the city.

1942 All Japanese civilians are moved inland from the coast because of the war.

1957 Queen Elizabeth and Prince Philip make their first of many visits to the city.

1965 Simon Fraser University opens.

1976 The Museum of Anthropology at the University of British Columbia opens.

1986 Expo '86 opens and logs 22 million visitors in six months, making it one of the most successful World's Fairs in history.

1987 The BC World Trade and Convention Centre opens.

1987 Vancouver resident Rick Hansen completes his "Man-in-Motion" round-the-world tour in his wheelchair.

1990 The first Indy car race in Vancouver takes place on streets around BC Place Stadium.

Rock star Bryan Adams buys and restores Vancouver's oldest brick building, the Oppenheimer Brothers grocery store at Columbia and Powell.	1991
Vancouver is the venue for a summit meeting between U.S. president Bill Clinton and Russian president Boris Yeltsin.	1993
The NBA's Vancouver Grizzlies open their inaugural season in November at the new 20,000-seat General Motors Place stadium.	1995
Reconstruction begins on the old warehouse district, Yaletown.	
The new Vancouver International Airport terminal opens, and the Open Skies treaty between the United States and Canada makes travel to Vancouver easier.	1996
Vancouver is the site for the Asia-Pacific Economic Cooperation Group (APEC) conference; student protests ensue.	1997
Vancouver will host the World Figure Skating Championships.	2001

cently Vancouver has had a somewhat bland history—it has seen no major rebellions, no foreign occupation, and no wars (although hostilities almost broke out once between Canada and the United States over a pig that was shot on a nearby island). Enormous changes have taken place in Vancouver as it has transformed from a slice of Britain on Canada's West Coast to a colorful international mosaic.

The first permanent residents of the area were the Coast Salish Indians, split into a series of tribes that included the Musqueam, who lived by the mouth of the present-day Fraser River and along the shores of Burrard Inlet and English Bay, and the Kwantlen and Squamish tribes, who lived north and east of present-day Vancouver. In all, thousands of seasonal and permanent residents lived in the region long before the first Europeans arrived.

Spain sent three explorations into the area between 1774 and 1779, and during this time Spanish names were given to some of the waterways and islands. But Spain's primary interest was in the outcome of the American Revolution, so they gave the West Coast only cursory interest. During this time, however, the British were increasingly involved in fur trading in the area. In 1791 a Spanish explorer by the name of José Maria Narváez sailed into what is now English Bay; he was greeted and given a tour of the area by contingents of the Musqueam and Squamish people.

A year later, in the summer of 1792, Captain George Vancouver and Spain's Dionisio Alcala Galiano sailed together to the region and shared what they knew about the area with each other. Vancouver explored the area and named and staked claims on Point Grey, Burrards Inlet, and

Robert's Bank. Spain became a British ally during the French Revolution, but by 1795 the Spanish influence in the region had seriously diminished. Vancouver nonetheless relied on Spanish charts and never changed the area's Spanish names. So today the original names, like the Strait of Juan de Fuca and Quadra Island, still reflect Spain's former glories.

In 1808 a British explorer named Simon Fraser, in search of fur-trading routes, arrived at the mouth of what later became known as the Fraser River. While the native population quickly turned him back, his discovery managed to open the door for future European expeditions, and in 1827 the Hudson Bay Company arrived and built a trading post at Fort Langley.

Gold was discovered in Vancouver in 1856; however, the first group of gold seekers from San Francisco didn't arrive until two years later, in April 1858. The arrival of these 25,000 Americans frightened British Columbia's governor, James Douglas, into declaring the entire province a British colony (prior to this, only Vancouver Island was a colony) and into asking England to send a contingent of Royal Engineers to help maintain control of the area. The engineers, led by Colonel Richard Moody, arrived on November 25, 1858. Moody selected sites for the main roads and military

Captain George Vancouver

Vancouver's namesake was a man of Dutch descent who joined the British Navy at the age of 13 and eventually served with Captain Cook on his second and third voyages around the world. By 1791, Vancouver was on his own, captaining the HMS Discovery *around the Cape of Good Hope on commission from the British government to survey North America's northern Pacific Coast. He also, on behalf of the British admiralty, negotiated a land settlement with Spanish Captain Bodega-y-Quadra at Nootka, on what is now known as Vancouver Island.*

Vancouver didn't know that the Spanish had already charted the entire region well in advance of his arrival. Therefore he claimed all of the land he saw for King George III. Pleased with himself, in 1797 he returned to England, where he died three years later at age 40. The Spanish, meanwhile, were too involved with the Mexican Revolution to much notice what was going on, and they simply walked away from their claims to the Pacific Northwest.

reserves, and he chose present-day New Westminster as the mainland colony's capital.

The early 1860s saw the first significant influx of white settlers to the region. In 1862 Sewell Prescott Moody, hailing from Maine, established the area's first sawmill in Port Moody at the eastern end of Burrard Inlet, thereby setting in motion what continues even today to be a driving force of British Columbia's economy. It wasn't until 1886, however, that Vancouver was incorporated and the city really took off. That's when the Canadian Pacific Railway (CPR) linked British Columbia to the rest of Canada.

More than 10,000 Chinese were hired to come to Canada to build the railway. After the railway was completed, many of the Chinese settled in Vancouver, but in 1885 the federal government passed legislation restricting and taxing immigration. Racist city-housing policies forced those who did immigrate to settle together into one large neighborhood just south of Gastown—in present-day Chinatown. All of the racist laws have long since been eliminated; and with Asia in its heart, Vancouver has since served both as a link to the East and as a gateway to the continent of North America. The result has been almost continuous growth since the 1960s. Viewed as neutral territory between Asia and the United States, Vancouver is one of North America's busiest ports.

People of Vancouver

Vancouver used to be a prim, proper, and staid British enclave where a stiff upper lip was a sign of position. Not so any longer. Today Vancouver serves as an example of how varied cultures can live together in harmony, discover the best of one another, and apply what they learn from those discoveries to daily life. Because Vancouver is the Far East's major point of entry into Canada, the city has become a United Nations of languages, colors, costumes, and foods. After English and Chinese, the most common languages spoken here are Punjabi, German, French, Tagalog (Philippine), Italian, and Spanish. Perhaps because of this rich cultural mix, Vancouverites seem to be more tolerant of varying lifestyles and customs than are folks in many other cities.

This cultural variety is also the reason why the city, with little debate, has willingly accepted

A native Hiwus woman at Grouse Mountain

Grouse Mountain

Top 10 Languages Spoken by Vancouverites

1. English—1,165,270
2. Chinese—238,790
3. Punjabi—68,110
4. German—33,940
5. French—23,450
6. Tagalog—23,430
7. Italian—18,680
8. Spanish—16,720
9. Vietnamese—13,730
10. Polish—13,335

Source: Statistics Canada

shopping centers that have only Chinese writing on all of their signs and why a member of the Canadian Parliament won reelection in a landslide even after he announced he was gay. But diversity is also the reason why getting anything done in this city can be so infuriatingly slow. Whether constructing a new bridge, cutting down a neighborhood tree, or building a new shopping center, people almost always take care not to offend anyone's sensibilities, lifestyle, or cultural heritage.

Vancouverites look outward—visitors are constantly surprised at how much residents know about Asia, Europe, and the United States. In fact, many of us have at least three favorite Tokyo or London restaurants we're willing to recommend—either because we've been to them or because we have simply heard them mentioned in conversation.

Weather

Moderated by Pacific Ocean currents, Vancouver's weather is the mildest in Canada, with daytime temperatures averaging 20 degrees Celsius (68 °F) in summer and 2.4 degrees Celsius (36.3 °F) during the coldest periods of win-

TRIVIA

When you account for all immigrants living in British Columbia, 44 percent are Asian and 40 percent are European born.

ter. Every 10 years or so we get a monster snowstorm that lasts two or three days. We don't really know how to handle snow, so we generally just wait for the rain to melt it.

OK, so it rains. A lot. But rumors about permanent soakings are unfounded. And we like to think that our 144 centimeters (approximately 56 inches) of annual rainfall doesn't just mean wetness. Rather, that rainfall translates into good skiing conditions on local mountains in winter and green shrubs in spring and summer.

Waterlogged half the year, Vancouver gets 45 days of fog, 168 days of rain, and 80 days without measurable sunshine, usually between the end of October and April. June, July, August, and September are the driest. There can be as many as 45 to 60 straight days of sunshine in the summer, and fall is usually gorgeous, with a combination of fresh, fog-shrouded mornings; sunny afternoons; and clear, crisp evenings. Monthly hours of sunshine average 305 in July and 44 in December.

Because of its oceanic and mountain influences, the area experiences huge variations in average hours of sunshine, rainfall, snow, and temperature, sometimes over short distances. For example, the average yearly precipitation in White Rock, a small community just south of Vancouver, is 1,092 millimeters (approximately 43 inches). Less than 50 kilometers (about 31 miles) away, in North Vancouver, the North Shore mountains force clouds to

Weather Statistics

	Ave. Low/High Temps (°F)	Precipitation in (cm)	Hours of Sunlight
January	2 (35.6)/5 (41)	21.8 (55.4)	55
February	4 (39.2)/7 (44.6)	14.7 (37.3)	93
March	6 (42.8)/10 (50)	12.7 (32.3)	129
April	9 (48.2)/14 (57.2)	8.4 (21.3)	180
May	12 (53.6)/18 (64.4)	7.1 (18)	253
June	15 (59)/21 (69.8)	6.4 (16.3)	243
July	17 (62.6)/23 (73.4)	3.1 (7.9)	305
August	17 (62.6)/23 (73.4)	4.3 (10.9)	255
September	14 (57.2)/18 (64.4)	9.1 (23.1)	188
October	10 (50)/14 (57.2)	14.7 (37.3)	116
November	6 (42.8)/9 (48.2)	21.1 (53.6)	70
December	4 (39.2)/6 (42.8)	22.4 (56.9)	44

To convert degrees Celsius to Fahrenheit, multiply by 1.8 and add 32. To convert centimeters to inches, multiply by 2.54.

rise and release their moisture, producing yearly rainfall averaging 1,859 millimeters (approximately 73 inches). On the other hand, Vancouver airport records about 100 centimeters (39 inches) of rain each year.

This varied climate, combined with the varied landscape, creates a wide array of outdoor-sports opportunities, including superb skiing just 20 minutes from Downtown, with sailing and motorboat cruising possible on the same day.

Vancouver's Climate

Average daily low and high temperatures in degrees Celsius (Fahrenheit in parentheses), monthly precipitation in centimeters (inches in parentheses), and hours of sunshine.

Dressing in Vancouver

This is the West Coast, so lighten up. Anything goes in Vancouver, as long as you're neat about it. Restaurants do not require a tie or a jacket, and although some nightclubs have dress codes, you'll find most of those simply prohibit cutoffs, tank-tops, or bare feet. If you're a golfer, check with the pro shop about appropriate dress—some courses won't allow jeans and ask that you wear a collared shirt. Businesspeople in Vancouver dress like businesspeople in most cities, so if you're in town to cut a deal, your normal office attire is still the standard.

Otherwise, Vancouver's a city in which you can feel comfortable wearing jeans to the opera or dressing in an outlandish combination of colors and cuts, because in Vancouver, style is an individual statement, and what may seem bizarre in other places might look great in Vancouver. Because the downtown area encompasses office towers and many of Vancouver's major tourist and entertainment sites, you'll see a wide variety of dress. Just make sure you bring along a light jacket or sweater in the summer (evenings can be cool), rain gear year-round, and light winter wear for December through March. If you want to get into the nearby North Shore mountains, bring hiking boots and all-climate wear. If you arrive during the rainy season, take along a waterproof jacket.

When to Visit

Every season in Vancouver has its own character; this is a year-round city marked by great skiing in winter, sailing and music festivals in summer, and a rich blend of arts and entertainment throughout the year.

In winter, come prepared to swoosh down the slopes. Not only do the local mountains provide superb ski runs just 20 minutes from Downtown, but for most of the '90s nearby Whistler Resort was voted the finest ski facility anywhere in North America.

If it's blossoms you want, visit in March and April, when a succession of ornamental cherry and plum trees bloom. From May onward it's simply glorious, with the rhododendrons and azaleas in full bloom. Remember,

Top 10 Ways to Keep Happy When It's Raining in Vancouver
by Phil Reimer, popular television and radio weatherman

1. Walk the entire seawall around Stanley Park. Very few bikers or in-line skaters will be around—you'll have the wall to yourself.

2. If the wind is up with the rain and it's not too cold, rent a small sailboat and race across English Bay.

3. Walk the trails around Spirit Park on the UBC lands. There's lots of old-growth forest to keep you at least partially dry.

4. Play golf on any of the public courses. The locals won't be there, and you can finish a game in fewer than four hours.

5. If it's winter, head up to the local mountains. Chances are if it's raining in the city you might find some fresh snow for skiing or snowshoeing.

6. Visit Long Beach on the west side of Vancouver Island. It offers miles of beach for walking in the fresh wind off the Pacific.

7. Find a Starbucks, sit near the window, and watch the world go by.

8. Linger over coffee and a calorie-laden cinnamon bun at one of the host of great places on Fourth Avenue.

9. Sit inside the Vancouver Library atrium, where lots of neat little food places provide the best people watching in town.

10. Get on the SkyTrain and head to Metro Town. You can eat in a jungle restaurant and play games in the palladium. Before you leave, chase the blues away by buying a whole bunch of stuff just for yourself.

however, that while June may be warm and sunny in many parts of the world, in Vancouver it's cool and wet.

Vancouverites love festivals. Give us a theme and we'll plan a celebration around it. We spend 15 percent less time at work than do citizens of the average Canadian city . . . and that's just fine by us. Some of the events are fairly small. Others, like the Vancouver International Children's Festival or the Bard on the Beach Shakespeare Festival—both located at Vanier Park in Kitsilano—are major events that attract visitors from throughout the Pacific Northwest. Some events, such as the Brewmasters Festival held in June, are primarily just for fun. Others, like the well-attended Women in View Festival in February, have important artistic and sociological significance. The following Calendar of Events tells you what's happening when and where.

Calendar of Events

JANUARY
Canadian Airlines International Chinese New Year Festival (Chinatown, Downtown, 604/687-8330)
Polar Bear Swim (West End, False Creek, Downtown, 604/665-3424)

FEBRUARY
BC Outdoors Show (BC Place Stadium, Downtown, 604/294-1313)
BC Spring Home Show (BC Place Stadium, Downtown, 604/433-5121)
Chinese New Year (Chinatown, Downtown, 604/687-8330)
Women in View Festival (Granville Island, Uptown, 604/685-6684)

MARCH
Vancouver Golf Show (BC Place Stadium, Downtown, 604/536-7878)
Vancouver Storytelling Festival (Roundhouse Community Centre, Downtown, 604/876-2272)

APRIL
Vancouver Playhouse International Wine Festival (Vancouver Trade and Convention Centre, Downtown, 604/873-3311)

MAY
Cloverdale Rodeo (Surrey, Southern Suburbs, 604/576-9461)
Hyack Festival (New Westminster, Eastern Suburbs, 604/522-6894)

Music West Festival (Vancouver East Cultural Centre, East Vancouver, 604/684-9338)

Vancouver International Children's Festival (Vanier Park, Point Grey, 604/708-5655)

Vancouver International Marathon (Downtown, 604/872-2928)

JUNE

Bard on the Beach Shakespeare Festival through September (Vanier Park, Point Grey, 604/737-0625)

Brewmasters Festival (Plaza of Nations, Downtown, 604/290-4268)

Canadian International Dragon Boat Festival (False Creek, Uptown, 604/688-2382)

Du Maurier International Jazz Festival (various locations, 604/872-5200)

VanDusen Flower and Garden Show (VanDusen Botanical Garden, Uptown, 604/878-9274)

JULY

Benson & Hedges Symphony of Fire (English Bay, Downtown, 604/688-1992, sometimes takes place in August)

Summer is a good time for a dinner cruise on the MPU Constitution.

Sea Snaps/Maria Steernberg

Vancouver Holidays

January 1—New Year's Day
Late March/early April—Good Friday
May 24 (or preceding Monday)—Victoria Day
July 1—Canada Day
August 1—BC Day
First Monday in September—Labor Day
Second Monday in October—Thanksgiving Day
November 11—Remembrance Day
December 25—Christmas Day
December 26—Boxing Day

Canada Day (July 1) Celebrations (Canada Place, Downtown, 604/666-7200)

Dancing on the Edge Festival (Firehall Arts Centre, Downtown, 604/689-0926)

Enchanted Evenings at the Dr. Sun Yat-Sen Gardens (Chinatown, Downtown, 604/687-8330)

Salmon Festival (Steveston, 604/277-6812)

Vancouver Chamber Music Festival (Crofton House School for Girls, Point Grey, 604/602-0363)

Vancouver International Comedy Festival (Granville Island, Uptown, 604/683-0883)

Vancouver International Folk Festival (Jericho Beach Park, Point Grey, 604/602-9798)

AUGUST

Abbottsford International Airshow (Abbottsford, Eastern Suburbs, 604/857-1142)

Pacific National Exhibition (Pacific National Exhibition Grounds, East Vancouver; changing to an as-yet-unnamed location in another two years, 604/253-2311)

Powell Street Festival (Oppenheimer Park, East Vancouver, 604/682-4335)

SEPTEMBER

Air Canada PGA Tournament (Northview Golf Club, Surrey, Southern Suburbs, 604/687-8330)

Fringe Theater Festival (various venues, East Vancouver, 604/257-0350)
Molson Indy (Downtown, 604/684-4639)

OCTOBER
BC Fall Home Show (BC Place Stadium, Downtown, 604/433-5121)
Vancouver International Film Festival (several locations, 604/685-0260)
Vancouver International Writers and Readers Festival (Granville Island, Uptown, 604/681-6330)

NOVEMBER
Christmas Fair at Hycroft (Hycroft Manor, Uptown, 604/731-4661)

DECEMBER
Christmas Carol Ship Parade (English Bay and Burrard Inlet, 604/878-9988)
Christmas under the Sails at Canada Place (Canada Place, Downtown, 604/666-8477)
Festival of Lights (VanDusen Botanical Garden, Uptown, 604/878-9274)

Business and Economy

Vancouver's financial roots can be seen growing out of the ground—trees. Although the logging business is in decline, it still employs more people in British Columbia than any other industry.

Over the past couple of decades, the city has made a conscious effort to diversify the economy and has generally succeeded. Tourism brings in a whopping $3 billion to the city each year. The high-tech industry, too, is on the move and growing at a spectacular 22 percent each year. Throughout the province high-tech companies employ 60,000 people and generate about $7 billion yearly in revenue. Vancouver's film industry is huge; in 1998 it brought in $807 million.

In some ways Vancouver is a branch-plant city, with the head offices of many corporations found in places like Toronto and Montreal. That's not surprising, considering that the economic center of the nation resides east of Manitoba. Nonetheless, greater Vancouver is home to the headquarters of some 160 major corporations, and all told they

TRIVIA

In what seems to have been a sign of things to come, the first meeting of Vancouver's City Council in 1887 was delayed because no one had paper and pencil.

account for more than $60 billion in revenue a year. A majority of the town's top employers (55 percent) are headquartered within the city boundaries, while others are in Burnaby (13 percent) and Richmond (11.8 percent). Most firms are in the forestry business (13 percent), followed by food distribution (8.1 percent), mining (6.2 percent), construction and development (6.2 percent), retail (5.6 percent), and financial services.

In part because Burrard Inlet—one of the world's largest natural harbors—is deep and ice-free all year, Vancouver serves as a major North American port. The city handles more tonnage annually than does any other municipality on the West Coast, and it is among the top five ports in the Western Hemisphere. Freighters anchored in English Bay, awaiting their cargoes of grain, sulfur, coal, potash, iron ore, forest products, and copper, are as much a part of the Vancouver landscape as the mountains and city skyline.

The average cost of living in the city is about the same as in other major cities in North America. However, the Canadian dollar makes things considerably cheaper for the traveler in Vancouver than in Chicago, New York, and San Francisco, as well as Tokyo and London.

Here's an estimate of what you can expect to pay in Vancouver:
- Eight-kilometer (five-mile) taxi ride: $12
- Downtown hotel double room: $110
- Dinner for two: $50
- Movie admission: $8.50
- Daily newspaper: $.75/$1.25 weekends

Housing

Dig into your wallet if you plan to stay. This is a city of high rent and even higher purchase costs—the highest in Canada. It hasn't always been that way—only for the past 30 years or so. In Vancouver a quarter-million dollars will buy you a starter home, and your house or condo isn't just a place to live but also an investment and a guaranteed retirement plan.

T I P

Taxes include the BC provincial sales tax (6 percent), hotel tax (10 percent), and a 10-percent sales tax added to liquor consumed in bars and restaurants. The federal General Sales Tax is 7 percent, but you can get that money back upon filling out a rebate form if you buy more than $100 worth of goods.

Canadian Currency

Like the United States, Canada uses the decimal system and the dollar. However, if you're from the United States, remember that the numbers can be misleading. The Canadian dollar is worth less than the U.S. dollar (between 30 and 37 cents less)... so a dollar isn't always a buck. And while money machines are everywhere—including many grocery stores and hotels—and your VISA, MasterCard, and bank cards should work in them, always try to make your money exchanges at a bank, where you'll get the best rate of exchange.

Canadian bills, like most European currencies, are colored according to their value. The five-dollar bill is blue, the 10 is purple, the 20 is green, the 50 is red, and the 100 is beige. We also have one-dollar coins (nicknamed loonies) and two-dollar coins (nicknamed twonies).

How much you pay will of course depend on what you're looking for. Do you want to live at a prestigious address? Be close to the ocean? Have a view? Be part of the trendiest neighborhoods? Do you like the pulse of the downtown core or prefer the burbs? How about being near the horse paths along the Fraser River or owning a house on leased Indian land? It's all here, and each has its price.

Below is a list of housing prices in the Vancouver region from the Real Estate Board of Greater Vancouver (604/730-3000). Although figures change monthly, the relationship between districts for the cost of housing remains roughly the same.

	Detached House	Condominium
Vancouver West Side	$608,452	$177,004
West Vancouver	$549,368	$301,562
Richmond	$364,944	$130,661
North Vancouver	$359,374	$158,600
Burnaby	$349,597	$142,420
Vancouver East Side	$332,679	$131,220
Port Moody	$288,842	$129,508
Coquitlam	$267,330	$130,965
New Westminster	$256,904	$136,911
Port Coquitlam	$247,158	$117,339

Business Organizations in Vancouver

- **Asia Pacific Foundation of Canada** (666-999 Canada Pl., 604/684-5986) helps Canadians operate and be successful when doing business in Asian countries. (DV)
- **BC Trade and Investment Office** (World Trade Centre, 999 Canada Place, Suite 730, 604/952-0607) is an information source for potential buyers and investors interested in innovative products, services, and technologies. (DV)
- **Downtown Vancouver Business Improvement Association** (789 W. Pender St., Ste. 1250, 604/685-7811) promotes downtown Vancouver as a place to do business, live, visit, and enjoy. (DV)
- **The Fraser Institute** (626 Bute St., 604/688-0221) is an independent research center whose objective is to present the position of business in competitive markets. (DV)
- **The Real Estate Board of Greater Vancouver** (2433 Spruce St., 604/730-3028) is an association of realtors offering research and general real estate information. (UV)
- **Retail Merchants' Association of BC** (1758 W. Eighth Ave., 604/736-0368) represents independent retailers and lobbies the government on retail-business issues. (UV)
- **Vancouver Board of Trade** (World Trade Centre, 999 Canada Pl., Ste. 400, 604/681-2111) serves as the city's chamber of commerce. (DV)
- **Vancouver Trade and Convention Centre** (200-999 Canada Pl., 604/482-2225) is the major exhibition site for conventions in the city. (DV)

Schools

Vancouverites are learning freaks. Whether you're looking for a course on sailing, computers, or muffin making, you can find it at any number of adult-education locations that range from universities to the local "Y."

The city has two universities. The biggest and the province's primary

The Vancouver Aquarium houses over 8,000 species of aquatic life.

seat of higher learning is the University of British Columbia (UBC), located on the westernmost tip of Point Grey. Simon Fraser University (SFU), known for its innovative programs, sits atop Burnaby Mountain in Burnaby. SFU also has a downtown campus, located one block south of Gastown. The Lower Mainland has five colleges providing technical and general courses of study. Trinity Western University, located five miles south of Fort Langley, specializes in religious studies and theology.

The public-school system is outwardly similar to that of virtually any other community, with neighborhood elementary schools (grades one through eight) and high schools (grades 9 through 12). But there's a substantial difference once you're inside the hallowed halls: The greater Vancouver schools deal with a population that's expected to reach 307,000 by the year 2004—with about 25 percent of those students born elsewhere.

The high number of students for whom English is a second language means most districts have intensive ESL (English as a Second Language) programs. In addition, there's an ongoing battle between the public-school systems and the provincial and federal governments over who should pick up the bill. Since education is a provincial jurisdiction, the federal government claims the provinces should pay. The provincial government counters that since the federal government is responsible for immigration they should be footing the bill. In the middle are cash-strapped school boards that are forced to cope regardless.

Because many parents believe that public-school systems devote too much time to matters other than curriculum, private schools have enjoyed a huge growth in recent years. Private schools—some with religious affiliations—also receive government funding, a situation that has stirred an ongoing philosophical debate among educators.

© John Elk

2

GETTING AROUND VANCOUVER

The greater Vancouver area consists of the city itself (population 521,000) plus the suburbs of Richmond, Surrey, Burnaby, Delta, North Vancouver, West Vancouver, New Westminster, Coquitlam, Port Moody, and White Rock. Taken together, their populations add up to more than 1.9 million.

Despite the mountains, rivers, and harbors, it's relatively easy to get in and out of Vancouver. Drive south along Oak Street and onto Highway 99 and you can be in the United States in 45 minutes; by crossing the Lion's Gate Bridge, you're at Whistler Resort in two hours (watch out for speed traps); and all of the suburbs are within a half hour of the downtown core. The integrated public transit system is well established and makes it easy to get from place to place within the city.

City Layout

Vancouver proper spreads out between the Fraser River to the south and Burrard Inlet to the north. Beyond its borders are the southern bedroom communities of Richmond (location of Vancouver International Airport), Delta, Ladner, Surrey, Crescent Beach, and White Rock. To the east are Burnaby, New Westminster, Coquitlam, Port Moody, Port Coquitlam, Langley, Fort Langley, and Maple Ridge. North of Downtown, along the mountainsides, are North Vancouver and West Vancouver. Collectively, the communities in and around the city are called the Lower Mainland; this region extends, roughly, to the Port Mann Bridge that crosses the Fraser River just beyond New Westminster. Beyond that are the Lower and Upper Fraser

TRIVIA

The 1,368-kilometer Fraser River, which separates Vancouver from Richmond, Surrey, and Delta, is the longest of British Columbia's rivers. It begins near the Alberta border, cuts the deep gorges of The Fraser Canyon, then spills through Vancouver and into the Pacific Ocean.

Valleys, farmland that extends eastward about 150 kilometers to the community of Hope. There is no "Upper" Mainland.

Public Transportation

The Lower Mainland maintains an integrated system of buses, rapid-transit computerized trains, and a ferry service for crossing Burrard Inlet. All told the system covers nearly 1,800 square kilometers of land. About 50 percent of all Vancouver buses have wheelchair ramps; look for the wheelchair symbol on the front of the bus. For more information, call TransLink (the name for the Greater Vancouver Transportation Authority) at 604/521-0400.

SkyTrain is an elevated system connecting downtown Vancouver with Burnaby, New Westminster, and Surrey, stopping at 20 stations along the way. It's a safe and inexpensive ($1.50) way to see the general layout of the city. But don't look for a conductor—there isn't one; the entire system is computerized.

Seabus is a passenger-only ferry service that connects downtown Vancouver with North Vancouver via a 12-minute ride. Terminals are located in Vancouver at the foot of Granville in the old Canadian Pacific terminal and in North Vancouver at the Lonsdale Quay, where you can shop at the farmer's market or enjoy the view from a waterfront café. You can transfer to a bus at either end.

The British Columbia Ferries Corporation (888/223-3779) operates a series of large vehicle and passenger ferries between the Lower Mainland (from Horseshoe Bay in West Vancouver and the Tsawwassen ferry terminal in Delta) and Vancouver Island, the Gulf Islands, Bowen Island, and the Sechelt Peninsula, directly north of Vancouver. It also operates a passenger ship that sails between Port Hardy at the northern tip of Vancouver Island to Prince Rupert along the Inside Passage. Onboard facilities (except for on the smaller Bowen Island vessels) include restaurants, gift shops, snack bars, business centers with data ports, and comfortable lounges.

The corporation recently introduced high-speed service between Horseshoe Bay in West Vancouver and Nanaimo, on Vancouver Island. Built in 1998, the high-speed catamaran, called *Pacificat Explorer*, is the first of three planned "Cats" on the route. It carries 250 passengers and makes the crossing at 37 knots, cutting 20 minutes from the usual one-and-

one-half-hour trip. Amenities include a restaurant, a lounge, a snack bar,
a gift shop, an elevator, a video arcade, a play area for children, tele-
phones, lap-top friendly work stations, video screens, a washroom for
people with disabilities, and tourist information.

For the purpose of determining fares, TransLink splits the Lower
Mainland into three zones; with cross-zone travel, there's an increase in
prices. Travel within one zone costs $1.50, two zones $2.25, and three
zones $3.00. There are deep discounts for seniors (over age 65),
Vancouver's high-school students, and all children between the ages of 5
and 13. Children under the age of five travel free if accompanied by an
adult. On the *Pacificat,* fares between the Lower Mainland and Vancouver
Island in high season (June 30–September 12) are $32 for a car plus $9 for
each adult passenger and $4.50 for children between the ages of 5 and 11.
Children under the age of five ride for free. *Pacificat* fares do change
according to the season, the size of the vehicle, and the destination.

Driving in Vancouver

If you're arriving by car from the south, out of Seattle, you'll likely travel via
Interstate 5 through the border crossing at Blaine, Washington. This road
becomes Highway 99 on the Canadian side and will take you into Vancouver
via the Oak Street Bridge. Be prepared for long lines at the border on weekends and holidays—you may have to wait as much as an hour.

Watch the signs at the bridge for directions. The most direct route into
Downtown is via Granville Street. Although Oak Street is a six-lane thoroughfare, it ends at False Creek, short of the downtown core. (You won't
get lost following Oak Street, but you will need to navigate a few side

© PhotoNet

The Seabus ferries passengers between Downtown and North Vancouver.

routes.) A sign will direct you to turn west at 19th Avenue. From there you'll go to Hemlock Street, where you'll turn right, continue down the hill and across Broadway, and cross the Granville Street Bridge into Downtown.

Downtown has no freeways. In fact, if Vancouverites had their way, downtown streets would be replaced by bicycle lanes. In the 1960s and '70s Vancouver's citizens successfully fought city planners to keep out large streets. Even without freeways, however, Vancouver doesn't experience much rush-hour gridlock, though the streets do get crowded.

Downtown is laid out on a grid system, with a series of one-way streets to ease the flow of traffic. Many neighborhoods have blocked some streets to control traffic and have placed roundabouts in strategic spots. The result is an on-road civility that's a cross between British tradition and contemporary necessity. When three lanes of traffic merge into two, cars alternate like a line of dancers who all know their place. There's no ramming into a vacant spot and no horn blowing (it's illegal in Vancouver except in emergencies), and obscene gestures are as rare in the city as snow in winter. In fact, you're expected to give a friendly wave back to the driver who allowed you into the line.

Parking isn't quite so friendly. If you park in a no-parking area, your car could be impounded. Downtown has tough on-street parking regulations, and prime shopping and business streets are always full. Expect to pay between $1.50 and $3 an hour for parking garages and $1 for 40 minutes on the street.

One of the least popular items in British Columbia is photo radar. You don't know whether you've gone through a speed trap until you receive a ticket—along with a photo of your car—in the mail. The owner of the vehicle—not the driver—pays the fine. If you're renting a car and are caught by photo radar, you will receive a bill in the mail.

Vancouver leads the country in number of auto break-ins. Make sure your car is secure. If you have a lock on your trunk release switch, use it.

Biking in Vancouver

In decent weather, bikes are a major mode of transportation in Vancouver. In fact, the city is a cycling mecca. Biking is a great way to explore the city's neighborhoods, where wide thoroughfares and cycling lanes make it safe and enjoyable. Headgear is mandatory: you'll get a $25 ticket if you're caught without a helmet.

If you'd like to take a bicycle tour of the area, check out one of the following companies: By Cycle Tours Ltd., 955 Alderson Ave., Coquitlam, 604/936-2453 (Eastern Suburbs), or Velo-City Cycle Tours, 2256 Chapman Way, North Vancouver, 604/924-0288 (North Shore).

Air Travel

Getting to Vancouver is easier than it was prior to 1995, now that more air-

---

Bicycle Rental Companies

- *Alley Cat Rentals*, 1779 Robson St., 604/684-5117 (Downtown)
- *Bayshore Bicycles and Rollerblade Rentals*, 745 Denman St., 604/688-2453; or at the Westin Bayshore hotel, 604/689-5071 (Downtown)
- *Bike 'n' Blades Rentals*, 718 Denman St., 604/602-9899 (Downtown)
- *Cambie Cycles*, 3317 Cambie St., 604/874-3616 (Uptown)
- *Lo-Cost Camper and Bike Rentals*, 1835 Marine Dr., N. Vancouver, 604/986-1266 (North Shore); or 5551 No. 3 Rd., Richmond, 604/303-9970 (Southern Suburbs)
- *Spokes Bicycle Rental and Espresso Bar*, 1798 W. Georgia St., 604/688-5141 (Downtown)
- *Stanley Park Cycle*, 1741 Robson St., 604/608-1908 (Downtown)
- *Stanley Park Rentals*, 1798 W. Georgia St., 604/688-5141 (Downtown)
- *Steveston Bicycle*, 3731 Chatham St., Richmond, 604/271-5544 (Southern Suburbs)
- *West Point Cycles*, 3771 W. 10th Ave., 604/224-3536 (Point Grey)

---

lines, more flights, and more cities are available through the new Open Skies Treaty, which allows any airline to schedule direct flights between U.S. and Canadian cities.

Vancouver International Airport, located in Richmond—about a half-hour

Vancouver International Airport

In just three years, Vancouver International Airport (YVR) has been transformed from the DC-3 of North America's airports to what business travelers now say is the continent's Boeing 777 of facilities. A recent survey of international business passengers by the International Air Transport Association (IATA) rated Vancouver first among 14 major North American airports, including airports in New York, Chicago, San Francisco, Toronto, and Los Angeles. Prior to May 1996, when the new terminal opened, YVR was little more than a crowded bus depot. Built in the 1960s to handle 3 million passengers a year, its main terminal building was serving triple that number.

That ugly duckling changed into a swan with the opening of YVR's new $456-million International Terminal. The terminal, which serves both transborder (Canada/United States) and overseas passengers, combines state-of-the-art technology with traditional art, reflecting both contemporary Vancouver and the culture and lifestyle of the Musqueam, the aboriginal peoples who have lived at the mouth of the Fraser River near the airport for more than 8,000 years. While Native Canadian art is everywhere, the terminal's centerpiece—and perhaps its most interesting work—is the massive, $1.3-million Spirit of Haida Gwaii, *a jade-green patina bronze casting by the late Bill Reid.*

In designing YVR, architect Clive Grout distilled the best ideas from existing and proposed airports around the world, and then he gave those ideas a new, West Coast flavor. Such stylistic and functional features as skylights, glass walls, an outdoor strolling area, retail "streets," and a business center set YVR apart from other major airports. For more information contact Airport Operations at 604/276-6101 or check out their Web site: www.yvr.ca.

drive from Downtown—is now served from anywhere in North America via the usual collection of North American airlines. Vancouver is also served by a series of international and Canadian lines, such as Singapore Airlines, Japan Airlines, British Airways, Lufthansa, and Air Canada.

The airport's new International Terminal, built in 1997, is—unlike many airports—logical, easy to access, and laid out so that you can actually find your way along concourses and terminals that have human dimensions. Airport parking is simple, and long-term lots are on the property itself. Expect to pay $8.50 a day for long-term and $4 an hour for short-term parking, with special rates at designated lots for Air Canada and Canadian Airlines International patrons.

Taxis from the airport are plentiful. The fare for a trip Downtown runs about $25. You can expect to pay about $5 to $8 for a ride to the hotels in the vicinity of the airport.

Besides Vancouver International, the city has several other air gateways. The seaplane terminal, near the Westin Bayshore hotel, services a number of communities; a helicopter service is located next to the convention Centre between downtown Vancouver and Victoria; and the old terminal at Vancouver International offers both land and seaplane service to communities, lodges, and resorts.

Train Service

Vancouver is served by Amtrak (604/585-4848) from Los Angeles, Portland, and Seattle, and by Via Rail (800/561-8630) from eastern Canada. The terminus for both is the old Canadian National Railway station on the edge of Chi-

The Pacific Starlight *Dinner Train*

B.C. Rail

T I P

Entering Canada and going through Canada Customs and Immigration is a relatively speedy process, with very few entry restrictions. Make certain that you have proof of citizenship. The only guns allowed into the country are those permitted by hunting laws. Liquor is limited to one liter, and cigarettes are limited to 200.

natown. It's here that you also leave for and return from Alberta via the super-luxurious *Rocky Mountaineer* (800/665-7245).

Trips into the interior and to Whistler Mountain are taken from the B.C. Rail (604/631-3500) terminal in North Vancouver, also the home of the spectacular *Pacific Starlight* dinner ride (604/984-5500 or 604/631-3500) along Howe Sound. North Vancouver is also the departure point for the Royal *Hudson* (604/984-5246), a B.C. Rail–run historic steam train that goes up Howe Sound to Squamish.

The Westcoast Express (800/570-7245) is a commuter train service that travels between Mission, in the Lower Fraser Valley, and Vancouver twice daily; it leaves from the Canadian Pacific station in Gastown.

Bus Service

Bus service into and out of Vancouver arrives at and departs from the Pacific Central Station (1150 Station Street), the former western terminus for Canadian National Railway. The station, located at the southwest end of Chinatown, also serves Amtrak and Via Rail, as well as Greyhound, Maverick, and Pacific Stage Coach Lines. It's a short walk (about one block) from the station to the Main Street SkyTrain station.

The Airporter to Vancouver Airport (604/899-8589) is a scheduled service from hotels in the downtown area to Vancouver International Airport, with service every 45 minutes.

Gray Line of Vancouver (604/879-3363), one of the city's largest tour operators, has a variety of package tours of the city and outlying areas.

Greyhound Canada (604/482-8717) travels to points throughout the United States, Canada, and British Columbia.

Maverick Coach Lines (604/662-8051) is one of the regional bus lines and travels to Whistler, Vancouver Island, and Squamish. In addition, it has package tours to select U.S. destinations, such as Las Vegas.

Pacific Coach Lines (604/662-8074) is the bus service you'd likely take to visit Victoria. It has direct Vancouver–Victoria service, as well as tours of Victoria and Vancouver Island.

Call the Quick Shuttle (604/899-8588) bus line if your flight is leaving directly out of either Seattle or Bellingham. They'll pick you up at your hotel and drop you at Seattle's SeaTac Airport or Bellingham Airport.

© Rob Melnychuk

3

WHERE TO STAY

Prince or pauper? No matter, because there's no limit to the variety of lodging available to Vancouver's visitors. Greater Vancouver currently has over 18,000 rooms—more than 10,000 of them in the downtown core alone. While the average rate is just over $100, rooms can go for as little as $60 and for as much as $1,000. The city has three five-diamond hotels in the downtown core and scores of four-diamond lodgings. Boutique hotels abound, and bed-and-breakfasts can be found in every neighborhood—including the West End and Downtown. Virtually every U.S. chain hotel is represented in the city, and several Canada-only chains offer wonderful accommodations with a full range of rates and varying degrees of luxury.

One important word of advice: Don't even think of visiting between May and October without a reservation. Vancouver is one of North America's leading convention sites, and the high season is prime tourist time. During this time, many tourists spend a couple of days sightseeing before they embark on cruise ships to Alaska. The result is that most hotels are booked to the hilt. Show up unannounced and you'll likely be directed to a suburban hotel. Not a tragedy, but it could make your stay less convenient.

As a general rule, the closer you are to Downtown, the more you'll pay. And while most travelers prefer to stay in or near Downtown, the airport area and nearby Richmond have many fine hotels and motels that are just a 30-minute drive from the heart of the city. This chapter focuses on accommodations that are closest to the downtown area. Prices given are for the lowest

Price rating symbols (Canadian dollars):

$	**$75 and under**
$$	**$76 to $115**
$$$	**$116 to $155**
$$$$	**$156 to $199**
$$$$$	**$200 and up**

rates available. Most hotels have a wide selection of rooms that fall into separate price categories.

DOWNTOWN

Hotels

BARCLAY HOTEL
1348 Robson St.
Vancouver
604/688-8850
$$

This European-style hotel, located on one of the city's hottest streets, allows you to witness all the downtown action without paying typical downtown rates. Near Stanley Park, it's a cordial family place with a casual restaurant and lounge. Because it's at the quieter end of Robson Street, it offers the best of both worlds—fantastic location without constant noise from the street activity. It's especially good for anyone expecting to stay more than a couple of days. The continental breakfast buffet is enormous, the piano lounge is a wonderful place to spend a couple of hours in the evening, and the hotel's Marbella Restaurant features tapas-style Spanish cuisine. (Downtown)

BLUE HORIZON
1225 Robson St.
Vancouver
604/688-1411
$$$

Great views and moderately priced meals aren't the only reasons for staying at this West End hotel. It's just a pleasant place to be, especially since it recently underwent an extensive renovation. Every room has a view. And the best part is that you're right on Robson Street, a mix of weird-looking people, yuppies,

and incredible energy. A family plan and spacious units make this long-established hotel a good choice. ♿ (Downtown)

BUCHAN HOTEL
1906 Haro St.
Vancouver
604/685-5354
$$

This three-story 1930s apartment hotel rests on a tree-lined cul-de-sac in the residential area of the West End, next to Stanley Park. The great location and character of the place are somewhat offset by the fact that there are no telephones in any of the 64 rooms. However, kids under 12 stay for free, there's cable TV and in-house bicycle and ski storage, and restaurants and excellent shopping are only a block away. The hotel's walls are decorated with interesting, museum-quality photos of old-time Vancouver. Take a room on the east side—they're brighter and overlook a small park. The largest rooms are the four front-corner executive suites. The hotel has no parking—you'll have to leave your car on the street, and open spots are rare in this high-rise part of town. No elevator, nonsmoking only. ♿ (Downtown)

CENTURY PLAZA HOTEL
1015 Burrard St.
Vancouver
604/687-0575
$$$

The Century Plaza is directly across the street from the luxurious Wall Centre Hotel, but it's also next to St. Paul's Hospital, so you might hear the occasional siren during the night. That minor irritation aside, this all-suites hotel is one of downtown Vancouver's better values, with reasonable daily, weekly, and monthly

While most of Vancouver's downtown hotels are expensive, off-season rates can make your stay surprisingly affordable. Come in February for some of the city's best bargains.

rates. Originally built as an apartment building, it offers 235 suites, a restaurant, a lounge, a nightclub, a cappuccino bar, and an indoor pool. Some floors are nonsmoking. Tour groups often stay here. & (Downtown)

COAST PLAZA AT STANLEY PARK
1733 Comox St.
Vancouver
604/688-7711
$$

Stay here for a taste of Hollywood—film-industry people tend to pick this place over the others when they're in town (the stars, of course, stay elsewhere.) This is also a great location for anyone staying a week or so. The 267-room former apartment building has 170 suites, 12 of which have two bedrooms. A block away from the main West End streets, the hotel is next to Stanley Park and only a short walk from the tennis courts. All of the rooms have balconies, and some include great views of the park. Many also have kitchen facilities to augment the round-the-clock room service. & (Downtown)

CROWNE PLAZA HOTEL GEORGIA
801 W. Georgia St.
Vancouver
604/682-5566
$$$$

If you want both old-fashioned charm and up-to-date innovations, and you prefer to stay in the heart of the city,

try this place. Built in 1927, this 12-story stone hotel across from the Vancouver Art Gallery received a complete facelift in 1998 and now combines the look and feel of a first-class business hotel with the casual aura of a tour stop. All the rooms have custom-designed furniture, fabrics, and artwork that reflect the hotel's original era. On the mezzanine level, the meeting place has been restored to its original grandeur, and conference rooms now include refurbished woodwork, moldings, and ornate chandeliers. The regal ballroom—which is perfect for large social functions—has had its unique interior balcony restored. The lobby includes modern furnishings on original tile floors, ornate woodwork, marble accents, and a fireplace. & (Downtown)

DAYS INN VANCOUVER DOWNTOWN
921 W. Pender St.
Vancouver
604/681-4335
$$

The Days Inn is arguably one of the best values in the downtown area. One block from the waterfront, it's located in the middle of everything—shopping, restaurants, museums, Gastown, and theaters. A recently refurbished European-style hotel, it offers 85 guest rooms and business-friendly facilities that include

DOWNTOWN VANCOUVER

Centennial Pier

CORDOVA ST

MAIN ST

UNION ST

Main Station

EAST COMMISSIONER

COLUMBIA ST

QUEBEC ST

Seabus to North Vancouver
(Burrard Inlet passenger Ferry)

Heliport

HASTINGS ST

PENDER ST

EXPO BLVD

GEORGIA VIADUCT

1ST AV

9

GM Place

43

Canada Place

24

Burrard Inlet

CANADA PLACE WAY

8

BC Place Stadium

EXPO BLVD

CAMBIE ST

BEATTY ST

18

31

Cambie St. Bridge

CAMBIE ST

PACIFIC BLVD

38 36

7

DUNSMUIR ST

42

29

HOMER ST

SMITHE ST

19

NELSON ST

False Creek

Seaplanes

26

6 22

17

18

HASTINGS ST

PENDER ST

MELVILLE ST

GEORGIA ST

39

HOWE ST

GRANVILLE ST MALL (buses and taxis only)

16

32

Dead Man's Island

WEST COMMISSIONER

23

ROBSON ST

2

34

20

BURRARD ST

THURLOW ST

HELMCKEN ST

4

Coal Harbour

28

27 21

JERVIS ST

PENDRELL ST

Nelson Park

37

13

Lost Lagoon

41

1

BROUGHTON ST

40

10

HARO ST

CARDERO ST

Granville Island

Granville St. Bridge

LAGOON DR

PARK LN

CHILCO ST

DENMAN ST

NELSON ST

11

PENDRELL ST

DAVIE ST

15

BURNABY ST

33

PACIFIC ST

BEACH AV

3

12

5

COMOX ST

35

BROUGHTON ST

Sunset Beach

Burrard St. Bridge

English Bay Beach

English Bay

Vanier Park

BURRARD ST

CHESTNUT ST

1 KILOMETER MILE

0

Where to Stay in Downtown Vancouver

1 Barclay Hotel
2 Blue Horizon
3 Buchan Hotel
4 Century Plaza
5 Coast Plaza at Stanley Park
6 Crowne Plaza Hotel Georgia
7 Days Inn Vancouver Downtown
8 Delta Vancouver Suite Hotel
9 Dominion Hotel
10 Empire Landmark
11 English Bay Inn
12 Executive Inn Downtown Vancouver
13 Four Seasons
14 Georgian Court
15 Hostelling International
16 Hotel Dakota
17 Hotel Vancouver
18 Hyatt Regency Vancouver
19 Kingston Hotel
20 La Grande Residence
21 Listel Vancouver

22 Metropolitan
23 Pacific Palisades
24 Pan Pacific Hotel
25 Parkhill Hotel
26 Renaissance Vancouver Hotel Harbourside
27 Riviera Hotel
28 Robsonstrasse City Motor Inn
29 Rosedale on Robson Suite
30 Rosellen Suites
31 Sandman Hotel
32 Sheraton Wall Centre
33 Sunset Inn Travel Apartments
34 Sutton Place
35 Sylvia Hotel
36 Terminal City Club Tower Hotel
37 Travelodge
38 Waterfront Centre
39 Wedgewood
40 West End Guest House
41 Westin Bayshore
42 Westin Grand
43 YWCA

voicemail and data ports, in-room safes, and coffeemakers. The executive suites have harbor views. The Chelsea Restaurant serves three meals daily, and the Bombay Bicycle Club is a warm, English-style lounge that is popular among Vancouver's businesspeople. (Downtown)

DELTA VANCOUVER SUITE HOTEL
550 W. Hastings St.
Vancouver
604/605-8880
$$$

Located across the street from the Simon Fraser University downtown campus, this new property is one block from the old Canadian Pacific Terminal and on the edge of everything. An all-suites establishment, it has 227 rooms, 24-hour room service, in-room movies, and all the extra amenities one usually associates with a major hotel. Each room also includes a full array of useful business tools. Want a printer? Ask at the front desk and they'll get one for you. The hotel's Manhattan Restaurant—serving up a delicious meld of Asian and West Coast cuisines—is destined to become one of Vancouver's favorite dining spots. ᕕ (Downtown)

DOMINION HOTEL
210 Abbott St.
Vancouver
604/681-6666
$$

This golden oldie—one of Gastown's greatest and most historic buildings—has enjoyed a long life since its construction in 1899, but it's more than just a dusty museum piece. In fact, on weekends it's one of Vancouver's most popular gathering spots—its Lamplighter Pub attracts youthful energy like a candle does moths. The pub, located downstairs, was the first

Crowne Plaza

Crowne Plaza Hotel Georgia, p. 34

in Vancouver to acquire a beer license (1925) and the first to serve women—a fact that hasn't been forgotten either by women or the young dudes chasing them. The 68 units in the hotel includes private or shared baths. Nonsmoking rooms are also offered. The rooms are comfortable, ski packages are available, and pets are permitted. (Downtown)

EMPIRE LANDMARK HOTEL
1400 Robson St.
Vancouver
604/687-0511
$$

The 358-room Empire Landmark has been a Vancouver institution for several decades. In all that time, it has never lost its character or its importance as a major West End property. It's one of the tallest hotels in the city and caters to large conventions, but it has remarkably intimate public rooms. It also has nonsmoking floors and a fitness center, and the revolving restaurant atop the hotel, Cloud 9, features Continental and West Coast cuisine and some of the city's best views. As is true of many rooftop eateries, though the scenery is better than the food. ᕕ (Downtown)

EXECUTIVE INN DOWNTOWN VANCOUVER
1379 Howe St.
Vancouver
604/688-7678
$$

This property—located next to Yaletown, the city's latest historical redevelopment area—is just one block away from False Creek and the passenger ferries to Granville Island. With terrific views of the Vancouver South Slope and Point Grey, the hotel has everything you'd expect in a businessperson's facility, including same-day turnaround on laundry and a business center with fax machines and data ports. Complimentary shuttle service within the downtown core is provided on request. ᕕ (Downtown)

FOUR SEASONS HOTEL
791 W. Georgia St.
Vancouver
604/689-9333
$$$$$

La crème de la crème! The Four Seasons has been a five-star establishment since the day it was built some 25 years ago. Everything about it is impeccable. Amenities include complimentary shoeshines, hair dryers, bathrobes, and 24-hour valet service. Kids are welcomed with complimen-

tary milk and cookies. Voicemail is in English, French, or Japanese. Some of the city's best shopping is right beneath your room. While it may seem hard to determine where the shopping center ends and the hotel begins, you'll have no trouble adapting once you get into the place. To get there, drive south alongside the Pacific Centre Shopping Mall, on Howe St. (it's one-way.) The entrance is through an alcove on the side of the mall. Adjacent to the Hotel Georgia, it's across the street from the Vancouver Art Gallery. ᕕ (Downtown)

GEORGIAN COURT HOTEL
773 Beatty St.
Vancouver
604/682-5555
$$$

This is a surprisingly inexpensive facility, especially considering its intimate and luxurious stature. The 180-room European-style building is located directly across the street from BC Place Stadium and the stadium plaza. It's also the location for one of the city's finest restaurants, William Tell. (See Chapter 4, Where to Eat.) Be sure to spend in the restaurant what you save on the accommodations. All of the immaculate rooms have terrific reading lamps, turn-down service on request, desks, and three telephones. ᕕ (Downtown)

HOTEL DAKOTA
645 Nelson St.

Vancouver
604/605-4333
$

Clean and efficient, this 100-unit property is close to everything Downtown and is a couple of blocks from the Queen Elizabeth Theatre, the BC Place Stadium, and the General Motors Place Stadium. Originally built in 1904, the hotel has since been renovated many times—the current look dates to the 1950s, and includes chrome banisters and neon signs. The wonderful array of photos on the walls dates back to when this end of Granville was the center of the city. The hotel also features a restaurant, dining lounge, and tavern, as well as nonsmoking rooms and convenient parking. Because of the nightclub downstairs, it's not a particularly quiet place, but rooms are well priced, and the '50s feel gives the hotel a certain charm. (Downtown)

HOTEL VANCOUVER
900 W. Georgia St.
Vancouver
604/684-3131

$$$$

This hotel has been a local landmark since it was built in 1939. It's at the core of downtown Vancouver, across the street from the Vancouver Art Gallery, one block from the courthouse complex, three blocks from the Orpheum Theatre, and five blocks from the BC Place Stadium and the GM Place Stadium. A multi-million-dollar makeover in 1996 has not only brought the hotel up to modern standards (the hotel was beginning to look its age), but has also exposed the wonderful stone arches and other designs that had been covered up by previous renovations. The hotel's 555 rooms feature décor that's traditional and elegant. Standard rooms are spacious and have either king- or queen-size beds and business amenities that include voice mail, a data port, a computer jack, and a well-lit, spacious desk area. The hotel also has a well-equipped fitness club, a large swimming pool, a Jacuzzi, and a sun deck. An "Entre Gold" floor provides its own concierge service, a fruit

Poolside at the Four Seasons Hotel, p. 37

Four Seasons

buffet, complimentary breakfast, fresh flowers in the rooms, complimentary newspapers, and an upscale atmosphere. The first floor has two restaurants (the casual Griffins and the more formal 900 West), and afternoon tea—including scones and a dessert buffet—is held daily in Griffins from 2:30 p.m. to 4:30. On the basement floor are a business center, a shoe shine service, and a travel agent. ⅃ (Downtown)

HYATT REGENCY VANCOUVER
655 Burrard St.
Vancouver
604/683-1234
$$$$

OK, so it's a Hyatt—there aren't any real surprises here. But if you ask for a north-facing corner room with a balcony, you'll be rewarded with spectacular views of the city. Located directly above and next to the Royal Centre Mall complex and just two blocks north of Robson Street, this hotel is in the heart of the action. It has 645 rooms and a large convention space, and the massive lobby is always busy. Just off the lobby is the Gallery bar, one of the city's great post-work meeting places. Next door, the quieter Peacock Lounge offers respite from the bustle. Bill Clinton stayed here during his 1996 meeting with Russian President Boris Yeltsin. ⅃ (Downtown)

KINGSTON HOTEL
757 Richards St.
Vancouver
604/684-9024
$

This clean, no-frills, 60-room backpacker's special stands out for its European-style continental breakfast. The facade includes cut granite and heavy wood along with Tudor-style windows. A lot of the usual hotel amenities, like TVs, have been eliminated. The four-story building has no elevator, and not all of the rooms have private baths. But despite its shortcomings, the Kingston is in a great location, and with senior discounts and off-season rates, it won't break your bank account. It's close to the theater, the GM Place, and the BC Place Stadium. A neighborhood pub, the Rose and Thorn, is on the main floor. (Downtown)

LA GRANDE RESIDENCE
855 Burrard St.
604/682-5511
$$$$

This 18-story luxury apartment building, attached to and run by the Sutton Place Hotel (see below), serves as a home-away-from-home for those staying in Vancouver for a week or more and in need of a good address in the heart of the city. The property's 162 one- and two-bedroom suites all have dishwashers, microwaves, and balconies. The west side of the building is quiet and has the best views. Guests have access to all of the Sutton Place facilities, as well as free use of bicycles. A minimum stay of seven days is required. ⅃ (Downtown)

LISTEL VANCOUVER
1300 Robson St.
Vancouver
604/684-8461
$$$

This former Best Western O'Doul's is a decidedly upscale property, with 130 nicely appointed rooms, a restaurant, and a lounge. It's within walking distance of both Stanley Park and the main shopping area of Robson Street. The real story here, however, is the artwork. Almost 40 percent of the guest rooms double as gallery space. The hotel is "curated" by the nearby Buschlen-Mowatt gallery, one of the city's finest art galleries. O'Doul's restaurant, which opens onto the sidewalk, is one of the better places along Robson to watch the crowds stroll by. & (Downtown)

METROPOLITAN HOTEL
645 Howe St.
Vancouver
604/687-1122
$$$$

Located across from the Pacific Centre shopping Mall, this place has had more lives than a lucky cat. It began as the Mandarin Hotel (built for Expo '86), was sold to Delta Hotels, and is now owned by the Metropolitan chain. Over the years, however, this 197-room hotel has never lost its edge as a top-of-the-line facility. It still has a touch of the Mandarin influence, with Chinese art tastefully placed throughout the lobby and in rooms. Down quilts and marble bathrooms are standard, and visitors can expect first-class concierge service, a full-scale business center, limousine service, and one of the best health clubs in town. Though the generous use of marble would suggest otherwise, this place has a wonderfully understated and quiet elegance—you want to lower your voice the minute you enter the lobby. The hotel restaurant (Diva at the Met) is a culinary delight and a popular hangout for yuppies. & (Downtown)

PACIFIC PALISADES HOTEL
1277 Robson St.
Vancouver
604/688-0461
$$$$

The Pacific Palisades, located across the street from the Listel Vancouver,

has always been one of Vancouver's finest hotels, but it became an even classier establishment when the prestigious Shangri-La chain bought it back in 1991. Klimpton Hotels of San Francisco recently purchased the hotel from Shangri-La, and they're planning further renovations. The hotel is a favorite among those in the movie industry, mainly because its 300 spacious one- and two-bedroom suites have well-equipped kitchens replete with microwaves and refrigerators. The hotel's Monterey Grill is one of Robson Street's best eateries. & (Downtown)

PAN PACIFIC HOTEL
300-999 Canada Pl.
Vancouver
604/662-8111
$$$$$

Even if you don't stay here, take time out of your schedule to walk through the lobby of this 503-room hotel. In a city of exceptional accommodations, The Pan stands out as an opulent dwelling of thick carpets, marbled commons, waterfalls, and floor-to-ceiling windows. Rooms and suites are exquisitely decorated with tasteful art and leather furniture, and all rooms include burnished bronze lamps, ample desks, and data ports. The superb fitness center has a running track and massage facilities, and four restaurants keep everybody well fed. & (Downtown)

PARKHILL HOTEL
1160 Davie St.
Vancouver
604/685-1311
$$

This high-rise hotel, located in the heart of the West End, is perfectly situated for access to the beaches and Granville Island. Some of the hotel's

Pan Pacific Hotel's Opal Suite

192 studio suites offer views of the city, while others look out over False Creek or English Bay. Amenities include exercise facilities, a dining room and lounge, a heated outdoor pool, and underground parking. Several Japanese restaurants are nearby, including one in the hotel. Davie Street feels more like a residential neighborhood than does nearby Robson, and it is certainly less glitzy. (Downtown)

RENAISSANCE VANCOUVER HOTEL HARBOURSIDE
1133 W. Hastings St.
Vancouver
604/689-9211
$$$$$

This is probably downtown Vancouver's most Asian hotel—in fact, Renaissance Hotels was originally a Hong Kong–based chain with 50 hotels in 38 countries. The chain was bought out in 1997 by Marriott, but the Hong Kong influence still dominates. The decor features dark wood, Asian art, and lacquered bamboo room separators. Large Asian tour groups come here, and a variety of Chinese dialects and Japanese are constantly spoken in the lobby. A rooftop revolving restaurant makes one complete cycle per hour, providing a great way to see the waterfront from all perspectives. The Renaissance Vancouver is close to most of the downtown action—including the Convention Centre (three blocks away)—but just far enough from the sometimes-frantic cruise-ship facilities to qualify as an off-the-beaten-path establishment. ♿ (Downtown)

RIVIERA HOTEL
1431 Robson St.
Vancouver
604/685-1301
$$

The Riviera, located a short walk away from Stanley Park, is exceedingly popular and, as a result, often doesn't have enough rooms available to meet demand. Perhaps it's the free parking for all guests, or maybe it's the balcony views of the mountains, harbor, and city. Possibly, it's the fully equipped kitchenettes or the easy access to Robson Street and prime shopping. Each of the one-bedroom suites is brightly decorated and roomy, as are the large family suites. Overall, The Riviera maintains the look and feel of an apartment block, and its exceptional staff members always do their best to make guests feel at home. (Downtown)

ROSEDALE ON ROBSON SUITE HOTEL
838 Hamilton St.
Vancouver
604/689-8033
$$$

You have to love Rosie's. That's the name of the New York–style restaurant attached to the hotel, but it's also what Vancouverites call the property itself. Right next to the public library, two blocks from the theater district, near Yaletown, and a 20-minute walk from Chinatown, it's one of those places where you feel comfortable the second you walk in. The bright and functional hotel offers everything a long-stay client might need, including business facilities and a good fitness room with a pool and sauna. The rooms are somewhat small, the bay windows and the light furnishings make them seem larger. The corner suites offer the most space. &
(Downtown)

ROSELLEN SUITES
2030 Barclay St.
Vancouver
604/689-4807
$$

It may look plain, but this West End suite hotel is one of the city's best-kept secrets, just a few hundred yards from Stanley Park and two blocks from the action. It was converted from an apartment block to a suite hotel in the 1960s, but it has un-

dergone expensive renovations since then. It just so happens that Katherine Hepburn, who was once a frequent visitor to Vancouver, called this her favorite hotel—probably because of its homey feel and its location off the beaten path. The Rosellen caters to the film industry, families, and executive travelers, and it requires a minimum stay of three nights. Free health facilities are in the neighborhood, and all suites are spacious. Although the hotel has no lobby to speak of, the manager's office is decked out with autographed photos of some of the luminaries who've stayed here in the past. (Downtown)

SANDMAN HOTEL
180 W. Georgia St.
Vancouver
604/681-2211
$$

The Sandman chain is British Columbian to the core. Originally established to serve the province's smaller communities, it has since spread into virtually every BC city. Its purpose today is to offer functional and clean downtown facilities at affordable prices. And that's what you'll get here—unpretentious good value and the potential for a lot of fun. The popular Shark Club and Grill, located on the ground floor, is well known for its sports bar, pool tables, and wide-screen TVs. It's across the street from the Queen Elizabeth Theatre and one block from BC Place Stadium and GM Place Stadium. When you stay for 12 days, you get the 13th free. Senior-citizen discounts are available, and pets are allowed. & (Downtown)

SHERATON WALL CENTRE HOTEL
1088 Burrard St.
Vancouver
604/331-1000

$$$$$

Imagine waking up one morning and saying, "I'm going to build the city's best hotel," and then doing it. That's exactly what one of the city's most prominent financiers and arts patrons, Peter Wall, did about five years ago—and he's still at it. The result is an exceptional property that has quickly vaulted to near the top of Vancouver's quality-hotels list. In addition to the current 455-room facility, another tower is scheduled to open sometime in 2000. The Sheraton-managed facility is located on downtown Vancouver's highest point (114 feet above sea level), and a full acre of the land is devoted to gardens. For such a large complex, it has a relatively small and intimate lobby. Try to get a one-bedroom corner suite—the floor-to-ceiling windows offer views of Grouse Mountain. ♿ (Downtown)

SUNSET INN TRAVEL APARTMENTS
1111 Burnaby St.
Vancouver
604/688-2474
$

If you're the type who might be bothered by an occasional high C, this is not the place for you. This tall, gray, concrete structure is the accommodation of choice for many opera singers and actors. Located in the heart of the West End residential area, two blocks off one of the neighborhood's major streets, it's an exceptional bargain. In fact, with its kitchen facilities, balconies, free parking, and easy access to the beaches and Stanley Park, it is, for many of its guests, a sort of home-away-from-home. The decor can best be described as twentieth-century miscellaneous, but the rooms are spacious, with large closets and pri-

vate balconies. The fitness center on the first floor is a bit cramped, but it's never crowded. (Downtown)

SUTTON PLACE HOTEL
845 Burrard St.
Vancouver
604/682-5511
$$$$

This five-star hotel has the most comfortable, homey feel of all of Vancouver's "best." Originally a Le Meridien property, it still has a decidedly French decor and manner. Located one block south of Robson and one block from the key shopping areas, the hotel is elegant and warm, with small but richly appointed rooms. Suites include French doors separating the bedrooms from the sitting areas.The amenities include thick terrycloth bathrobes, in-room movies, and all business-traveler facilities, as well as twice-daily maid service. The nearby towers serve as suites for long-term guests. Friday evenings are chocolate nights, when some 30 different chocolate items are served at remarkably low prices in the Fleuri restaurant. ♿ (Downtown)

SYLVIA HOTEL
1154 Gilford St.
Vancouver
604/681-9321
$$

Want a piece of the old Vancouver? The venerable Sylvia—an official Vancouver heritage site—is an ivy-covered building overlooking English Bay (the beaches are across the street) on the south side of the West End, two blocks from both Stanley Park and Denman Street (the West End's main thoroughfare). Originally built as an apartment complex in 1912, the hotel has be-

TRIVIA

The 45-story, 455-room Sheraton Wall Centre Hotel stands on the highest point in downtown Vancouver and is two floors higher than the Sheraton Centre Hotel in Toronto, making it Canada's tallest.

come an English Bay landmark. Its 119 rooms are comfortable (though some are quite small), and many have kitchenettes. Families should ask for the one-bedroom suites that sleep four and have a living room and kitchen. A good choice for anyone looking for the best combination of price and setting, the hotel has a comfortable restaurant and a lounge with views of the beaches. ₺ (Downtown)

TERMINAL CITY CLUB TOWER HOTEL
837 W. Hastings St.
Vancouver
604/681-4121
$$$
The Terminal City Club, set near the waterfront on West Hastings Street, has acted as a beacon for Vancouver's Old Boy network since it was founded in 1892. The club's new tower, opened in 1998, has five floors devoted to hotel rooms. And for such well-heeled accommodations, they're a bargain. With off-season discounts, the 60 studio and one-bedroom apartments go for as low as $120, and all of the club's amenities and privileges are extended to hotel guests. This is a perfect location for any businessperson (it's no longer restricted just to men) spending a few days in the city. Take a look at the club's billiards room—some of the tables date back to the turn of the last century. ₺ (Downtown)

WATERFRONT CENTRE HOTEL
900 Canada Pl.
Vancouver
604/691-1991
$$$$$
If hotels were people, this one would be the Rodney Dangerfield of Vancouver. Right across the street from the Pan Pacific and a mere block from Downtown, this jewel in the Canadian Pacific chain just doesn't get the press of its rival the Pan Pacific. Nonetheless, it has a collection of amenities not typically found in city hotels. The ground-floor Herons Restaurant, for example, is one of the city's finest. The third-floor rooms have small terraces. For a premium, guests can book a room on one of the two "Entre Gold" club floors, which cater to every whim and include a resident concierge, continental breakfast, nightly hors d'oeuvres, and a private conference room. And, as you'd expect from a five-star hotel, The Waterfront has all the technological gadgets a business traveler could need. ₺ (Downtown)

WEDGEWOOD HOTEL
845 Hornby St.
Vancouver
604/689-7777
$$$$
If you see a collection of dark suits sitting in the warm and friendly Bacchus Lounge after five, don't worry—

they're just lawyers, judges, and court clerks unwinding after a long day on the job. This European-style boutique hotel is directly across the street from the British Columbia Supreme Court buildings and is a favorite hangout for those in the legal profession. Located half a block from the Vancouver Art Gallery, the 93-room Wedgewood is a downtown gem. The well-appointed rooms are large and meticulously decorated, the dining room specializes in excellent Continental cuisine, and The Bacchus is the most cordial lounge in the city. This is definitely one of Vancouver's finest luxury facilities. ♿ (Downtown)

WESTIN BAYSHORE
1601 W. Georgia St.
Vancouver
604/682-3377
$$$$
If you don't have time to go to an island resort while you're in the area, the Westin Bayshore is the next best thing. Located adjacent to Stanley Park and on the waterfront facing the Royal Vancouver Yacht Club docks,

Sutton Place Hotel, p. 43

Sutton Place Hotel

the 517-room hotel offers easy access to the Coal Harbour marina and to the downtown seaplane airport. A 15-minute walk along the newly developed Coal Harbour waterfront leads to downtown shopping. The hotel tower—which served as Howard Hughes' headquarters for more than a month in the 1980s—has been totally renovated, and now each room has a balcony. The hotel's Kids' Club program is a hit with children, and its superb health club is equally popular with adults. ♿ (Downtown)

WESTIN GRAND
433 Robson St.
Vancouver
604/684-9393
$$$$
Opened in April 1999, Vancouver's newest luxury hotel is located directly across the street from the Vancouver Public Library and next door to the Ford Theatre; it's within walking distance of Yaletown, Gastown, the Vancouver Art Gallery, the Queen Elizabeth Theatre/Playhouse complex, and all downtown shopping areas. The 45 "office suites" in this 207-room, all-suite establishment feature kitchenettes, ergonomically designed desk chairs, laser printers, fax and copy machines, and speakerphones with data ports. Light colors and modern furnishings provide a cheery atmosphere, especially when it's raining. (Downtown)

Motels

ROBSONSTRASSE CITY MOTOR INN
1394 Robson St.
Vancouver
604/687-1674
$$
Because German immigrants who

came to Vancouver after World War II established German restaurants and specialty shops on Robson Street, the street has been nicknamed Robsonstrasse. This property has recently been renovated and caters to both family and business clients. The 41 kitchenette suites have facilities for computers (including data ports); the hotel provides free, monitored parking and in-house laundry; and you're within walking distance of all downtown activities. The studio and one-bedroom suites are spacious. (Downtown)

TRAVELODGE VANCOUVER CENTRE
1304 Howe St.
Vancouver
604/682-2767
$$

Though the Travelodge is located in quite an unconventional place—at the north end of the Granville Street Bridge next to the on-ramp—it's close to everything and the traffic noise is surprisingly low. The motel includes cable TV, an elevator, and a restaurant and lounge, and it's just a couple of blocks from the False Creek waterfront and water taxis. Getting to the front door, however, can be tricky: As you approach via Howe Street, stay in the right lane—otherwise, you'll end up on the wrong side of False Creek. (Downtown)

Bed-and-Breakfasts

ENGLISH BAY INN
1968 Comox St.
Vancouver
604/683-8002
$$$

A stay in this romantic, five-bedroom establishment guarantees more than just a good night's sleep. Owner Bob

Wedgewood Hotel

The European-style Wedgewood Hotel, p. 44

Chapin has made the B&B into a place that reflects his own attitudes about old-world charm and class. From the Louis Phillipe sleigh beds, thick down comforters, private baths, terrycloth robes, and evening ports or sherries to the dining room complete with a fireplace and a wonderful old grandfather clock, the intricacies of the place are enough to make any couple fall in love all over again. The top-story, two-level suite includes a fireplace, and a garden is accessible from two of the rooms. (Downtown)

WEST END GUEST HOUSE
1362 Haro St.
Vancouver
604/681-2889
$$

This early 1900s Victorian-style home, a long-standing Vancouver landmark, is located one block from Robson Street. Its pink exterior sets it apart from the surrounding houses and offers a hint of the unusual warmth to be found inside. Each of the eight rooms is superbly furnished, comes with a private bath (and robes), and includes a bed with feather and lambskin comforters. Antiques are scattered throughout the house. For breakfast, guests can choose between a family-style feast and a private meal in the comfort of their own rooms. The legendary service of this bed-and-breakfast makes it very easy to get spoiled. (Downtown)

Hostels and Budget Accommodations

HOSTELLING INTERNATIONAL—DOWNTOWN
1114 Burnaby St.
Vancouver
604/684-4565
$
This newest of Vancouver's two hostels is bright, basic, and an incredible value in the most expensive part of town. In addition to its 16 triples and 44 quadruples, this hostel has seven double rooms—an unusually high number for a hostel—a fully equipped kitchen, and a large dining area. In all, it can handle about 240 people at any one time. A free shuttle service is offered between this hostel and the one at Jericho Beach. Every guest is provided a key card. In the lobby there's a full travel service and a place to plan activities and tours. (Downtown)

YWCA
733 Beatty St.
Vancouver
604/895-5830
$
You won't find inexpensive accommodations this clean and secure anywhere else Downtown. The YWCA has 155 rooms on 12 floors, all built with security in mind—keys are provided for parking, the front door, guest rooms, private bathrooms, and hall bathrooms. Rooms are immaculate and functional, and there's a communal kitchen, laundry room, and lounges. And the location, well—it couldn't be better: it's within a couple blocks of the Queen Elizabeth Theatre complex, BC Place Stadium, GM Place Stadium, and The Orpheum. It is also within a few blocks of the main business section of Downtown. Guests receive full use of the Y's pool, steam room, exercise rooms, and fitness classes as well. (Downtown)

UPTOWN

Hotels

GRANVILLE ISLAND HOTEL AND MARINA
1253 Johnston St.
Vancouver
604/683-7373
$$$
Tired of sailing around the world? Dock your boat outside this place and spend a couple of nights. The Granville Island Hotel and Marina is, to the say the least, unusual. Part sailor's shanty, part big-city meeting place, it's located on the eastern tip of Granville Island and comes with unmatched views of False Creek, the North Shore Mountains, and the highrise condos that climb to the sky from the old Expo '86 fairgrounds. It's also within walking distance of the Granville Island Market, a perfect place to pick up a morning snack of bread and cheese before heading out to explore the neighborhood. The hotel's 54 units include marble floors and oversized bathtubs, and some have balconies. The dockside lounge

UPTOWN/PT.GREY

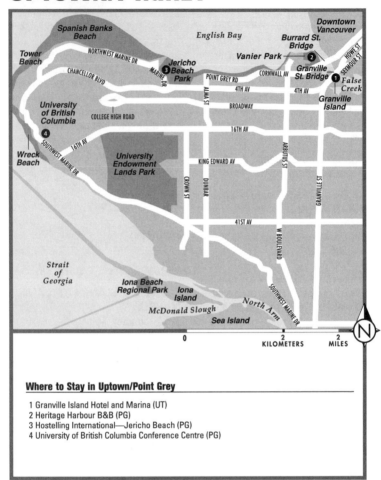

Spanish Banks Beach
English Bay
Downtown Vancouver
Burrard St. Bridge
Vanier Park
Tower Beach
NORTHWEST MARINE DR
Jericho Beach Park
MARINE DR
POINT GREY RD
CORNWALL AV
Granville St. Bridge
HOWE ST
SEYMOUR ST
False Creek
CHANCELLOR BLVD
ALMA ST
4TH AV
4TH AV
Granville Island
University of British Columbia
COLLEGE HIGH ROAD
BROADWAY
16TH AV
Wreck Beach
16TH AV
SOUTHWEST MARINE DR
University Endowment Lands Park
KING EDWARD AV
CROWN ST
DUNBAR
ARBUTUS ST
GRANVILLE ST
41ST AV
W BOULEVARD
Strait of Georgia
Iona Beach Regional Park
Iona Island
McDonald Slough
North Arm
SOUTHWEST MARINE DR
Sea Island

0   2   2
KILOMETERS   MILES

N

Where to Stay in Uptown/Point Grey

1 Granville Island Hotel and Marina (UT)
2 Heritage Harbour B&B (PG)
3 Hostelling International—Jericho Beach (PG)
4 University of British Columbia Conference Centre (PG)

is one of Vancouver's hottest gathering spots for singles. ♿ (Uptown)

POINT GREY

Bed-and-Breakfasts

HERITAGE HARBOUR B&B
1838 Ogden Ave.

Vancouver
604/736-0809
$$

This quiet waterfront home in the heart of Vanier Park is located directly across from English Bay, near the Kitsilano beaches and the Vancouver Maritime Museum. The view of False Creek, the West End skyline, and the mountains in the distance is simply spectacular. In the mornings there's a sweetness in the air from the fresh salty dew that comes in from English Bay and the smell of fresh-cooked eggs, sausage, and baked delights. Because museums and beach activities are just steps from the front door and tennis and hiking are nearby, summers can be quite busy in this neighborhood. This B&B has only two units, but many amenities are included—private baths, a balcony, full gourmet breakfast, and a guest lounge with fireplace, TV, VCR, and fridge. Smoking is not allowed, and neither pets nor credit cards are accepted. (Point Grey)

Hostels and Budget Accommodations

HOSTELLING INTERNATIONAL—JERICHO BEACH
1515 Discovery St.
Vancouver
604/224-3208
$
Every hostel in the world should be so well located. In the middle of Jericho Park just off the Point Grey strip of beaches, this hostel's only 20 minutes to Downtown by car (35 minutes by bus) and right next to Jericho Beach. The view of downtown Vancouver is stunning. Facilities are open to individuals and families but off-limits to children under five and pets. Bring your own sleeping bag or rent linens on the spot. If you're planning to be there between June and September, you'll have to post a one-night advance deposit. (Point Grey)

UNIVERSITY OF BRITISH COLUMBIA CONFERENCE CENTRE
5961 Student Union Blvd.
Vancouver

604/822-1010
$
UBC opens its resident housing to nonstudents every summer. The move to the mainstream attracts a variety of clients, including businesspeople hoping to keep their budgets in line. The location is great: nearby you'll find the UBC Museum of Anthropology, the UBC Botanical Gardens, and Wreck Beach—a nude beach at the western tip of Point Grey. Dormitory rooms with two beds (and a bath down the hall) go for about $25 a night. The University also has some studio apartments and one-bedroom apartments that sleep four with a pullout couch bed. Parking is free during the summer, and the primary residence building, the Walter Gage, is only a short bus trip from Downtown. ♿ (Point Grey)

EAST VANCOUVER

Hotels

ATRIUM INN
2889 E. Hastings St.
Vancouver
604/254-1000
$$
This hotel, located a few blocks from Exhibition Park on the east edge of Vancouver near the Burnaby border, offers a variety of rooms in a wide range of prices. While its drawback is

that it's on one of Vancouver's main thoroughfares, it's also a delightfully airy and bright property. The three-storied, glass-domed Atrium is a regular setting for concerts and, often, weddings. Complimentary shuttle service is offered to Downtown—about 20 minutes away—and the airport. Rooms include business peripherals and cable TV, and they are decorated with houseplants. The on-site Caffe Florian is a fine restaurant serving Mediterranean and West Coast cuisine, and locals gather at the Grand Garage Pub for darts and big-game sporting events. ♿ (East Vancouver)

NORTH SHORE

Hotels

PARK ROYAL HOTEL
540 Clyde Ave.
West Vancouver
604/926-5511
$$$

In a community that has few hotels, this 30-room Tudor inn, covered in ivy and painted in traditional Tudor brown and white, fits nicely into its background along the Capilano River. Rooms are small and cozy, and an outdoor patio offers pleasant views of the river and the surrounding woods. Guests often take strolls along the riverbank. Located only 15 minutes from downtown Vancouver, the hotel has a restaurant (with both indoor and outdoor dining) and a small pub. Still, it can be a bit tricky to find: Cross the Lion's Gate Bridge and take the first right onto Taylor Way, then take an immediate right at Clyde Avenue. ♿ (North Shore)

Motels

GROUSE INN
1633 Capilano Rd.
North Vancouver
604/988-7101
$$
The Grouse Inn is one of the more

10 Biggest Hotels in Greater Vancouver

1. Hyatt Regency Vancouver (645 rooms)
2. Hotel Vancouver (555 rooms)
3. Westin Bayshore (517 rooms)
4. Pan Pacific Hotel (503 rooms)
5. Waterfront Centre Hotel (489 rooms)
6. Sheraton Wall Centre Hotel (455 rooms)
7. Renaissance Vancouver Hotel Harbourside (439 rooms)
8. Delta Pacific Resort and Conference Centre (438 rooms)
9. Delta Vancouver Airport Hotel and Marina (415 rooms)
10. Sutton Place Hotel (397 rooms)

EASTERN SUBURBS

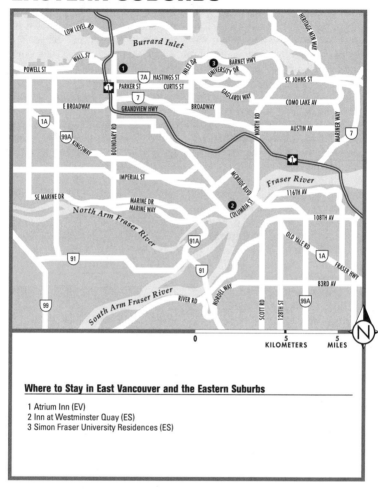

Burrard Inlet

Fraser River

North Arm Fraser River

South Arm Fraser River

0   5   5
KILOMETERS   MILES

N

Where to Stay in East Vancouver and the Eastern Suburbs

1 Atrium Inn (EV)
2 Inn at Westminster Quay (ES)
3 Simon Fraser University Residences (ES)

charming motels serving Grouse Mountain and North Shore businesses. It includes 80 spotless units (each family unit houses up to seven people), free in-room movies, a restaurant, and a heated pool. The North Shore's two major golf courses are nearby, as is the Upper Levels Highway, which leads to Whistler Resort. Because the motel is close to the Grouse Mountain Skyride and the Capilano Suspension Bridge, it caters to a lot of tourist groups. ♿ (North Shore)

Bed-and-Breakfasts

THISTLEDOWN HOUSE
3910 Capilano Rd.
North Vancouver

604/986-7173
$$

This exceptional B&B, located near Grouse Mountain and set on 100 acres of orchards and fields, includes five rooms with individual themes. The Under the Apple Tree room has a private patio and a fireplace in a sunken sitting area; Mulberry Peak has a view of the gardens and a private balcony; Sweet Tibby's features a giant sleigh bed; Memories has traditional European charm; and The Snuggery has Persian carpets and stained glass. In the afternoon guests can enjoy European pastries, chocolates, fresh fruit desserts, teas, and coffee by the fire. One of the ThistleDown's owners operated a family hotel in Switzerland; the other has been in the hospitality industry for years, so you can expect sophistication and attention to detail. & (North Shore)

Campgrounds and RV Parks

CAPILANO RV PARK
295 Tomahawk Ave.

North Vancouver
604/987-4722
$

In most cities, you can expect any RV parks to be located well outside city limits. That's why this one is so special. The Capilano RV Park, set on the Capilano River across the water from Stanley Park, is only 10 minutes from downtown Vancouver. It offers excellent views, caters to a lot of young families, and has a pool, playground, and Jacuzzi. Both tenting and full-hookup facilities are available. Reservations are required for all vehicles in summer. Tent campers are first-come, first-served. Daily fee: $22–$32. (North Shore)

EASTERN SUBURBS

Hotels

INN AT WESTMINSTER QUAY
900 Quayside Dr.
New Westminster
604/520-1776
$$$

ThistleDown House, located near Grouse Mountain

ThistleDown House

NORTH SHORE

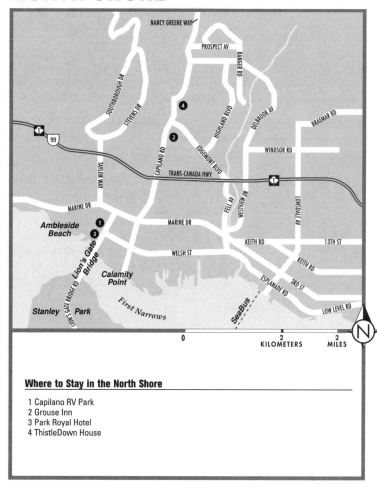

Where to Stay in the North Shore

1 Capilano RV Park
2 Grouse Inn
3 Park Royal Hotel
4 ThistleDown House

The Inn at Westminster Quay, located in central New Westminster, is only a few feet from the Westminster Quay Market, one of greater Vancouver's most diverse public markets. The rooms are decorated in soft earth tones and include such amenities as individually controlled air-conditioning, a refreshment center, a coffee maker and Starbucks coffee, and in-room movies and Nintendo. A newspaper is delivered every morning, and you'll find chocolates by your bed every night. The inn has nonsmoking floors, executive suites, honeymoon suites with Jacuzzis, and hospitality rooms for receptions. All 126 rooms in this dramatic facility face the Fraser River, and a wonderful boardwalk runs along the front of the hotel and

Richmond plans to open nine new hotels (with 2,400 rooms) between 1998 and 2000. A total of 3,300 new rooms will be available in downtown Vancouver by the year 2003.

past condos, small restaurants, and even an old Russian submarine that's open for tours. The inn is near the SkyTrain entrance, which means you can be in downtown Vancouver in just 20 minutes. A wide range of discounts and weekend rates makes this an attractive alternative to downtown hotels. & (Eastern Suburbs)

Hostels and Budget Accommodations

SIMON FRASER UNIVERSITY RESIDENCES
McTaggart-Cowan Hall, Room 212
Burnaby
604/291-4503
$
Like UBC (see above), Simon Fraser University opens its mountaintop residences to the public from May to August. Located atop Burnaby Mountain, the university was hailed as an architectural marvel when it was constructed in the 1960s. No room-catering services are offered, but the campus cafeteria is open and provides a chance to mingle with summer students. Guests have access to kitchen facilities, laundry rooms, a TV lounge, and plenty of parking. The one disadvantage is that it's 12 miles east of Downtown. The big advantage is that it's cool in summer and offers spectacular views of the mountains. & (Eastern Suburbs)

SOUTHERN SUBURBS

Hotels

BEST WESTERN ABERCORN INN
9260 Bridgeport Rd.
Richmond
604/270-7576
$$
You'd hardly expect to see a country-style British inn this close to the airport, but that's exactly what The Abercorn is. This Lower Mainland landmark stands out even amidst its high-rise neighbors. As you walk into the lobby, you're greeted by an open sitting area, beamed ceilings, a fireplace, and plenty of deep-cushioned chairs and couches. All 100 units are decorated in dark Tudor browns and are provided with complimentary coffee and tea. Located next to the Oak Street Bridge, this inn provides easy access to the heart of Downtown and, like most hotels in the area, offers complimentary shuttle service to the airport. & (Southern Suburbs)

DELTA PACIFIC RESORT AND CONFERENCE CENTRE
10251 Edwards Dr.
Richmond
604/278-9611
$$
The Delta Pacific is as close as any accommodation in the Vancouver area comes to a theme-park hotel. Located just south of the Oak Street

Bridge and east of Highway 99, this is a facility that pays special attention to families with children. Kids under 18 stay free in their parents' room; children eight and under eat free in the restaurants. This high-rise also has tennis courts, indoor and outdoor swimming pools, a 225-foot waterslide, a children's center, squash courts, and in-room Nintendo, in addition to a health club, restaurants, and lounges. Among the 438 units are quite a few nonsmoking rooms. ♿ (Southern Suburbs)

DELTA VANCOUVER AIRPORT HOTEL AND MARINA
3500 Cessna Dr.
Richmond
604/278-1241
$$$

Not only is this the closest major hotel to Vancouver International Airport, it's also on the middle arm of the Fraser River. So if you want to be close to the airport (this is a good place for a layover), you can still be in a waterfront environment, with the marina right at your doorstep. You can ride a bike or walk along the top of the dike that keeps the Fraser River from drowning Richmond. A bus will take you to the nearby Delta Pacific Resort where you can play indoor tennis under the bubble. Kids under six eat free in the hotel's dining rooms. ♿ (Southern Suburbs)

RADISSON PRESIDENT HOTEL AND SUITES
8181 Cambie Rd.
Richmond
604/276-8181
$$$$

The real charm of this luxurious 184-room hotel is in its location—the heart of the new Richmond Chinatown. Next to it is a Buddhist temple

and one of the most fabulous Chinese grocery stores this side of Shanghai. Around the corner is a Japanese food center, and nearby is an Asian mall. The hotel is 25 minutes from downtown Vancouver and just 10 blocks from the airport. Rooms are tastefully understated rather than opulent but very comfortable. The hotel restaurant, Gustos Eurobistro, specializes in Continental-fusion cuisine. Small pets are allowed in this almost-new four-diamond property. ♿ (Southern Suburbs)

STEVESTON HOTEL
12111 Third Ave.
Richmond
604/277-9511
$

This 25-room hotel—the only accommodation in this part of Richmond—has character. The Steveston Hotel was established in 1898, and the southern part of the present hotel was home to the Duke of Connaught's troops, who camped here during July 1900 to break up the

The kid-friendly Delta Pacific Resort and Conference Centre

Robert Plowman

SOUTHERN SUBURBS

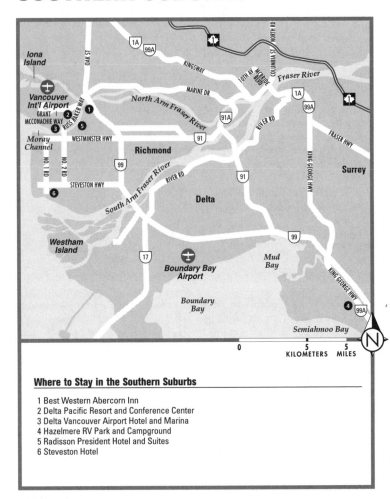

Where to Stay in the Southern Suburbs

1 Best Western Abercorn Inn
2 Delta Pacific Resort and Conference Center
3 Delta Vancouver Airport Hotel and Marina
4 Hazelmere RV Park and Campground
5 Radisson President Hotel and Suites
6 Steveston Hotel

unpopular fishing strike of that year. It was then called the "Sockeye Hotel" and was one of many hotels that flourished in Steveston at the turn of the last century, catering mostly to fishermen. It is the only hotel, however, to survive the fires that have ravaged the town during the last 100 years. The north wing was added in the 1950s, and in 1986 the hotel underwent extensive renovations.

The Steveston Hotel is located about 20 minutes from the airport, in the heart of historic Steveston, which is to Vancouver what Sausalito is to San Francisco, but with a little more of a rough edge. The hotel has a beer and wine store, a pub, and a restaurant. The pub is popular among the lo-

Many of the region's provincial parks and recreation areas have RV and tent sites during the summer season. For information contact Tourism British Columbia at 800/663-6000 and ask for their Parks Guide.

cals, mainly working-class fishermen in search of a good time. The selection of rooms ranges from basic accommodation (one or two beds, television, no phone, private or shared bath, and daily maid service) to luxurious (queen-size bed, television, phone, daily maid service, private bath, kitchen unit, in-room Jacuzzi, and a complimentary bottle of sparkling wine). (Southern Suburbs)

Campgrounds and RV Parks

HAZELMERE RV PARK AND CAMPGROUND
11843 Eighth Ave.
Surrey
604/538-1167

$
If you're a golfer, this is the place for you. Two of the areas finest golf courses—Hazelmere and Peace Portal—are right next door. The Campbell River runs through this tranquil, parklike setting, and the campground includes a laundry room, showers, a recreation room, and a covered picnic area. A store is on site, and cable hookups are available. Beaches and shopping are nearby. You can take your pick of the 150 sites and choose to pay by the day, the week, or the month. Daily, $18–$24; weekly, $108–$144; monthly (RVs only), $335. (Southern Suburbs)

4

WHERE TO EAT

Vancouver's restaurants are more than places to eat; they're cultural experiences. What are you in the mood for? Sushi? Wontons? Italian sausage? Or how about grilled salmon or venison? A plate of fiddleheads? You name it, Vancouver's got it. Apart from the wonders of Chinatown, the city offers a wealth of culinary West Broadway—past Granville and on the way to UBC—has numerous Greek restaurants, Commercial Drive has more Italian restaurants than anywhere else in the city, and Robson has multicultural restaurants on every block. Take a stroll down any one of these streets and you'll find yourself faced with an array of tantalizing choices.

Since Vancouver is the melting pot of Canada, many of its cuisines have begun to fuse. With the vast increase in Asian immigration, markets and restaurants are now regularly filled with once-exotic foods, and European and Asian culinary traditions have started to integrate. The "West Coast cuisine" takes France's sophistication and Asia's inventive spirit and applies them to Canada's own indigenous foodstuff (venison, moose, salmon, and fiddleheads), with delicious results.

This chapter begins with a list of restaurants organized by cuisine type. Restaurants names are followed by zone abbreviations (see page v) and the page numbers where you can find descriptions. The descriptions are organized alphabetically within each zone. The dollar symbols indicate the price of a typical entrée.

Price rating symbols: (Canadian dollars)
$ $10 and under
$$ $11 to $19
$$$ $20 and up

RESTAURANTS BY CUISINE TYPE

Burgers
Earl's (UV, NS, SS), p. 73
Griffins (DV), p. 65
Hamburger Mary's (DV), p. 65
Milestone's (PG), p. 80
The Red Onion (PG), p. 82
Sophie's Cosmic Cafe (PG), p. 83
Steamworks Brewing (DV), p. 71
White Spot (EV, NS, ES, SS), p. 87

"Character"
Benny's Bagels (PG), p. 79
S'il Vous Plait (DV), p. 71
The Tomahawk (NS), p. 88
Uncle Herbert's Fish & Chip Shop (SS), p. 91

Chinese
Floata Seafood Restaurant (DV), p. 65
Imperial Chinese Seafood Restaurant (DV), p. 67
Kirin Mandarin (UV), p. 75
The Pink Pearl (DV), p. 70
Shanghai Chinese Bistro (DV), p. 71
Sun Sui Wah Seafood Restaurant (EV), p. 85
Top Gun Chinese Seafood Restaurant (SS), p. 91

Fine Dining
Bishops (PG), p. 79
Chartwell (DV), p. 63
Diva at the Met (DV), p. 64
The Five Sails (DV), p. 65
Star Anise (UV), p. 77
Teahouse at Ferguson Point (DV), p. 72
William Tell (DV), p. 72

First Nations
Liliget Feast House (DV), p. 69

French
Café de Paris (DV), p. 63
Le Crocodile (DV), p. 68

Le Gavroche (DV), p. 69
Lumière (PG), p. 80

Greek
Le Grec (EV), p. 84
Meli Taverna (PG), p. 80
Ouzerie (PG), p. 81
Stepho's Souvlakia (DV), p. 72
Vassilis Taverna (PG), p. 83

Italian
Bacchus Ristorante (DV), p. 61
Bianco Nero (DV), p. 61
Il Giardino di Umberto (DV), p. 67
Primavera Ristorante (SS), p. 91
Quattro on Fourth (PG), p. 81
Settebello (DV), p. 70
Sortino's Restaurante (EV), p. 85

Japanese
Aki (EV), p. 83
Chiyoda (DV), p. 64
Daimasu (UV, ES, SS), p. 75
Ichibankan (DV), p. 67
Kamei Royale (DV), p. 67
Misaki (DV), p. 70
Mito (UV), p. 76
Shijo (PG), p. 82
Shiro (UV), p. 77
Tojo's (UV), p. 77

Pizza
Boston Pizza (UV, NS, ES, SS), p. 73
The Flying Wedge (DV ,PG, UV), p. 65
Minerva Pizza and Steak House (PG), p. 81
Yaletown Brewing (DV), p. 73

Mediterranean
El Patio Mediterranean Restaurant (DV), p. 64
Las Tapas (DV), p. 68

Mexican/Southwestern
Las Margaritas Restaurante y Cantina (PG), p. 79
Mescalero (DV), p. 69
Primo's (UV), p. 76

Tio Pepe's Restaurante Mexicano
(EV), p. 85

Seafood
Amorous Oyster (UV), p. 73
Aqua Riva (DV), p. 61
Beach House (NS), p. 87
Bridges (UV), p. 73
The Cannery (EV), p. 83
Cardero's (DV), p. 63
The Creek (UV), p. 75
The Fish House (DV), p. 64
Horizons on Burnaby Mountain (ES),
p. 89
Monk McQueen's (UV), p. 76
The Only Seafood Cafe (DV), p. 70
The Salmon House on the Hill (NS),
p. 88
Steveston Seafood House (SS), p. 91

Southeast Asian
Annapurna (PG), p. 77
Phnom Penh (DV), p. 70
Sami's (UV), p. 76
Sawasdee (EV), p. 85

Steak and Ribs
Anderson's (DV), p. 60
Giraffe (SS), p. 89

Vegetarian

Capers (NS), p. 87
Isadora's (UV), p. 75
Naam (PG), p. 81
Tomato Fresh Food Cafe (EV), p. 86

Special
Harbor Ferries (DV), p. 66
Pacific Starlight Dinner Train (NS),
p. 88

DOWNTOWN

ANDERSON'S
1661 Granville St.
Vancouver
604/684-3777
$$
Located directly under the Granville
Street Bridge, which crosses False
Creek from Granville Island, Ander-
son's offers prime viewing of boats
sailing out of False Creek. The clien-
tele is a mix of in-the-know business
types and locals who come for the
view. The menu consists of a mix of
standard meat fare and fresh seafood
items, all of which are presented with
care. But frankly, you'll be spending
more time looking out the glass-
walled waterfront restaurant than at

"Character" Restaurants

*We don't call them greasy spoons, diners, or anything else that
might be associated with the onset of painful bouts of gas. No, we
call them "character" restaurants. And yes, we're proud of them.
"Character" restaurants might come without a pedigree, but they
do include mama-style stick-to-the-ribs cookin'. The "character"
restaurants included in this chapter are really one-of-a-kind es-
tablishments—places you'd go to for the style as much as the food.*

Always try to make a reservation. If a restaurant won't take reservations, ask for your name to be put on the wait list.

your plate. Boats float by, and at night, the lights from the island flicker like fireflies. Lunch Mon–Fri, dinner Mon–Sat. & (Downtown)

AQUA RIVA
200 Granville St.
Vancouver
604/683-5599
$$
Until recently Vancouver did not have a downtown on-the-water restaurant worth mentioning. Then along came this place, located on the ground floor of the high-rise tower that houses both of Vancouver's daily newspapers and right across the street from the Canadian Pacific Waterfront Hotel. The cuisine is a cross between northern Italian and Pacific Northwest, including such items as wood-fired pizza with house-smoked duck, shiitake mushrooms, bocconcini; and cilantro oil, and a cioppino of local seafood. If you'd prefer something more familiar, the menu also includes many standard meat and fish items. Enter the tower via the plaza for a great view of the mountains. Lunch and dinner Mon–Sat. & (Downtown)

BACCHUS RISTORANTE
Wedgewood Hotel
845 Hornby St.
Vancouver
604/689-7777
$$$
If you're here for lunch, chances are you'll hear a lot of lawyer-speak—the

restaurant is right across the street from the courthouse complex, and it's a favorite with the local barristers. The flavor of the place is "luxury": from the moment you enter, you're surrounded by a sense of opulence. The cuisine is northern Italian with an emphasis on British Columbian products, such as salmon. The restaurant combines a lounge and café with a high dining room. Try afternoon tea in front of the fireplace, especially on a rainy winter's day. The evening menu changes often, but the tuna carpaccio is a constant. Behind a set of elegant doors is a cigar room stocked with fine Cuban cigars. Breakfast, lunch, and dinner daily. & (Downtown)

BIANCO NERO
475 W. Georgia St.
Vancouver
604/682-6376
$$
If you're looking for a place within a block of the Queen Elizabeth Theatre, the library square, and the Ford Centre for the Performing Arts, try this one. The problem is you may not want to leave. The stark black and white decor with brushed steel accents and the dramatic lighting will immediately overpower you with its theatricality. The surroundings are indicative of the style of the food presentation: high visual appeal with substance. It seems that there's every kind of Italian dish on the menu, but you won't go wrong with the tortellini alla nonna (sole in

DOWNTOWN VANCOUVER

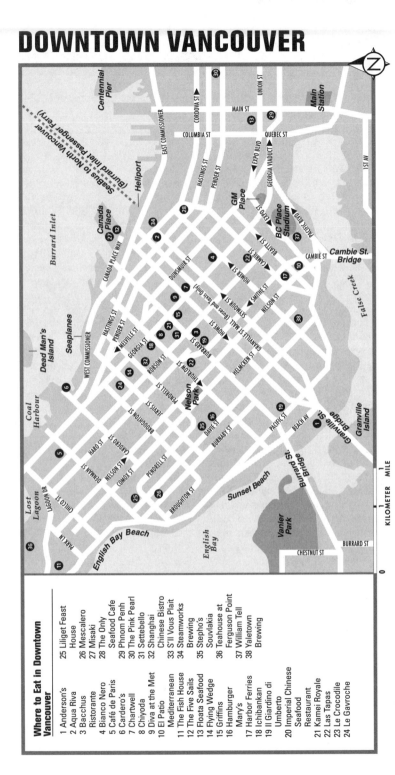

Where to Eat in Downtown Vancouver

1 Anderson's
2 Aqua Riva
3 Bacchus Ristorante
4 Bianco Nero
5 Café de Paris
6 Cardero's
7 Chartwell
8 Chiyoda
9 Diva at the Met
10 El Patio Mediterranean
11 The Fish House
12 The Five Sails
13 Floata Seafood
14 Flying Wedge
15 Griffins
16 Hamburger Mary's
17 Harbor Ferries
18 Ichibankan
19 Il Giardino di Umberto
20 Imperial Chinese Seafood Restaurant
21 Kamei Royale
22 Las Tapas
23 Le Crocodile
24 Le Gavroche
25 Liliget Feast House
26 Mescalero
27 Misaki
28 The Only Seafood Cafe
29 Phnom Penh
30 The Pink Pearl
31 Settebello
32 Shanghai Chinese Bistro
33 S'il Vous Plait
34 Steamworks Brewing
35 Stepho's Souvlakia
36 Teahouse at Ferguson Point
37 William Tell
38 Yaletown Brewing

aquavit). The wine bar is exceptional. Lunch Mon–Fri, dinner Mon–Sat. ♿ (Downtown)

CAFÉ DE PARIS
751 Denman St.
Vancouver
604/687-1418
$$

This comfortable bistro is a West End favorite with a long list of regulars. Little wonder. The atmosphere—set by the lace curtains on the windows and wooden chairs—is decidedly cozy and somewhat informal; the waiters are dressed in black pants, white shirts, and long aprons; and the music is by Edith Piaf. In fact, the Café de Paris is about the closest thing you'll find in this town to a Left Bank bistro. The food is a combination of North American (New York steak) and French (orange-glazed salmon slices perfumed with tarragon). Lunch Mon–Fri, dinner daily. ♿ (Downtown)

CARDERO'S
1583 Coal Harbour Quay
Vancouver
604/669-7666
$$

This casual bar and dining room is known for its seafood and steaks. Its position on the downtown waterfront, right next to the Westin Bayshore inn, allows for spectacular views of the Coal Harbour marina and the mountains. If the patio is open, it's one of the city's prime porches for eating, drinking, and viewing. The menu consists primarily of seafood and inventive meat entrées. The reasonably priced grilled fish is succulent, and the braised lamb shank is a bargain. The value-oriented wine list is basic but well chosen. Lunch and dinner daily. ♿ (Downtown)

CHARTWELL
Four Seasons Hotel
791 W. Georgia St.
Vancouver
604/689-9333
$$$

The Chartwell is THE downtown dining place. Despite its look and feel of a corporate power-meal headquarters (high-backed leather chairs, ex-

Chartwell at the Four Seasons Hotel

Four Seasons

pensive china), it is surprisingly comfortable once you settle in, and the warm, attentive service is more typical of that found at an elegant neighborhood restaurant. The Continental cuisine is supplemented by Asian dishes such as Szechwan roasted pork tenderloin with cashew plum sauce. Breakfast and dinner daily, lunch Sun–Fri. (Downtown)

CHIYODA
200-1050 Alberni St.
Vancouver
604/688-5050
$$
Of all the Japanese restaurants in town, this is the one many claim to be the closest to a typical place in Japan. If you like to see your food cooked in front of you, then you'll love this place. The bar is designed in a series of concentric circles. A wood counter displays the day's selections. Order from a relatively simple menu of snapper, squid, scallops, and eggplant, then watch a chef prepare your meal. When it's ready, he'll pass you the finished item across the bar on the end of a long wooden paddle. It's a popular lunch spot for downtown businesspeople and a favorite of Japanese tourists in the evening. Lunch and dinner daily. & (Downtown)

DIVA AT THE MET
645 Howe St.
Vancouver
604/602-7788
$$$
Many of Vancouver's best restaurants are attached to a hotel, and this one, connected to The Metropolitan, is no exception. It's an airy space, with a decidedly businesslike atmosphere during lunch. Brunch includes a delicious Alaska black cod hash

topped with poached eggs, and the rack of lamb is a house specialty. For a starter, try the chilled tomato martini. Wrap things up with a delicious slice of Stilton cheesecake. Lunch and dinner daily. & (Downtown)

EL PATIO MEDITERRANEAN RESTAURANT
891 Cambie St.
Vancouver
604/681-9149
$$
A couple of blocks away from the main entertainment area of Downtown, this comfortable two-level place is designed for group eating. Order a selection of small items and then reach over to the middle of the table and share. Try the patatas la bodega (potatoes served with a mild, spicy sauce)—they're excellent. When it rains, the interior seems sunny; on hot days, the rich, Mediterranean colors tend to cool things down. Both the downstairs and upstairs rooms are cozy, and the staff is exceptionally friendly. Lunch Mon–Fri, dinner Mon–Sat. & (Downtown)

THE FISH HOUSE
2099 Beach Ave.
Vancouver
604/681-7275
$$
The Fish House is located in an old house on the edge of Stanley Park, next to the tennis courts, a croquet lawn, and a pitch-and-putt golf course. From the dining room you'll have views of English Bay or the spectacular gardens and forests of Stanley Park. The menu, mainly seafood, features such unusual items as poached sockeye salmon on a potato pancake with crème fraiche and, the Pacific Northwest Seafood Bowl—fresh clams, mussels, scal-

lops, tiger prawn, and other fresh fish in a tomato-saffron broth on creamy polenta. There's also an oyster bar. The wide range of white wines and selection from local microbreweries will make you want to linger. Lunch and dinner daily. ♿ (Downtown)

THE FIVE SAILS
999 Canada Pl.
Vancouver
604/662-8111
$$$

The Five Sails, located in the Pan Pacific Hotel, serves up a perfect fusion of European elegance and robust Asian flavors. On top of that, it also offers impeccable service and a splendid view of Coal Harbour and the North Shore Mountains. The smoked Alaska black cod chowder is delectable, as is the seared scallop in wasabi sauce. The clientele is primarily traveling businesspeople, but that doesn't prevent locals from eating here on special occasions. Dinner daily. ♿ (Downtown)

FLOATA SEAFOOD RESTAURANT
400-180 Keefer St.
Vancouver
604/602-0368
$$

This 1,000-seater, Vancouver's largest restaurant, is surprisingly cozy for its size. Floor-to-ceiling partitions divide the space into a number of smaller rooms. The menu is similar to that at other Cantonese seafood restaurants (fresh ingredients and plenty of spice) and to the restaurant's sister operation at Parker Place (4380 No. 3 Rd., Richmond, 604/270-8889). Be sure to try the lobster in cream sauce or the braised mushrooms with mustard greens. Lunch and dinner daily. (Downtown)

THE FLYING WEDGE
244-1055 W. Georgia St.
Vancouver
604/681-1233
$

The Flying Wedge does not serve alcohol, and they don't take credit cards or checks either. All they do here is make marvelous pizza. This franchise, with outlets at the airport, in the library square, and in Point Grey, has a loyal following. Name the ingredient and it's a potential topping. Deep Purple is an old standby (marinated eggplant and spicy chicken) for those who want adventure without getting too far from the basics. The crust is thin, the decor, bright. Lunch and dinner daily. ♿ (Downtown)

GRIFFINS
Hotel Vancouver
900 W. Georgia St.
Vancouver
604/662-1900
$$

The upscale Hotel Vancouver doesn't advertise the fact that it has one of the best burgers in the downtown area. You have a choice for lunch— off the menu or the buffet. If you order the special burger off the menu, you won't be disappointed—even though it's pricier than your typical burger. In addition to burgers, you'll find a wide range of West Coast choices. Griffins is usually hopping, especially at lunch because it's a favorite of lawyers who pop in from the nearby courthouse complex. Lunch and dinner daily. ♿ (Downtown)

HAMBURGER MARY'S
1202 Davie St.
Vancouver
604/687-1293
$

The mother of all burger joints, Mary's

Japanese Flair

Whether you're a sushi junkie or you prefer your dinner grilled and coated in a savory teriyaki sauce, you won't have any problem finding just the right Japanese restaurant for your palate. Vancouver is filled with sushi bars, soba (noodle) houses, and tempura dens. In fact, there are now upwards of 80 Japanese restaurants in the Greater Vancouver area.

If you've never tried Japanese cuisine before, you've come to the right place—unless, of course, your next stop is Tokyo! Dining in a Japanese restaurant in Vancouver is more than just going out for fish, chicken, and rice. About 900 years of art, history, and culture are all presented as an inseparable part of your meal. The traditional presentation begins as soon as you enter the front door and are greeted with a welcome (sometimes boisterous, sometimes subtle) and a bow. You'll be offered a hot towel to cleanse your hands as soon as you're seated, and service is almost always efficient, friendly, and attentive.

And then there's the food. How a meal looks is equally as important as how it tastes, and the intricate methods of cutting, arranging, and serving are ceremonially attended to. Ordinary white rice, for example, served in a black lacquer bowl, is an artistic treat. Raw fish (sashimi) presented in colorful surroundings and carefully placed on the tray—as a bouquet of flowers on a table—is truly an art form.

is the place to go after everything else has closed. People come here for the big burgers 22 hours a day. The really hungry order the double-sized Banquet Burger with the Works if they can't decide which of the many toppings to use. The place used to be grungier, and regulars worried that things would deteriorate when Mary's went upscale with a bloc-glass and chrome decor. But it's still a great place. The chips with gravy are real artery pluggers. Vegetarian meals are available, too. Breakfast, lunch, dinner, and late-night snacks. ♿ (Downtown)

HARBOR FERRIES
North Foot of Denman St.
Vancouver
604/687-9558
$$$
What a wonderful way to spend an evening in Vancouver. Board the

MPV *Constitution* paddle wheeler and take a pleasant journey back in time. The Sunset Dinner Cruise combines a large dinner with a three-and-a-half-hour sightseeing cruise of the harbor. The cruise, which lasts from 6:30 to 10, includes an onboard buffet with baron of beef, poached salmon, salads, a variety of veggies, and a wide selection of desserts. Evenings May–Oct. ♿ (Downtown)

ICHIBANKAN
770 Thurlow St.
Vancouver
604/682-3894
$

If you like your food served on a conveyor belt, this is the place for you. Sit around the long sushi bar and watch as the chefs go to work. A variety of sushi items are prepared, placed on color-coded dishes, then set on a moving conveyor belt. As the food rounds the bar, diners just snatch whatever catches their fancy. A waitress collects your dishes before they get too high and keeps a running tally of what you've eaten. Be careful about the colors. You might be surprised when you get the bill and realize you should have had the green instead of the black. It may resemble an assembly line, but it's really a good time. Lunch and dinner daily. (Downtown)

IL GIARDINO DI UMBERTO
1382 Hornby St.
Vancouver
604/669-2422
$$$

Owner Umberto Menghi was born in Tuscany in 1946 and came to Vancouver in the late 1960s. He opened his first restaurant, Umberto's, in 1973, and has since opened a number of other eateries—of which Il Giardino di Umberto is one—in Vancouver and Whistler. If Vancouver has a consistently "in" place where people go to see and be seen, this is it. The ambiance at Il Giardino di Umberto is custom-made for talking and looking. Ask for the wonderful table above the intimate dining area just to the right of the entrance. High above the main floor, it's in a small cove that can't be equaled for romantic intimacy anywhere in the city. The menu is Tuscan and emphasizes pasta and game, although farm-raised pheasant is a specialty. The veal, with a melange of lightly grilled wild mushrooms, is also delicious. Lunch Mon–Fri, dinner Mon–Sat. ♿ (Downtown)

IMPERIAL CHINESE SEAFOOD RESTAURANT
355 Burrard St.
Vancouver
604/688-8191
$$

This decidedly upscale Chinese restaurant, perhaps the grandest dining room in town, is located in the historic Marine Building at the north end of Burrard Street, in the middle of hotel row. Most opulent is the grand staircase that looks like it came out of the nineteenth century and the two-story windows that tower over the dining room, allowing fantastic views of Burrard Inlet and the North Shore Mountains. Classical music and Dom Perignon accent the menu of lobster, pan-fried scallops, pan-smoked black cod, and more. In all, there are nearly 100 items on the menu, each fetching $15 and up. Lunch and dinner daily. (Downtown)

KAMEI ROYALE
1030 W. Georgia St.
Vancouver
604/687-8588

Vancouver's Coffee and Tea Shops

"The whole town is on a caffeine jag," said Bette Midler during a Vancouver performance. And she was right. Everywhere you go you'll find coffee bars and stores devoted only to coffee and tea. Bean Bros., Murchies, Starbucks outlets—we've got them all. Here's a brief lesson in coffee terminology.

Espresso: A two-ounce shot of strong, dark coffee
Cappuccino: A shot of espresso mixed with foamed milk
Caffe Mocha: Espresso with cocoa and steamed milk
Caffe Americano: Espresso diluted with hot water
Caffe Latte: One-third espresso mixed with two-thirds steamed milk

$$

This is where you'd go with a special guest, a great client, or even by yourself for a wonderful time. Located on the second floor of the Burrard Building (West Georgia and Burrard Sts.), the Kamei Royale employs a fulltime staff of about 55. The decor is bright, modern, and traditional, and individual privacy is maintained even with an open-air layout. The private tatami rooms are exquisite examples of mixed traditional and modern interior design. Kamei Royale has seven sushi chefs, so you can expect a large and efficient staff, with waitresses in traditional kimonos and food that's as fresh as the latest salmon run. Lunch and dinner daily. ♿ (Downtown)

LAS TAPAS
760 Cambie St.
Vancouver
604/669-1624

$

This restaurant, located right across from the CBC Building, is a gathering place for many of Vancouver's familiar television personalities, producers, and directors. The first tapas bar in Vancouver, it retains its original appeal and its intensive Spanish character. The grilled portobello mushrooms are a must—they're cooked in a butter sauce with sherry. This is the perfect place to go after a performance at the Queen Elizabeth Theatre complex. Lunch Mon–Fri, dinner daily. ♿ (Downtown)

LE CROCODILE
100-909 Burrard St.
Vancouver
604/669-4298
$$$

For years this has been the French restaurant of choice among critics and aficionados. You won't find anything that's out of place here—neither on the table, nor on your plate. French is French, right? Well, not quite. The food is a delightful combination of Franco-German (Alsatian) cuisine. The lobster bisque is laced with cognac; the warm goat cheese with balsamic vinegar is encrusted with sesame seeds. A favorite is Barbarie duck, served with a dark citrus sauce. A wide range of good-value wines is offered. Lunch Mon–Fri, dinner Mon–Sat. க் (Downtown)

LE GAVROCHE
1616 Alberni St.
Vancouver
604/685-3924
$$$

This is, bar none, the most romantic French restaurant in the city. Why? Well, first of all, consider the ambiance: Picture a cool rainy night with you and your significant other sitting in a discreet upstairs room beside a cozy fireplace, the harbor seeming to rest just outside the window. Then there's the gracious service, the incredible wine cellar, and the host, Manual Ferreira. This place has been in business for 20 years, and some of the original staff members are still here. The menu consists of lighter French fare, with the accent on delicate herb flavors rather than on heavy sauces. You'll also find an emphasis on seafood. For dessert be sure to try the almond and hazelnut meringue with an almond crème anglaise. Lunch Mon–Fri, dinner Mon–Sat. (Downtown)

LILIGET FEAST HOUSE
1724 Davie St.
Vancouver
604/681-7044
$$

If you're looking for a culinary experience that you're likely never to have again, head to the West End and this Native restaurant—the only one in Vancouver. Walk down the stairs and enter a world you won't find anywhere else. Dining takes place in a simulated longhouse of poles and beams, graveled walkways, and sunken tables. Haida folk songs accompany oolichan, bannock bread, caribou, salmon cheeks, and whipped soapberries. First designed by architect Arthur Erickson in the early 1970s, the restaurant was originally known as the Muckamuck. Later, it became the Quilicum. Still later, the current owner, Dolly Watts, a Native caterer reopened it as Liliget. Try the Liliget Platter for Two, a heaping feast of grilled salmon, buffalo smokies (buffalo sausage), rabbit, halibut, and smoked ooligans. You might also try the Hagul Jam Soup, a combination broth of salmon and vegetables. Dinner daily. (Downtown)

MESCALERO
1215 Bidwell St.
Vancouver
604/669-4155
$

This West End eatery, just off Davie Street, caters mostly to a young, local crowd that sometimes looks as though they're taking time out from their Internet surfing. The Southwestern menu is matched by a rustic interior that could well have come right out of an Italian Western set. Specialties like the tequila-marinated roasted duck offset a tapas menu that includes halibut and crab cakes with a red-chili-and-rough-mustard aioli, and a lamb-and-chorizo tamale with papaya and black-bean salsa. They also have a good beer and wine list. Lunch and dinner daily, brunch Sun. க் (Downtown)

MISAKI
300-999 Canada Pl.
Vancouver
604/891-2893
$$$

Misaki is a high-end restaurant where Japanese businesspeople are wined and dined by locals trying to impress new or potential clients. In the Pan Pacific Hotel, on the level just above the lobby, it has a menu that manages to please both traditional and experimental palates. You'll find traditional items like udon, chawan mushi, and sushi, but you'll also see a West Coast influence in dishes like the Dungeness crab–stuffed tofu, barbecued black cod, and barbecued salmon wrapped around asparagus and served with prawns. Lunch and dinner daily. & (Downtown)

THE ONLY SEAFOOD CAFE
20 E. Hastings St.
Vancouver
604/681-6546
$

The oldest restaurant in Vancouver, the Only Seafood Cafe dates from 1912, when loggers came to town to eat and booze. This unpretentious eatery is situated in the heart of downtown's pawnshop and cheap-taverns territory. With two booths and a counter, the decor is decidedly diner. When you sink your teeth into the perfectly cooked fish and chips, you'll understand why this place is always busy. No alcohol, credit cards, or checks. Lunch and dinner Mon–Sat. & (Downtown)

PHNOM PENH
244 E. Georgia St.
Vancouver
604/682-5777
$

This place was once just for locals.

Then the blasted *New York Times* declared it one of the city's best restaurants. Now it's constantly busy, and the menu has diversified from its Cambodian roots to include Chinese and Vietnamese, in keeping with Vancouver's ethnic diversity. The result is a cuisine tempered by a West Coast culinary sensibility—especially in the toning down of spices. The sautéed baby shrimp in prawn roe and slivers of salted pork over hot steamed rice cakes is a masterpiece. The garlic-chili squid and the oyster omelet are unique items. Lunch and dinner Wed–Mon. & (Downtown)

THE PINK PEARL
1132 E. Hastings St.
Vancouver
604/253-4316
$$

You had better arrive early on weekends, because the Chinatown locals know a good thing when they taste it. The Pink Pearl is always packed. The reason? It serves what is arguably the finest dim sum in the city. The most spectacular dish on the regular Cantonese menu is crab sautéed with rock salt and chilies. When you're done eating, the waiter grabs the corners of the top plastic tablecloth sheet, gathers everything, including the dishes, and scoops up any evidence of your meal. Since the restaurant is located on the far edge of Chinatown, you'll have to take a cab or a bus from the downtown core. Breakfast, lunch, and dinner daily. & (Downtown)

SETTEBELLO
1131 Robson St.
Vancouver
604/681-7377
$$

This is another of the establishments

in Vancouver owned by Tuscan Umberto Menghi. A great place to come in warm weather, Settebello has a second-floor dining patio that's perfect for watching people strolling down Robson Street. You'll find a wide selection of Italian cuisine, including pizza. The service reflects the easygoing and friendly ambiance, which, consequently, attracts a fairly young crowd. The pastas are first-rate, including tortellini and fettuccini served in a spicy tomato sauce. Lunch and dinner daily. ᴆ (Downtown)

SHANGHAI CHINESE BISTRO
1128 Alberni St.
Vancouver
604/683-8222
$

A meal is not the only thing you'll get at this place. You'll also get quite a show: sometime around 7:30 each evening, the noodle chef enters the L-shaped dining room with a lump of dough and proceeds to string it out into long noodle strands. The food here embraces virtually all Chinese cuisine—Mandarin, Szechwan, Can-

Settebello's dining room

Settebello

tonese, and Shanghai. Try the finger-lickin'-good salt-and-chili crab. Dim sum, served from midnight to three in the morning, provides a refreshing alternative to the pizzas and stale pastries that are more typically available late-night in the downtown area. And it would be tough to find a cheerier collection of waiters. Lunch, dinner, and midnight snacks daily. (Downtown)

S'IL VOUS PLAIT
500 Robson St.
Vancouver
604/688-7216
$

If you want an old-fashioned diner with vinyl-covered stools and tough-on-the-butt booths, come here. This is the place where you bring your newspaper—preferably the *New York Times* or *Guardian*—order your meal, then try to look casually intense. The clientele here consists of true West Enders, a varied mix of characters ranging from those making unconventional fashion statements to members of the upper class purposefully dressing down. Expect the usual diner fare of burgers and corned beef, but with oh-so-much-more character. Serving late breakfast, lunch, and dinner Mon–Sat. ᴆ (Downtown)

STEAMWORKS BREWING
375 Water St.
Vancouver
604/689-2739
$

Combining the best beer selection in town with a location adjacent to the old Canadian Pacific Terminal on the edge of Gastown, Steamworks is a two-story restaurant that serves great burgers and everything-on-it pizzas, as well as Continental and Pacific Northwestern items that

Wear whatever clothing makes you feel comfortable when you go out to eat. Vancouver's eateries are relaxed; few places have a dress code. Let common sense prevail.

could easily be served in trendier restaurants. All kinds of activity take place at once here. Upstairs is a pub and lounge that has become, interestingly, an unofficial boy-meets-girl-on-their-respective-lunchhours kind of place. (It's also popular among the after-work set, who come to unwind.) Downstairs are three more dining rooms. Since the restaurant is next to and below The Landing mini-mall, it attracts a lot of youngish, upscale shoppers. Lunch and dinner daily. & (Downtown)

STEPHO'S SOUVLAKIA
1124 Davie St.
Vancouver
604/683-2555
$
This little West End jewel is both inexpensive and enjoyable. Dollar for dollar it's one of the city's best combinations of substance and value. The portions are generous and tasty, and the wine list is well priced. If you've been to more than one Greek restaurant, you'll find no surprises on the menu except the fact that everything is humongous. What separates Stepho's from the others is the casual, friendly way the staff treats its customers. Lunch and dinner daily. & (Downtown)

TEAHOUSE AT FERGUSON POINT
7501 Stanley Park Dr. (in Stanley Park)

Vancouver
604/669-3281
$$
Thanks to its unequaled view of Point Grey and English Bay, this place is a magnet for tourists. But the fact is that it's an exceptional dining experience as well, especially in the evening. Salmon here is always a good bet, but try the lamb in a fresh herb crust, a meal that locals have favored for years. The appetizers are big enough to be served as main courses in most other places. Try the Teahouse stuffed mushrooms (crab, shrimp, and Emmentaler) or the steamed mussels in saffron-anchovy broth. Lunch Mon–Fri, dinner daily. & (Downtown)

WILLIAM TELL
765 Beatty St.
Vancouver
604/688-3504
$$$
Across from the BC Place Stadium and attached to the Georgian Court Hotel, "The Tell" is a longtime Vancouver institution that has never lost its edge and remains, even after a quarter century, the place for special-occasion dining. Because it's close to the Ford Theatre and the Queen Elizabeth Theatre complex, this Old World Swiss restaurant is convenient for a preconcert dinner. The ambiance is upscale, with thick, lush carpeting; fine china; and crystal glasses. The menu ranges from standards like

Chateaubriand for two to veal scallopini with morel mushrooms in cream sauce such as arctic char; and a variety of unique salmon dishes. And the desserts, well—they're to die for; try the crêpes. Lunch Mon–Fri, dinner daily. & (Downtown)

YALETOWN BREWING
1111 Mainland St.
Vancouver
604/688-0039
$$

This character-heavy brewpub is Yaletown's best place to go for pizza and beer. Far from traditional, Yaletown Brewing is known for its odd pizzas (sour cream and cilantro?) and six delicious homebrews. Try washing down a couple slices with a pint of Frank's Nut Brown Ale or Red Brick Bitter. Purists may find this place leans a little too far toward yuppie. Lunch and dinner daily. & (Downtown)

UPTOWN

AMOROUS OYSTER
3236 Oak St.
Vancouver
604/732-5916
$$

One of the keys to this restaurant's more than 16 years of success is its affordable menu and wine list. It started out as a dependable neighborhood restaurant that caught on as a tourist destination. As you might expect, oysters are the specialty, but that's not all they offer. You might try the salmon in a light mustard sauce or one of the other seafood selections. The decor is casually elegant, projecting the radiant simplicity also characterizes the food. Dinner Mon–Sat. & (Uptown)

BOSTON PIZZA
1333 W. Broadway
Vancouver
604/730-2822
$

No, you won't find this place in Boston. Boston Pizza is a homegrown Vancouver franchise, with outlets spread across the Lower Mainland. If you happen to be craving pizza, stop at any one of the 15 outlets for quality—if standard—food. Lunch and dinner daily. & (Uptown)

BRIDGES
1696 Duranleau St.
Vancouver
604/687-4400
$$

Come to this wharf-side restaurant on a sunny day and you'll never want to leave. Across the dock from the Granville Island Market, it's the quintessential West Coast eatery, with views of the boats, the mountains, the sea, and the West End. It simply couldn't be a more perfect place to spend a couple of hours over wine and a seafood salad. If the patio is full, try the vaulted second-story dining room. The innovative menu changes often, but seafood is the name of the game. Lunch and dinner daily, brunch Sun. (Uptown)

BROADWAY EARL'S
901 W. Broadway
Vancouver
604/734-5995
$$

A casual dining experience with a "fresh" twist is what you'll have at any of Earl's four locations. No canned sauce here—each item served is made from scratch in their kitchens. An eclectic menu offers up a taste for all palates from Italian-style pizza (prepared in a wood-burning oven) to

UPTOWN VANCOUVER

Where to Eat in Uptown Vancouver

1 Amorous Oyster
2 Boston Pizza
3 Bridges
4 Broadway Earl's
5 The Creek
6 Daimasu
7 The Flying Wedge
8 Isadora's
9 Kirin Madarin
10 Mito
11 Monk McQueen's
12 Primo's
13 Sami's
14 Shiro
15 Star Anise
16 Tojo's

N

MAIN ST
KINGSWAY
1A
MAIN ST
2ND AV
MANITOBA ST
7TH AV
19TH AV
6
14
Cambie St.
Bridge
CAMBIE ST
7
False Creek
COMMODORE RD
9
12TH AV
16TH AV
BROADWAY
11
6TH AV
Heather
Park
Douglas Park
WILLOW ST
WILLOW ST
Charleson
Park
False Creek
4
13
OAK ST
16
RICHELIEU AV
1
Granville
Street
Bridge
ALDER ST
Granville
Island
5
8
JOHNSTON ST
CARTWRIGHT ST
OLD BRIDGE ST
DOUGLAS CR
OSLER ST
TECUMSEH AV
2
FORESTORE WALK
3
99
HEMLOCK ST
15
McRAE AV
THE CRESC
Shaughnessy
Park
MATTHEWS AV
GRANVILLE ST
12
To 10

0   .5
KILOMETER   MILE
0   .5

Hunan-style Kung Pao, to a meaty grilled salmon (filleted and de-boned on premises) and, of course, a good old-fashioned hamburger. This spot is popular with business lunchers, families, and young professionals. Lunch and dinner daily. ᶘ (Uptown)

THE CREEK
Granville Island Hotel
1253 Johnston St.
Vancouver
604/685-7070
$$

The Creek, located at the eastern tip of Granville Island, occupies most of the Granville Island Hotel's ground floor. Large and boisterous, it's not the ideal spot for intimate dining. It is, however, a terrific place from which to watch the sailboats on False Creek, and the perfect choice for those hoping to put up their feet for a spell. The decor is a combination of factory-funk modernism and West Coast brashness, with huge hanging mobiles. The menu is all-inclusive, but seafood is a specialty, and the lamb—served with a succulent cassoulet—is divine. Lunch and dinner daily. ᶘ (Uptown)

DAIMASU
16B-525 W. Broadway
Vancouver
604/875-0077
$

For Japanese-style fast food, you can't go wrong at this bustling Uptown joint. In fact, you'll find few Japanese restaurants in the city that provide such good food for so little money. The menu, which also lists Vietnamese and Chinese items, includes sushi, scrumptious prawn gyozas (wrapped and fried in meat), and filling combination plates. The soba, served only on the late-night menu, is

as good as it is anywhere in town. Lunch and dinner daily. ᶘ (Uptown)

THE FLYING WEDGE
3499 Cambie St.
Vancouver
604/874-8284

See listing for The Flying Wedge under Downtown heading.

ISADORA'S
1540 Old Bridge St.
Vancouver
604/681-8816
$

This popular place is great for families. In fact, kids will love it. Kid-friendly features include a children's play area near the entrance, and the special kids' menu includes, among other entertaining items, clown-faced pizzas. Adults, too, enjoy Isadora's, and with organic salads and nut burgers on the menu, who could blame them? It's on Granville Island near the water, and the outdoor café is an absolute delight during summer. Lunch and dinner daily, brunch Sun. ᶘ (Uptown)

KIRIN MANDARIN
1166 Alberni St.
Vancouver
604/682-8833
$$

Beijing-style cuisine makes liberal use of bold vegetables and spices, such as peppers, garlic, ginger, leeks, and coriander; it also features dumplings (jiaozi) and bread rather than rice. The menu at this post-modern restaurant focuses on northern Chinese specialties—meats from Shanghai, for example, and braised items such as sea cucumber with prawn-roe sauce and crispy Peking duck pastry. Kirin Madarin also tries to embrace the styles of several other regions in China—Shanghai, Canton, and Sichuan. Desserts like the red bean pie—a crêpe rolled around a sweet bean filling and crisp-fired—will surprise you. Lunch and dinner daily. You'll find another Uptown location, at 201-555 W. 12th Ave., 604/879-8038. (Uptown)

MITO
8369 Granville St.
Vancouver
604/263-7412
$

An intimate, family-operated restaurant, Mito is a great place to go for everything from a full meal in a bowl (beef or chicken on a bed of rice with a rich sauce) to sushi. The menu consists mostly of traditional Japanese cuisine, the kind of food that Japanese eat after a hard day at work. Like most family restaurants, there's little overhead to pass on to the customer. Located on the way to the airport, near Granville and 70th Avenue. Lunch and dinner Mon–Sat. & (Uptown)

MONK MCQUEEN'S
602 Stamp's Landing
Vancouver
604/877-1351
$$

A terrific view of the Vancouver skyline accents a menu that provides something for both the casual and formal diner. On the water near the east end of False Creek's south side, McQueen's is in the heart of the city's boating community. The ambiance is light and spacious—patrons can choose between an upstairs room for more formal dining and a downstairs oyster bar for casual slurping. In reality, both rooms are easygoing—leave your tie at home. The salmon braised in prawn sauce—served upstairs, of course—is worth the splurge. Lunch and dinner daily. & (Uptown)

PRIMO'S
1509 12th Ave.
Vancouver
604/736-9322
$

Primo used to be a place-kicker with the BC Lions football team, but you won't find any jock-related stuff in this place. Vancouver's original Mexican restaurant, Primo's has been in this same spot since the 1960s. Located just off south Granville's main shopping area, the restaurant's three rooms are both intimate and colorful, with Mexican memorabilia hanging on all the walls. The most intimate room is on the second level, with a few tables for two. A nice touch is the live music from guitarists and singers on weekends. Primo's still makes the best margaritas in town. Lunch Mon–Sat, dinner daily. & (Uptown)

SAMI'S
986 W. Broadway
Vancouver
604/736-8330
$$

When Sami Lalji (the same man who made Star Anise one of the city's finest eateries) opened this place in June 1998, he brought many of his Star Anise clients with him. Sami's high-quality menu combines Southeast Asian cuisine with West Coast specialties, and, all things considered, it's a bargain. Beef short ribs braised in ginger and seafood poached in coconut nectar are just two of the many inventive meals that are offered. Lunch and dinner Mon–Sat. & (Uptown)

SHIRO
3096 Cambie St.
Vancouver
604/874-0027
$

You have to like a Japanese restaurant that has a Tex-Mex item on its menu. Then again, owner-chef Shiro Okano has his own ideas of how to attract customers to his tucked-away neighborhood restaurant in a small business alcove on Cambie Street. This tiny spot is one of Vancouver's treasures—customers try for seats at the central sushi bar, where Shiro cheerfully holds court as he cuts his fish. Expect fresh sushi, the best homemade gyoza in town, deep-fried squid, and value-packed bento box specials—like the spicy chicken donburi. The Tex-Mex? Sushi with a chili sauce. This is a happy place located at 17th Avenue. Lunch and dinner daily. & (Uptown)

STAR ANISE
1485 W. 12th Ave.
Vancouver
604/737-1485
$$$

The emphasis here is on local and fresh. The menu, in constant change, always includes a large selection of seafood as well as the house specialty: venison. Marinated in pepper and quince and served with potatoes flavored with just the right touch of garlic, it's absolutely delicious. The grilled Sonoma duck breast is a perennial favorite, as are the crab-and-shrimp cakes. On occasion you'll find roasted ostrich on the menu. Located across the Granville Street Bridge and in the-south Granville shopping area, Star Anise is well worth the short taxi ride from Downtown. Dinner daily. & (Uptown)

Tojo's sushi bar

TOJO'S
202-777 W. Broadway
Vancouver
604/872-8050
$$$

Tojo Hidekazu is probably the best known of Vancouver's sushi masters. He's been serving up his distinct brand of Japanese seafood for about 30 years. His popular place is located on the second floor of an office building, offering great views of the North Shore Mountains. Sit at the sushi bar to watch the man in action, or settle down in one of the tatami rooms. Try the steamed monkfish and sautéed halibut cheeks. Traditional dishes are moderately priced, but if you want the exotic, you'll have to pay for it. Dinner Mon–Sat. & (Uptown)

POINT GREY

ANNAPURNA
1812 W. Fourth Ave.
Vancouver
604/736-5959

POINT GREY

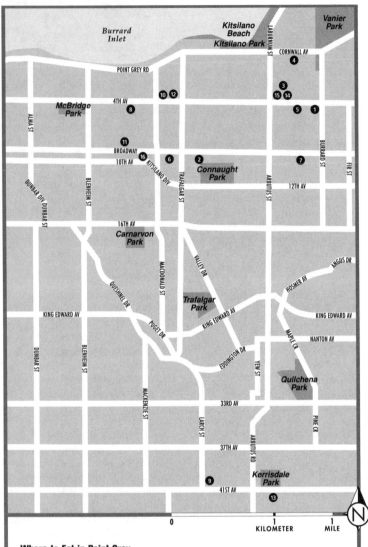

Where to Eat in Point Grey

1 Annapurna
2 Benny's Bagels
3 Bishops
4 The Flying Wedge
5 Las Margaritas
  Restaurante Y Cantina
6 Lumière
7 Meli Taverna
8 Milestones
9 Minerva Pizza and Steak
  House
10 Naam
11 Ouzerie
12 Quattro on Fourth
13 The Red Onion
14 Shijo
15 Sophie's Cosmic Cafe
16 Vassilis Taverna

$

Ever see a meatball without the meat? You will at this groundbreaking restaurant that was the first in Vancouver to explore Indian vegetarian foods. Today Annapurna is one of the very few restaurants in the city specializing in vegetarian cuisine. The food here—a far cry from standard meatless fare—is subtle and often mild, while maintaining a certain level of spiciness. Granted, the restaurant looks out over one of the city's busiest streets, but the decor, replete with lantern-covered ceiling, is restful. Among the entrées, bestsellers are curried spinach and navrattan korma—a mixed-vegetable dish. Or you might try the hard-to-forget pureed smoked eggplant and the malai kofta—meatballs without the meat. Lunch and dinner daily. & (Point Grey)

BENNY'S BAGELS
2505 W. Broadway
Vancouver
604/736-4686
$

Every Benny's outlet—and new ones are opening regularly—is unique in character. Toronto-style bagels and toppings are standard, yes, but the real reason for going is the atmosphere. In the original Benny's (1780 Cambie St., 604/872-1111), the decor is post-industrial rusted iron and wood. This Benny's is in the middle of one of Point Grey's busiest shopping areas. No matter what the weather, you'll find the patio swarming with bagel and coffee addicts. The bagel choices are astounding—plain, multigrain, pumpernickel . . . you name it. Great sandwiches are available, too; try the turkey, ham, or beef. Lunch and dinner daily. & (Point Grey)

BISHOPS
2183 W. Fourth Ave.
Vancouver
604/738-2025
$$$

Bishops consistently places near the top of everyone's "best" list. It has maintained its position as one of Vancouver's finest restaurants primarily because of its knack for simple presentation. Owner John Bishop has cooked for everyone from Bill Clinton and Boris Yeltsin to a long list of Hollywood stars (including Glenn Close, Robin Williams, and Robert DeNiro). Rack of venison is a house specialty, as are the pan-seared scallops scented with lemongrass. Dessert is a must: Try Death by Chocolate. Lunch and dinner daily. & (Point Grey)

THE FLYING WEDGE
1937 Cornwall St.
Vancouver
604/732-8840
$

See listing for Flying Wedge under Downtown heading.

LAS MARGARITAS RESTAURANTE Y CANTINA
1999 W. Fourth Ave.
Vancouver
604/734-7117
$$

A quick glance at the menu here won't yield any surprises: enchiladas, tacos, burritos, fajitas, nachos, and, of course, margaritas. Look closely, however, and you'll find more than a few twists to the usual Mexican fare, including vegetarian dishes and a surprising number of seafood selections. Tortillas filled with cilantro-and-pesto–marinated grilled salmon, and red snapper in a Veracruz sauce are the house favorites. The restaurant also offers an inexpensive children's

menu. Lunch Mon–Fri, dinner daily. &
(Point Grey)

LUMIÈRE
2551 W. Broadway
Vancouver
604/739-8185
$$$

The first thing you'll notice about this place is the minimal decor. In fact, it's downright spare. But that doesn't matter. At Lumière, a decidedly yuppie restaurant with one of the finest menus in town, it's the exquisite dishes that count. Think French cuisine gone twenty-first century and you'll begin to appreciate what's in store for you. Everything on the menu is prepared with painstaking attention to detail. The lamb, for example, is topped with shreds of preserved lemon and, at the last moment of its preparation, finely chopped Nicoise olives. The result is that the two flavors complement rather than clash. The appetizers are especially superb, and the choices are dizzying. Dinner Tue–Sun. & (Point Grey)

MELI TAVERNA
1905 W. Broadway
Vancouver
604/736-8330 or 604/736-8345
$

This neighborhood restaurant is set on one of Vancouver's busiest arteries. Yet, oddly enough, once you enter, it's easy to forget the activity just outside the window. No one hurries you; there's just a friendly sense that you're in for the evening. And in a town known for its inexpensive Greek restaurants, Meli is a bargain. The small, lunchtime pizzas here are more than large enough for one person, and all are Greek in flavor, topped with feta cheese, artichokes, tomatoes, and black olives. For a more traditional Greek dish, try the lamb with endive and artichoke hearts in an avgolemono (egg-lemon) sauce. The tartness of the sauce brings out the sweetness of the meat. Lunch Mon–Fri, dinner Mon–Sat. & (Point Grey)

MILESTONE'S
2966 W. Fourth Ave.

The William Tell, p.72

The William Tell

Vancouver
604/734-8616

The Milestone's chain has five restaurants, four in Vancouver and one in Burnaby, and each has essentially the same menu and fine service. Huge portions guarantee you won't walk away hungry—even if all you eat are the appetizers. Try the enormous breakfasts. For lunch, starters include baked goat cheese with roasted garlic, and southern-fried scallops with spicy Cajun cream, bacon, and green onions. You'll love the smoky charbroiled hamburgers—you can top one with mango chutney and cream cheese, guacamole, salsa, and Jack cheese. Breakfast, lunch, and dinner daily. ⅋ (Point Grey)

MINERVA PIZZA AND STEAK HOUSE
2411 W. 41st Ave.
Vancouver
604/263-1774
$

Sort of Italian, kind of Greek, mostly a combination of both, this neighborhood restaurant has been a West Side favorite for years, and with good cause. The family that runs it has merged a traditional Italian menu with big-city tastes. Expect pasta and beef in some unusual combinations, but, above all, prepare for stick-to-the-ribs homestyle cookin'. The interior is Mediterranean in character, and the menu spans that geographical area, but pizza's the specialty, with a selection of about 20 different topping combinations. Lunch and dinner daily. ⅋ (Point Grey)

NAAM
2724 W. Fourth Ave.
Vancouver
604/738-7151

$

As Vancouver's oldest vegetarian restaurant, Naam is the last survivor of Fourth Avenue's hippie days, the period between Haight-Ashbury and the arrival of developers in the mid-1970s. Everything inside the restaurant is laid-back, and you can still nibble on a bee-pollen cookie or drink dandelion tea. The decor is '60s funky, and portions are gigantic—especially the house salad and the veggie burrito. There is often a line to get into this no-reservations restaurant, so show up early. Breakfast, lunch, and dinner daily; brunch Sun. ⅋ (Point Grey)

OUZERIE
3189 W. Broadway
Vancouver
604/739-9378
$

A place of little pieces, this is where you go when you want a meal of appetizers. Like the trendy ouzeries in Greece, this restaurant offers both pre-dinner snacks and full-fledged entrées. The Kitsilano-style moussaka is vegetarian, and the prawns dressed with ouzo and mushrooms are tasty. A terrific place to spend 30 minutes or three hours. Lunch and dinner daily. ⅋ (Point Grey)

QUATTRO ON FOURTH
2611 Fourth Ave.
Vancouver
604/734-4444
$$

The spaghetti piga is advertised as being "for Italians only," but don't worry about your ethnic origins when ordering it. It's a crowd-pleaser that's guaranteed to warm—and fill—anyone's tummy. Quattro is known for its commitment to a quality menu at moderate

Food with a View

As everybody knows, nothing promotes good digestion better than a great view from your dinner table. Well, maybe that's not medically proven, but having a good view sure is nice. And Vancouver has plenty of oceanside, bayside, cityside, and mountainside restaurants to accommodate your viewing and dining desires.

Try Anderson's downtown for a view of False Creek. Beach House North Shore at Dundarave Pier looks out over English Bay from West Vancouver. From Granville Island, Bridges Uptown overlooks the docks, the West End, and the mountains. Or you can try The Cannery East Vancouver, where you can catch views of the city and the North Shore. The Five Sails Downtown offers plush surroundings and a great view of Coal Harbour and the North Shore, and Monk McQueen's Uptown displays all of Vancouver's West End and False Creek areas. And, from the Salmon House on the Hill North Shore, you can see just about everything—the city, the Gulf Islands, and Mount Baker.

prices, a policy that will surprise you once you taste the food. The list of antipasti is extensive, and each is worthy of a full meal in itself. Linguini with smoked salmon, black olives, fresh oregano, and tomato sauce is a favorite, as is the chicken in a sauce of white wine, bell peppers, broth, tomatoes, jalapeños, and vodka. Dinner daily. ♿ (Point Grey)

THE RED ONION
2028 W. 41st Ave.
Vancouver
604/263-0833
$
This wonderful burger joint in the heart of Kerrisdale is across the street and just east of a corner Mc-

Donald's. Try this lesser-known burger joint and you won't be disappointed—many of its regulars claim it has the best-tasting burgers and double dogs (twice the size of a normal hot dog) in town. The interior has a homey feel, and the service is attentive. The wieners and buns are made in-house. For breakfast try the baked-on-the-premises blueberry, chocolate chip, and cinnamon buns. Breakfast, lunch, and dinner daily. ♿ (Point Grey)

SHIJO
1926 W. Fourth Ave.
Vancouver
604/732-4676
$$
Some say the best part of the meal is

the ending, when you get an orange sherbet served in a hollowed-out orange. It's just one example of the care and attention given the customer in this Kitsilano restaurant. Shijo is certainly in the city's top tier of sushi restaurants. Begin with a sunomono salad, then try the shiitake foilayki (mushrooms sprinkled with lemony sauce and cooked in foil). The sushi, of course, is first-rate, and half the fun is in listening to the chefs and waiters cracking jokes. Lunch and dinner daily. & (Point Grey)

SOPHIE'S COSMIC CAFE
2095 W. Fourth Ave.
Vancouver
604/732-6810
$

When you walk past the leopard-skin sign and the huge knife and fork bracketing the doorway, you'll feel right at home in the room cluttered with childhood memorabilia—Roy Rogers lunch kits, baseball pennants, and hats. The burgers are huge and spicy, and the tasty chocolate shakes are as thick as glue. But it's breakfast—Mexican eggs with sausage, peppers, and onions spiced with pepper sauce—that's the real showstopper here. Breakfast, lunch, and dinner daily; brunch Sat–Sun. & (Point Grey)

VASSILIS TAVERNA
2884 W. Broadway
Vancouver
604/733-3231
$

Vassilis, located on a street chockfull of Greek restaurants, has maintained a three-decade-long reputation for excellence. While the menu is fairly traditional, the quality is consistently high. The Greek salad is a meal in it-

self, but try the house specialty, a juicy kotopoulo (chicken pounded flat and seasoned with lemon juice, garlic, and oregano). The moussaka, too, is exceptional. In the summer the restaurant windows open onto the sidewalk. The narrow room is often filled to capacity, so make sure you have a reservation. Lunch Tue–Fri, dinner Tue–Sun. & (Point Grey)

EAST VANCOUVER

AKI
374 Powell St.
Vancouver
604/682-4032
$

One of the originals in Vancouver in the early '70s, when Japanese restaurants were still "exotic," Aki remains what it always has been—an unpretentious place that delivers authenticity and a small check. The two-story restaurant is located in what used to be a mostly Japanese neighborhood but that is now—with the exception of a grocery store and a few restaurants—Japantown in name only. (The area is now primarily Chinese.) The restaurant is split into a series of screened tatami rooms upstairs and a somewhat grungy-looking smaller area downstairs. The same robust meals are available on either floor. The tempura has a delicate batter. Lunch Mon–Fri, dinner daily. (East Vancouver)

THE CANNERY
2205 Commissioner St.
Vancouver
604/254-9606
$$$

Isolated from the city on the industrial waterfront, The Cannery is not exactly easy to find. Yet while it's tucked be-

EAST VANCOUVER

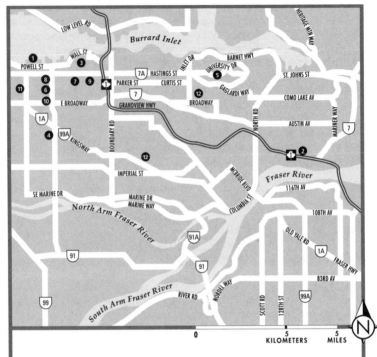

Where to Eat in East Vancouver and the Eastern Suburbs

1 Aki (EV)
2 Boston Pizza (ES)
3 The Cannery (EV)
4 Daimasu (ES)
5 Horizons on Burnaby Mountain (ES)
6 Le Grec (EV)
7 Sawasdee (EV)

8 Sortino's Restaurante (EV)
9 Sun Sui Wah Seafood Restaurant (EV)
10 Tio Pepe's Restaurante Mexicano (EV)
11 Tomato Fresh Food Cafe (EV)
12 White Spot (ES)
13 White Spot (EV)

hind railroad tracks near the warehouses, it has managed to remain a Vancouver seafood institution for nearly 25 years. The reason? All it does is produce satisfied customers. The rugged cedar restaurant looks out towards North Vancouver and to the downtown area, with views of fishing boats and freighters. The menu features almost anything that swims,

from marlin to monkfish. Lunch Mon–Fri, dinner daily. (East Vancouver)

LE GREC
1447 Commercial Dr.
Vancouver
604/253-1253
$
Big servings, a happy atmosphere, and a menu entirely of sub-nine-dol-

lar entrées make this restaurant in the middle of Vancouver's Little Italy one of the city's most enjoyable places. The three-level restaurant has an azure ceiling and white-washed walls typical of homes on the Greek Islands. The nice thing about the menu is that it introduces you to rare dishes like skordalia, a rich potato-based dip that screams garlic; and the Greek version of cod, bakaliaros. Portions are generous and meant to be shared. Reservations are not taken, so get there early or you'll have to wait. Lunch and dinner Mon–Sat. ♿ (East Vancouver)

SAWASDEE
4250 Main St.
Vancouver
604/876-4030
$

In a town with just a few Thai restaurants, Sawasdee is a mainstay. You won't find this place toning down its Thai cuisine to suit local palates. The menu, hailing from the central region of the country, includes green papaya salad with chili, chicken wings stuffed with noodles, and deep-fried marinated chicken wrapped in pandan leaves. The hot-sour soup with chicken or prawns, mushrooms, and lemongrass is a must-have. For something completely different, try the larb salad, made from minced and marinated beef, pork, or chicken, and accented with a tongue-searing splattering of chilies. Lunch and dinner daily. ♿ (East Vancouver)

SORTINO'S RESTAURANTE
1130 Commercial Dr.
Vancouver
604/253-5383
$$

Mama's cooking—that sums up this friendly neighborhood restaurant at the north end of Commercial Drive's restaurant row. Oddly, this wonderful little restaurant doesn't get the press that lesser restaurants seem to attract. Perhaps that's because the place is so unpretentious and the clientele is local. The room is softly lit with white tablecloths, parquet floors, and plaster walls. Most of Sortino's specialties are pasta-based, but the best item on the menu is as far away from noodles as you can get: chicken breast with Emmental cheese and Italian ham in a brown sauce. Try it. Lunch and dinner daily. ♿ (East Vancouver)

SUN SUI WAH SEAFOOD RESTAURANT
3888 Main St.
Vancouver
604/872-8822
$$

Sun Sui Wah was named the best Cantonese restaurant in the Lower Mainland by a Chinese-language radio poll. In fact, this is a great place for dim sum. On the menu you'll find such delicacies as steamed scallops on silky bean curd; live Alaskan king crab dressed in wine and garlic; lobster and egg noodles; and lightly sautéed geoduck paired with coconut milk in a fluffy crust. The atmosphere, set by a sail-like structure stretching across a glass-domed room, is turn-of-the-last century upbeat. This is a hotspot for Chinese weddings, so reserve early. Lunch and dinner daily. ♿ (East Vancouver)

TIO PEPE'S RESTAURANTE MEXICANO
1134 Commercial Dr.
Vancouver
604/254-8999
$

Come here for the flautas—corn

NORTH SHORE

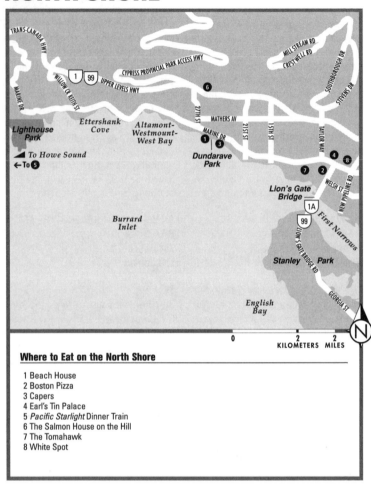

TRANS-CANADA HWY
MILL STREAM RD
CRESTWELL RD
SOUTHBOROUGH DR
WILLOW CR. KEITH ST.
CYPRESS PROVINCIAL PARK ACCESS HWY
UPPER LEVELS HWY
1 99
STEVENS DR
6
MARINE DR
27TH ST
MATHERS AV
21ST ST
15TH ST
TAYLOR WAY
Ettershank Cove
Altamont-Westmount-West Bay
MARINE DR
Lighthouse Park
1 3
4 8
To Howe Sound
←To 5
Dundarave Park
7 2
WELSH ST
NEW PIPELINE RD
Lion's Gate Bridge
1A
99
First Narrows
Burrard Inlet
LION'S GATE BRIDGE RD
Stanley Park
GEORGIA ST
English Bay

0   2   2
KILOMETERS MILES
N

Where to Eat on the North Shore

1 Beach House
2 Boston Pizza
3 Capers
4 Earl's Tin Palace
5 *Pacific Starlight* Dinner Train
6 The Salmon House on the Hill
7 The Tomahawk
8 White Spot

"flutes" crammed with chicken, beef, or veggies—and the egg-battered nopal. They're both delicious. The dining area at this popular local haunt is a long narrow room packed with tables. It does get crowded, but for good reason. Try the barbecued pork steak or the pork wrapped in banana leaf. If you'd rather have seafood, you'll find that here, too. Spanish speakers will find a couple of Spanish-language newspapers on hand. Dinner Mon–Sat. ප (East Vancouver)

TOMATO FRESH FOOD CAFE
3305 Cambie St.
Vancouver
604/874-6020
$
Here's a restaurant whose existence

is based on a single (well, almost) food item: the tomato, which appears in virtually everything that's served. But the theme doesn't seem to restrict the imagination of the chefs at this cross between a diner and a health-food café. Root beer floats and thick milkshakes served in metal containers make it easy to imagine you're back in the '50s. The menu includes mountain-sized sandwiches and, believe it or not, Campbell's tomato soup. Lunch and dinner daily. (East Vancouver)

WHITE SPOT
2518 W. Broadway
Vancouver
604/731-2434
$

This is a Vancouver original, homegrown and never forgotten, dating from 1958, when founder Nat Bailey (for whom the baseball stadium is named) opened his first restaurant. There are now 45 White Spots throughout British Columbia and 26 in the Lower Mainland. The menu is quite broad, but for a taste of what made the chain successful, try the legendary Triple "O" Burger with its special sauce (a secret recipe). In places with drive-in facilities (including this location) you'll be served in your car on a tray laden with your food. Breakfast, lunch, and dinner daily. & (East Vancouver)

NORTH SHORE

BEACH HOUSE
Dundarave Pier, 150 25th St.
West Vancouver
604/922-1414
$$$

The location is on everyone's most desired list—at the start of Dundarave Pier. Even locals come here to

photograph the dramatic views across English Bay. About six years ago Beach House was restored to its original 1912 character, with wooden floors, creamy-white walls, and a glass-walled front that allows everyone to look out. While the menu leans toward seafood, it also offers many traditional Italian favorites, as well as one of the best selections of British Columbian estate wines anywhere in the city. Lunch and dinner daily, brunch Sun. & (North Shore)

BOSTON PIZZA
1078 Marine Dr.
North Vancouver
604/984-0407

See listing for Boston Pizza under Uptown heading.

CAPERS
2496 Marine Dr.
West Vancouver
604/925-3374
$

A veggie restaurant that knows how to market itself is as rare as a cattle rancher eating an organic burger. But that's exactly what you'll find in this innovative restaurant in the fashionable Dundarave shopping section of West Vancouver. The vegetarian dishes served up at Capers are quite flavorful; the views of the water and city, wonderful. This restaurant's located atop a vegetable market by the same name, so patrons can either-shop for fresh produce while they wait or plan a picnic out of the variety of takeout dishes available. Breakfast and lunch daily, dinner Mon–Sat. & (North Shore)

EARL'S TIN PALACE
303 Marine Dr.
West Vancouver
604/984-4341

T I P

By law, all Vancouver restaurants and pubs are nonsmoking. A new regulation by the Worker's Compensation Board outlaws smoking in all public establishments.

See listing for Broadway Earl's under Uptown heading.

PACIFIC STARLIGHT DINNER TRAIN
B.C. Rail
West Vancouver
604/984-5500 or 604/631-3500
$$$

Imagine an entire train devoted to nothing but eating. Passengers choose their meals when they make reservations; the menu varies but generally includes beef, game, pork, and exceptional grilled salmon. The *Pacific Starlight* takes passengers up spectacular Howe Sound to the underwater park at Porteau Cove. Dinner is served on this leg of the trip, about an hour-and-a-half from the North Vancouver station. During a 45-minute break at Porteau Cove, passengers get out and walk, dance, or explore before reboarding for the return trip (when dessert is served). The ambiance is decidedly casual and friendly, and the staff goes out of their way to generate conversation. Choose to dine in a glass-domed viewing car or a regular dining car. Dinner May–Sept. ঙ (North Shore)

THE SALMON HOUSE ON THE HILL
2229 Folkstone Way
West Vancouver
604/926-3212
$$$

This restaurant, located 15 minutes from downtown Vancouver, offers spectacular views of English Bay, downtown, Stanley Park, and Point Grey from its perch on a bluff. The decor features West Coast Native carvings and art, and the lightly pungent and smoky aroma of burning green alder (used in cooking) fills the air. Their appetizer platter for two, $19.95, is outstanding—just make sure to request the potato, artichoke, and shrimp stack and the Dungeness crab dip. Main-course signature dishes include alder-grilled local salmon and house-smoked black cod with wasabi cream and mustard-seed vinaigrette. They have a strong, well-composed wine list that includes a nice selection of California whites and pinot noirs. Lunch and dinner daily. ঙ(North Shore)

THE TOMAHAWK
1550 Philip St.
North Vancouver
604/988-2612
$

You'll need the jaw hinge of a python to get your teeth around The Tomahawk's burgers. This North Shore greasy spoon—and its burgers—has been popular since the day it opened in 1926. Unless the sweet smell of bacon and grease is something you want to carry around with you, plan on changing your clothes after you eat. For a real tummy-filler, try topping your burger with a fried egg. Located adjacent to Native Capilano lands, this place is filled with First Nations artifacts. Lunch and dinner daily. ♿ (North Shore)

WHITE SPOT
2205 Lonsdale
North Vancouver
604/987-0024
See listing for White Spot under East Vancouver heading.

EASTERN SUBURBS

BOSTON PIZZA
4219 Loughheed Hwy.
Burnaby
604/299-7600
See listing for Boston Pizza under Uptown heading.

DAIMASU
106-4680 Kingsway
Burnaby
604/434-5687
See listing for Daimasu under Uptown heading.

HORIZONS ON BURNABY MOUNTAIN
100 Centennial Way
Burnaby
604/299-1155
$$
The road up Burnaby Mountain ends at this restaurant, a spacious room with plenty of windows and fine views of downtown Vancouver along Burrard Inlet. The menu is seafood oriented; alder-grilled salmon is the house specialty. You might also try the scallop and prawn risotto or the seafood bouillabaisse. The wine list includes a large selection of British Columbia wines. Lunch, dinner every day, Sunday Brunch, 11 a.m.-2 p.m. ♿ (Eastern Suburbs)

WHITE SPOT
5550 Kingsway
Burnaby
604/434-6669
See listing for White Spot under East Vancouver heading.

SOUTHERN SUBURBS

BOSTON PIZZA
50-8100 Ackroyd Rd.
Richmond
604/273-6151
See listing for Boston Pizza under Uptown heading.

DAIMASU
100-8111 Ackroyd Rd.
Richmond
604/270-4846
See listing for Daimasu under Uptown heading.

DAIMASU
8300 Granville Rd.
Richmond
604/273-7874
See listing for Daimasu under Uptown heading.

EARL'S LANSDOWNE
304-5300 No. 3 Rd.
Richmond
604/303-9702
See listing for Broadway Earl's under Uptown heading.

FLOATA SEAFOOD RESTAURANT
Parker Place
4380 No. 3 Rd.
Richmond
604/270-8889
See listing for Floata Seafood Restaurant under Downtown heading.

GIRAFFE
15053 Marine Dr.

SOUTHERN SUBURBS

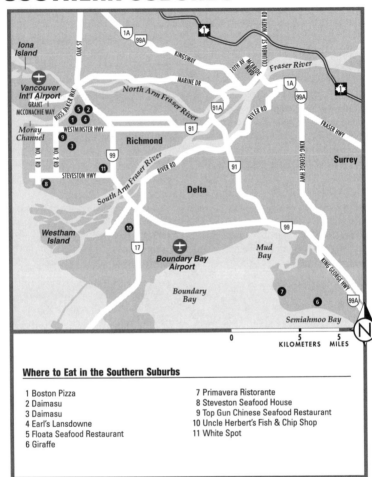

Where to Eat in the Southern Suburbs

1 Boston Pizza
2 Daimasu
3 Daimasu
4 Earl's Lansdowne
5 Floata Seafood Restaurant
6 Giraffe

7 Primavera Ristorante
8 Steveston Seafood House
9 Top Gun Chinese Seafood Restaurant
10 Uncle Herbert's Fish & Chip Shop
11 White Spot

White Rock
604/538-6878
$$

It may be as close to the United States as you can get without crossing the border, but if you're in the region, come to Giraffe and treat yourself to fine cuisine and a great view across Semiahmoo Bay to Blaine, Washington. Giraffe is a terrific place to graze on items such as sun-dried tomatoes or wonton skins filled with fresh crab, before digging into the superb lamb coated with a mustard herb sauce and caramelized onions or the boneless chicken breast with mixed berries. Lunch and dinner daily, brunch Sun. ꕤ (Southern Suburbs)

PRIMAVERA RISTORANTE
12211 Beecher St.
Surrey
604/536-5194
$$

If you drive out to Crescent Beach, at the northern end of the White Rock/Crescent Beach Peninsula, be sure to drop into Giuseppe Sfara's establishment. If it were in downtown Vancouver it would be one of the most popular places around. Just a block from the beach and a picturesque beachside walkway, this low-slung restaurant has both contemporary and traditional Italian cuisine. Live music on weekends and Sfara's personal touch (he frequently comes out of the kitchen to greet guests) make it feel like home. Try the grilled salmon in the chef's own special sauce. Dinner daily. & (Southern Suburbs)

STEVESTON SEAFOOD HOUSE
3951 Moncton St.
Steveston
604/271-5252
$$$

Once the only seafood restaurant in this gorgeous little community of fishing boats and seaside attractions, the Steveston Seafood House now has to compete with the semi–fast-food outlets in the nearby redeveloped Steveston dock area. Still, it continues to thrive, mainly because it's the best restaurant in the area. The mixed seafood platter is one of the most popular items on the menu, but don't let it get between you and the pan-fried halibut cooked with lemon butter. Fishing buffs will appreciate the nautical motif (overhead fishnets, glass floats, and seashells). Dinner daily. & (Southern Suburbs)

TOP GUN CHINESE SEAFOOD RESTAURANT
2110-4151 Hazelbridge Way
Richmond
604/273-4151
$$

This is really more than just a restaurant. Located in the Hong Kong–style Aberdeen Shopping Centre, Top Gun is also a lesson in multicultural living. It's in the area known as "Little Asia"—within several blocks are a Buddhist temple, a Chinese shopping center, a Japanese department store, and a series of Asian boutique shops and herbalists. You can expect a lineup every day. There's something special about this place, even though the service is a tad wanting. Don't be fooled by the prices—dishes are enormous. The pan-fried rock cod is a house specialty. Lunch and dinner daily. & (Southern Suburbs)

UNCLE HERBERT'S FISH & CHIP SHOP
4866 Delta St.
Ladner
604/946-8222
$

If you're coming or going to the Tsawwassen ferry terminal, turn off at Ladner and treat yourself to what is probably the best fish 'n' chips in the region. The interior is entirely British— one room is decorated with tea towels from every English town that prints one; another harbors piles of Royal memorabilia dating back to King George V. The pub food includes pork pies, Scotch eggs, sausage, and, most important, many British ales. Lunch Tue–Sat, dinner Tue–Sun. & (Southern Suburbs)

WHITE SPOT
14611 Steveston Hwy.
Richmond
604/271-7768

See listing for White Spot under East Vancouver heading.

Skip Young

5

SIGHTS AND ATTRACTIONS

Since Vancouver doesn't sprawl, getting about and seeing things is simple. Travel a couple of blocks in any direction and you'll find something worth experiencing—a building, a view, a garden. We like to brag that within sight of Downtown you can ski in the morning, play tennis in the afternoon, and sail in the evening. Some hearty souls actually do it.

You won't find many Disneyland-style theme parks in the region, though many of the gardens and museums have a specific focus. The result is that almost everything worth visiting is part of the local culture. Just pick a neighborhood—Gastown, Kitsilano, Chinatown, Yaletown, False Creek—and start walking. You'll find that the most popular tourist attractions are also important parts of everyday living.

Still, there are things you must see and do. For example, every visitor has to take the gondola ride to the top of Grouse Mountain for the greatest view this side of the moon—not to do so is like visiting Paris without ever going to see the Eiffel Tower. The five giant sails atop the downtown cruise terminal/convention center have become the city's symbol, drawing visitors to their unique design. A visit to the center during the cruise season—May through October—will give you a free, up-close view of the huge ships that cruise to Alaska.

Once you've seen the buildings, explored the hiking trails, and marveled at the mountains, walk the neighborhoods and absorb the atmosphere. That's an attraction in itself. Strolling through Chinatown, for example, will bring you just about as close to Hong Kong as you can get without actually flying there.

DOWNTOWN

BLOOD ALLEY SQUARE
Between Abbott and Carrall Sts.
Vancouver
In the late 1800s Blood Alley Square was a popular hangout for smugglers and opium (it was legal then) dealers. Thanks to the nature of the business, it was also a great place to find dead bodies. Today, fortunately, the square is much more civilized, and you're far more likely to find an interesting store or restaurant than a corpse. Still, drug deals do take place here, so stay on your toes. Police keep the square fairly well patrolled. (Downtown)

CANADA PLACE COMPLEX
Foot of Burrard St.
Vancouver
604/641-1987
The Canada Place complex—including the convention center, cruise ship terminal, Pan Pacific Hotel, Board of Trade, many restaurants, and good shopping—is easy to recognize. It's the city's landmark. Shaped like an enormous ship with five towering white sails, it's where more than 120 vessels drop anchor each year between May and October before they set sail for Alaska. You can walk around the complex and check out the docked ships or take dramatic photos of the harbor. The Pan Pacific

Hotel is the major tenant of the complex; if you take the escalator up the three stories to the lobby, the unfolding layers of the structure's interior will grab your attention. The convention center, built for Expo '86, faces the craggy North Shore Mountains. Next to the complex, to the east, is a heliport used by passenger helicopters providing service between Vancouver and Victoria. To the west is the seaplane docking area. &. (Downtown)

CANADIAN BROADCASTING CORPORATION BUILDING
700 Hamilton St.
Vancouver
604/662-6000
Up until April 6, 1964, CBC Radio 690 and Stereo 105.7 were operating from the Hotel Vancouver, and an old garage on West Georgia Street served as the CBC television studio. That changed in 1972 with the construction of what is now the CBC's western broadcast center. The first things you'll notice about this structure are the large pipes—actually air ducts used to cool the building—that cascade from the roof to the ground, giving the building an industrial look. The building houses six television studios, five large radio studios, several smaller radio studios, a screening theater, and a television rehearsal

You know you've come across a movie set when you see big, white trailers parked on city streets crowded with busy people wearing baseball caps and tennis shoes. You can find out about shootings ahead of time if you swing by the B.C. Film Commission Office at 375 Water Street. If that's too far out of your way, call the commission's hotline at 604/660-4790. They'll be more than happy to give you a list of what films are being shot where.

DOWNTOWN VANCOUVER

Sights and Attractions in Downtown Vancouver

1 Blood Alley Square
2 Canada Place Complex
3 Canadian Broadcasting Corporation Building
4 Canadian Pacific Railway Roundhouse
5 Chinese Cultural Centre
6 Christ Church Cathedral
7 East Pender Street
8 Granville Mall
9 Harbour Centre Tower
10 Hong Kong Bank Building
11 Hotel Europe
12 Library Square
13 Maple Leaf Square
14 Robson Square
15 Sam Kee Building
16 Steam Clock
17 Vancouver Aquarium
18 Vancouver Art Gallery
19 Waterfront Station

Centennial Pier
Seabus to North Vancouver (Burrard Inlet passenger ferry)
Heliport
Canada Place
Burrard Inlet
Seaplanes
Dead Man's Island
Canada Place Way
To Coal Harbour
Lost Lagoon
English Bay Beach
English Bay
Sunset Beach
Vanier Park
False Creek
Granville Island
Granville St. Bridge
Burrard St. Bridge
Cambie St. Bridge
Main Station
GM Place
BC Place Stadium

CORDOVA ST
MAIN ST
UNION ST
EAST COMMISSIONER
COLUMBIA ST
QUEBEC ST
HASTINGS ST
PENDER ST
EXPO BLVD
GEORGIA VIADUCT
EXPO BLVD
PACIFIC BLVD
BEATTY ST
CAMBIE ST
CAMBIE ST
DUNSMUIR ST
HOMER ST
SMITHE ST
NELSON ST
HELMCKEN ST
GRANVILLE ST MALL (buses and taxis only)
SEYMOUR ST
HOWE ST
BURRARD ST
THURLOW ST
PENDER ST
HASTINGS ST
MELVILLE ST
GEORGIA ST
ROBSON ST
PENDRELL ST
JERVIS ST
BROUGHTON ST
CARDERO ST
BIDWELL ST
NELSON ST
HARO ST
COMOX ST
DAVIE ST
BURNABY ST
PACIFIC ST
BEACH AV
PARK LN
CHILCO ST
LAGOON DR
WEST COMMISSIONER
Nelson Park
CHESTNUT ST
BURRARD ST
1ST AV

0 1 KILOMETER 1 MILE

Chinese and Japanese immigrants were not given full Canadian citizenship rights until 1949. Today Chinese immigrants control a large segment of Vancouver's economy.

hall, as well as offices. The CBC Plaza, on the corner of West Georgia and Hamilton Streets, features a totem pole entitled *Wild Woman of the Woods*, by native carver Richard Hunt. Tours are free, but call ahead, as tour times vary from day to day. ⚬ (Downtown)

CANADIAN PACIFIC RAILWAY ROUNDHOUSE
Davie St. and Pacific Blvd.
Vancouver
604/713-1800
This is all that remains of the once massive Canadian Pacific marshalling yard, where passenger trains were serviced. Built in 1888, it was where the large locomotives were driven in on a single track, turned around on a giant pivoting wheel, and sent off on one of several service tracks. It's now home for Engine 374, the steam locomotive that brought the first passenger train into Vancouver. The roundhouse was also the heart of the Expo '86 grounds, when the World's Fair was in town. It now houses a theater, restaurant, community center, and museum. Open daily. Free. ⚬ (Downtown)

CHINESE CULTURAL CENTRE
50 E. Pender St.
Vancouver
604/687-0729

Whatever Happened to Vancouver Expo '86?

More than 22 million people visited Expo '86, the World's Fair that thrust Vancouver into international prominence. Today most of the land on which the fair was held has been dedicated to high-rise condominium housing that will expand the size of downtown Vancouver by about one sixth. Located on the southern edge of Yaletown, the site will also include museums, a theater, and parkland. The most visible legacies of Expo '86 are Science World, BC Place Stadium, and the Roundhouse Community Centre, where the old CPR steam locomotive No. 374 is housed.

The architecture of this Chinatown building on East Pender Street (see listing, below) is a mix of modern glass and a traditional archway entrance. Just look for the big red arch. You'll find a variety of cultural exhibits and classes for tai chi and other Chinese arts. Attached to the building is the Dr. Sun Yat-Sen Garden (see Chapter 8, Parks and Gardens, and Recreation Areas). And be sure to visit the center's latest addition, the Chinese Museum, next door on Columbia Street; the two-story building features Chinese Canadian history exhibits on the second floor and Chinese art in the first-floor gallery. Open daily, hours vary. Free. & (Downtown)

CHRIST CHURCH CATHEDRAL
W. Georgia and Burrard Sts.
Vancouver
604/682-8441
Across from the Hotel Vancouver, this century-old sandstone Gothic Revival church with its gabled roof, buttresses, and stained-glass windows sticks out like a lush olive tree against the sterile high-rise skyline. You must go inside to see the rich, multicolored windows. The oldest surviving church in Vancouver, it was completed in 1895 and is at the heart of the Cathedral Place complex, a city block that houses several important buildings, including Cathedral Place Tower, the Canadian Craft Museum, and a lovely plaza that separates the buildings from one another. Open daily. & (Downtown)

EAST PENDER STREET
Vancouver
Located in the heart of the Chinatown, East Pender Street transports walkers thousands of miles in just a few blocks. Enter any of the crowded specialty shops and you'll find everything from mysterious herbal remedies to finely lacquered pots, jade, carved wood, and embroidered dresses. Mandarin, Cantonese, and Szechwan restaurants line the street, and nearby is the Chinese Cultural Centre (see listing, above), its entrance marked by an enormous red gate. (Downtown)

GRANVILLE MALL
Granville St. between the waterfront and Smithe St.
Vancouver
This banned-to-cars five-block stretch of Granville Street has been a work in progress since it was first proposed 25 years ago. It was once the glitziest stretch of roadway in Vancouver, with neon signs, nightclubs, and theaters. It was the place to be on a Saturday night. Today, while much more sedate, it still plays a major part in everyday downtown life. On it are Vancouver's major department stores, including Eaton's, The Bay, Holt Renfrew, and others. It's also the location of The Orpheum, home of the Van-

Vancouver Convention and Exhibition Centre

The British Columbia Pavilion Corporation

The Story of Pauline Johnson

Not far from Stanley Park's Teahouse restaurant—near the hollow tree at Third Beach—is a monument to Pauline Johnson, the Ontario-born writer of poetry, stories, and legends.

Pauline—whose Mohawk name was Tekahionwake—was the daughter of George Johnson, a Mohawk Chief, and a woman named Emily Johnson, who had come to Canada from Ohio. While Pauline had formal schooling for only seven years, her mother read her the works of famous English writers such as Sir Walter Scott, John Milton, and William Shakespeare. In addition, her grandfather told her Native legends and war stories—all of which would influence the stories, legends, and poems Pauline wrote.

In 1892, when she was 31, Pauline dressed as a Native princess and began reciting her poetry publicly. She retired from touring in 1909 and settled in Vancouver, where by this time she was well known. She continued to write, and her poem "The Song My Paddle Sings" captured the imagination of a whole generation of readers. She published the legends and stories of the Squamish people as told to her by her friend Chief Joe Capilano in a book called Legends of Vancouver *(1911). She also paddled her canoe around the bays of the city and entertained friends. She could often be seen canoeing in Lost Lagoon, a small body of water in Stanley Park that she named. She said it was there that she found tranquility.*

Pauline died on March 7, 1913, at the age of 52, and her funeral procession included all of the city's distinguished men and women, as well as representatives from every society and club and Native nation. Before her death, Pauline had asked to be buried in Stanley Park, her favorite place in Vancouver; she remains the only person to be buried there. Although she had requested that her grave site have no monument, a large stone decorated with her picture and Mohawk designs was placed there in 1922 by the Women's Canadian Club.

Top 10 Most Significant Buildings in Vancouver

by Edward Ratsoy, architect, developer, and keen student of Vancouver's cultural and social heritage

1. **Provincial Law Courts Building** (800 Smithe St.); Arthur Erickson, architect, 1979. This concrete building has some of the finest examples of cast-in-concrete work found anywhere, and it is a radical departure in courthouse design—from a building expressing law and order to one that is open and accessible. The sensitive blend of building and landscaping creates an oasis right in the heart of the city.

2. **Granville Island Public Market** (1689 Johnson St.); Norman Hotson, architect, 1980. The industrial windows and doors, heavy timber and steel, and natural lighting in this place stands in sharp contrast to the over-refined atmosphere found in similar markets such as Ghirardelli Square in San Francisco or Pioneer Square in Seattle. It is the centerpiece of the most successful urban people-place in Vancouver.

3. **Museum of Anthropology** (6393 NW Marine Dr., UBC); Arthur Erickson, architect, 1976. This dramatic concrete post-and-beam building, situated on an escarpment overlooking Georgia Strait, suggests the cedar longhouse structure of the coastal Natives.

4. **Vancouver Public Library** (360 W. Georgia St.); Moshe Safdie and Downs-Archambault, architects, 1997. This concrete low-rise with an associated tower is exotic, adventurous, and approachable. The structure is exceptionally well oriented to the street, with its ground-level configuration, boutiques, and grandiose entrance hall.

5. **Canada Place** (999 Canada Pl.); Zeidler Roberts Partnership/Musson Cattell Mackey Partnership/Downs-Archambault, architects, 1984. Natural lighting and a sail-like roof create an exciting, dramatic space suggestive of the waterfront. Although it encloses a very large space, the building is not at all obtrusive.

6. **Point Grey Townhouses** (3267–3293 Point Grey Rd.); Erickson and Massey, architects, 1970s. The choice of materials and style, along with special attention to natural lighting and the outdoors, makes these townhouses excellent examples of what has become known as "West Coast Vernacular."

7. **Cathedral Place** (925 W. Georgia St.); Paul Merrick, architect, 1991. This contemporary office tower relates well to the street and features an interesting neo-Gothic lobby that in turn relates to

the central courtyard and the Craft Museum behind it. The external detailing and ornamentation is exquisite, and the copper roof, in shape and finish, pays homage to the very important Hotel Vancouver across the street.

8. **Daon Building** (999 W. Hastings St.); Musson Cattell Mackey Partnership, architects, 1981. A concrete office tower with a reflective glass-curtain exterior, this building is carefully situated to allow the street end to remain open. The facade is stepped back, and the glass mirrors the waterfront and the surrounding buildings—especially the historically important Marine Building.

9. **Dominion Building** (207 W. Hastings St.); J. S. Helyer & Son, architects, 1910. This attractive nineteenth-century French classical building consists of a steel frame construction with terra-cotta exterior and elaborately decorated cornice and trims. It's a colorful and striking example of Vacouver's heritage.

10. **Canadian Pacific Railway Station** (601 W. Cordova St.); Barott, Backader, and Webster, architects, 1914; restored by Hawthorn, Mansfield, and Towers, architects, 1978. This building is important as the historical prime mover in establishing Vancouver as Canada's western seaport. A neoclassical, nineteenth-century building with ionic columns gracing Hastings Street, it has a magnificent interior with inspired detailing. It also offers glorious access to the city's harbor.

couver Symphony. While the street never did become the upscale fashion and arts model it was originally designed to be, it's still an enjoyable stroll for window-shoppers, especially between West Georgia Street and the waterfront. (Downtown)

HARBOUR CENTRE TOWER
555 W. Hastings St.
Vancouver
604/689-0421
The Harbour Centre Tower is home to a mix of stores and restaurants, and, most important, the downtown campus of Simon Fraser University. A former department store, it's one of the city's most energetic places, where shoppers, students, and tourists mix and mingle on a regular basis. Take the glass-encased Skylift up nearly 169 meters to the top of the tower for a spectacular view of the North Shore Mountains, the waterfront, the city and suburbs, and, on a clear day, the mountains of Washington State and Vancouver Island. While you're up there, stop in at the Top of Vancouver revolving restaurant (604/669-2230). The Harbor Mall, beneath the building, has more than 50 shops. Summer daily 8:30 a.m.–10:30 p.m.; winter daily 10–9. Skylift to the observation deck, $7 adults, $6 seniors, $4 students and children. & (Downtown)

ARCHITECTURAL HIGHLIGHTS

N

Centennial Pier

SeaBus to North Vancouver
(Burrard Inlet Passenger Ferry)

Heliport

EAST COMMISSIONER

MAIN ST

UNION ST

Main
Station

COLUMBIA ST

QUEBEC ST

CORDOVA ST

HASTINGS ST

PENDER ST

EXPO BLVD

GEORGIA VIADUCT

Canada
Place

Dominion
Building

GM
Place

Canadian Pacific
Railway Station

EXPO ST

BC Place
Stadium

PACIFIC BLVD

CANADA PLACE WAY

Daon
Building

Vancouver
Public
Library

BEATTY ST

CAMBIE ST

False Creek

WEST COMMISSIONER

DUNSMUIR ST

CAMBIE ST

HOMER ST

Cambie St.
Bridge

HASTINGS ST

Cathedral
Place

Provincial Law
Courts Building

SMITHE ST

NELSON ST

PENDER ST

MELVILLE ST

GEORGIA ST

HOWE ST

SEYMOUR ST

ROBSON ST

THURLOW ST

BURRARD ST

GRANVILLE ST MALL (buses and taxis only)

HELMCKEN ST

Nelson
Park

CARDERO ST

HARO ST

PENDRELL ST

JERVIS ST

BROUGHTON ST

DAVIE ST

BURNABY ST

PACIFIC ST

BEACH AV

Granville St.
Bridge

NELSON ST

COMOX ST

Burrard St.
Bridge

Granville
Island

DENMAN ST

Granville Island
Public Market

Sunset Beach

BROUGHTON ST

English Bay Beach

English
Bay

Vanier
Park

CHESTNUT ST

0   1   MILE

0   1   KILOMETER

HONG KONG BANK BUILDING
W. Georgia and Hornby Sts.
Vancouver
604/641-2973

You can't miss this building—it occupies the city's most central corner, directly across the street from the Vancouver Art Gallery. The Hong Kong Bank Building (the banking center is on the main floor) is much more than a bank: it's one of Vancouver's best unofficial art galleries. The main permanent attraction in the towering atrium lobby is the world's largest pendulum, designed by Vancouver artist and inventor Alan Storey. As the earth spins, it swings. Art exhibits, staged in the atrium, are always free and open to the public and include works by local and Native artists and schoolchildren. Mon–Sat 7:30–6. ⅙ (Downtown)

HOTEL EUROPE
43 Powell St.
Vancouver

If Gastown has a building that symbolizes the neighborhood's finest moments, this is it. Built in 1912 and modeled after New York City's Flatiron Building, the Hotel Europe was Vancouver's first steel-and-concrete structure. It had a lobby famous for its brass and marble detailing, and it was, at the time, the most lavish hotel in Vancouver. This grand lobby was gutted in the 1950s to expand the hotel's beer hall. (Unfortunately, the movement in the 1960s to save Gastown from the wrecking ball came a little too late.) Sadly, the hotel no longer accepts overnight guests and isn't open for tours—it's occupied by small businesses, including small antique stores. (Downtown)

LIBRARY SQUARE
350 W. Georgia St.

Vancouver
604/331-3670

In the winter of 1996, renowned Italian mezzo-soprano Cecilia Bartoli was in the Canadian Broadcasting Company (CBC) Building for a recording session. At one point, she looked across the street at the then newly constructed Vancouver main library complex. "Oh, we have one of these," she said, referring to the square's Roman Coliseum design. Completed in 1995, the postmodern seven-level library is an ambitious complex that also includes a nearby 21-story office tower. Within the circular cement walls of the building's massive atrium is a series of retail outlets, including restaurants, coffee shops, bookstores, and other small shops. The three-level parking garage offers the least expensive parking in the downtown area. The library itself, outfitted with computer terminals fully wired for access to the Internet, is designed for the future. Mon–Thu 10–8, Fri–Sat 10–5, Sun 1–5; closed Sun during summer. ⅙ (Downtown)

MAPLE LEAF SQUARE
Intersection of Water
and Carrall Sts.
Vancouver

Maple Leaf Square is the link between Chinatown and Gastown. It's also a miniature melting pot of economic and social zones, where yuppies, tourists, and Vancouver's less-affluent East Side residents mingle daily. Despite the fact that the square attracts both drug dealers and panhandlers, it's not a particularly dangerous place. A bronze statue of Gassy Jack Deighton, Vancouver's first nonnative resident, shown standing on a whiskey barrel, guards the intersection where Carrall Street, Alexander Street, and Powell Street

Stanley Park

Visiting Vancouver without ever seeing and walking through Stanley Park is like going to Manhattan and skipping Central Park—you can still have fun, but you'll have missed an important cultural icon. This 1,000-acre park opened in September 1888 and has been Vancouver's prime walking and doing place ever since. It's a mix of wilderness, sophisticated restaurants, and recreational facilities, with everything from an aquarium to an outdoor theater to hiking, cycling, and horse trails.

The best way to see the park (and the city) is by walking the 10.5-kilometer seawall that encircles it. The wall offers a magnificent view of Downtown, the North Shore, English Bay, and Point Grey. From the seawall one can branch out on side paths and roads. Bike rentals and maps are available at the park's entrance on Georgia and Denman Streets.

Along your journey you'll encounter lots of interesting attractions. For example, Deadman's Island, next to the Rowing Club, is where the Coast Salish Native Peoples buried their dead (it's now used as a naval training station). During the smallpox epidemic of 1888, it was also used to quarantine the ill, most of whom were prostitutes and Chinese. It's said that on misty nights the

intersect to become Water Street, the main thoroughfare of Gastown. Read the plaque on the wall of Miriam's Ice Cream Parlor, behind the statue, for a history of the corner and of Jack's second saloon. (Downtown)

ROBSON SQUARE
W. Georgia St., Howe St., Hornby St., and Robson St.
Vancouver
No place in Vancouver is more "downtown" than this. Robson Street, the busiest pedestrian thoroughfare

in greater Vancouver, separates the courthouse complex from the Vancouver Art Gallery (see listing, below). Robson Square begins with the massive slopes of glass covering the courthouse building opposite the Wedgewood Hotel. The courthouse opens up into a public space with a waterfall, trees, many stairs, and a ramp—the gathering place of young people in the summer—that descends to a lower level of restaurants, conference rooms, and a skating rink. Arthur Erickson, the occasional ghost walks across the causeway that connects Deadman's Island to Stanley Park.

Nearby is Malkin Bowl, an outdoor theater where, during the summer, you can watch popular Broadway shows staged by a local semiprofessional theater group, Theatre under the Stars. Local artists display and sell their work here. At Brockton Oval, you can sit on the grass and watch (or simply be confused by) a cricket match. The Nature Centre, near the entrance to the park, is a good place to learn about the area's fauna, flora, and other wildlife. Ask the staff to point you toward lily-covered Beaver Lake, a perfect place for peaceful contemplation.

Opposite Deadman's Island stand a number of totem poles carved by the Kwakiutl and Haida peoples. The poles are near the Nine O'Clock Gun, which was originally used to call fishermen home at night. (Today residents use the gun to check their watches and clocks. Beware, it's loud!) Nearby is the most popular spot in the park, the Vancouver Aquarium (see listing, below).

Keep walking on the seawall and you'll eventually come to Prospect Point, which overlooks the Lion's Gate Bridge and the North Shore. Continue on and you'll arrive at Ferguson Point, where among other things you can have a fine seaside meal at the Tea house at Ferguson Point.

complex's architect, designed this structure to be both functional and a testament to the idea that high-rises are not the only alternative for inner cities. After the courthouse was constructed, the classical-style former courthouse on Georgia Street at the north end of the site became the home of the art gallery. (Downtown)

SAM KEE BUILDING
Corner of Pender and Carrall Sts.
Vancouver
If you come across what looks like a building that has been on a diet for a long time, it's probably this place. Built in 1913, the Sam Kee is the narrowest building in the world, at a slim 1.8 meters wide, 30 meters long, and two stories tall. The building looks bigger than it really is because of the bay windows on the upper floor. A sidewalk made of small glass blocks and steel reinforcements forms a glass roof for the basement below it. Sam Kee (whose real name was Cheng Toy) was a poor immigrant who became a successful import merchant.

There's a real buried treasure somewhere in Stanley Park. In 1942 a bank robber is rumored to have buried $25,000 in a cluster of trees near the Brockton Point Oval. Treasure hunters are discouraged by the $500 fine that can be levied for digging in the park.

He began construction of his building after the street was widened, so he didn't have a lot of space with which to work. The building, once a store that sold gorgeous silks, now houses an insurance office. You can go inside, but you'll find yourself in a working office. (Downtown)

STEAM CLOCK
Corner of Water and Cambie Sts.
Vancouver

In 1977 clockmaker Ray Saunders decided that the underground steam pipes that heated the buildings in Gastown were a great source of power. He ended up building a steam-powered clock there simply because it could be done. Standing at five meters tall, the clock is an impressive item. It has a four-sided glass face, a 20-kilogram gold-plated pendulum, and a Gothic-style roof. The clock toots and erupts in a cloud of steam every 15 minutes. Saunders, who has built 12 other public clocks scattered throughout Vancouver, isn't alone in creating unusual time devices. In fact, Vancouver has some of the weirdest "clocks" in North America, including the Nine O'Clock Gun on the shore of Burrard Inlet; the clock on Canada Place that blasts out the first four notes of "O Canada"; and the world's largest functioning lunar tidal clock, located at the Bridgeport Building in Richmond near the Oak Street Bridge. (Downtown)

VANCOUVER AQUARIUM
Stanley Park
Vancouver
604/659-3474

Haida artist Bill Reid's massive bronze statue of a killer whale in its own reflecting pool marks Canada's largest aquarium. Inside the aquarium more than 8,000 species of aquatic life from around the world are on display in a variety of viewing rooms. The most popular creatures in the building are the killer whales, which eat up to 60 kilograms of fish a day. If you sit too close to the water's edge as the whales do their "big splash" routine you'll get drenched. Call for hours. $12.85 adults; $10.95 seniors; students, $8.55 ages 4–12; children under 3 free. (See also Chapter 7, Kids' Stuff.) & (Downtown)

VANCOUVER ART GALLERY
750 Hornby St.
Vancouver
604/662-4700

The Vancouver Art Gallery is located in the heart of the downtown core in the old Vancouver Provincial Courthouse. The courthouse was designed by Francis Rattenbury more than 90 years ago and was renovated in 1983 by noted architect Arthur Erickson. Here you'll find historical and contemporary exhibitions of painting, sculpture, graphic arts, photography, and video by distinguished regional, national, and international artists. A portion of the permanent collection, which covers four centuries of Canadian art, as well as Dutch paintings from the seventeenth and eighteenth centuries and modern British paintings and sculpture from 1933 to 1955, is always on view. So too are the paintings and drawings by Emily Carr—the gallery has the largest permanent collection of her work in Canada. (See also Chapter 6, Museums and Galleries, and Chapter 7, Kids' Stuff.) (Downtown)

WATERFRONT STATION
Canadian Pacific Building
601 W. Cordova St.
Vancouver
604/683-3266
The CPR railway station, meticulously restored in 1978 to its original 1914 beaux-arts style, is now a terminal for the Seabus and Sky Train transportation systems. The station lies next to Gastown and is adjacent to the Convention Centre and the Pan Pacific/Canadian Pacific Waterfront Hotel properties. The high ceilings and restored original woodworking and tile floor of the building's interior are very impressive. It's also a gathering place for young people—you'll find them sipping coffee and munching muffins at Café Zoom or Starbucks. (Downtown)

UPTOWN

GRANVILLE ISLAND BREWERY
1441 Cartwright St.
Vancouver
604/687-2739
If you're looking for a cold beer on a hot day, there's no better place to go than the Granville Island Brewery, one of Vancouver's most popular microbreweries. Stop in for a free 30-minute tour and sampling session. Granville Island Lager is one of the city's favorite local

Granville Island

Granville Island was once a giant industrial wasteland that spewed toxic pollutants into the air and the waters of False Creek. That changed in 1972, when the federal government created the Granville Island Trust and began leasing the land to city-backed businesses. In July 1979 the Granville Island Public Market opened and was an immediate success. Today the island still has some clean industry, but most of it is dedicated to other, user-friendly activities. Stop by the Granville Island Information Centre, across from the Public Market, for brochures, information, and a bit of history before venturing further onto the island. The center has a terrific map of the area, a money exchange, and a bank machine, as well as a couple of desk people available to answer questions.

UPTOWN/POINT GREY

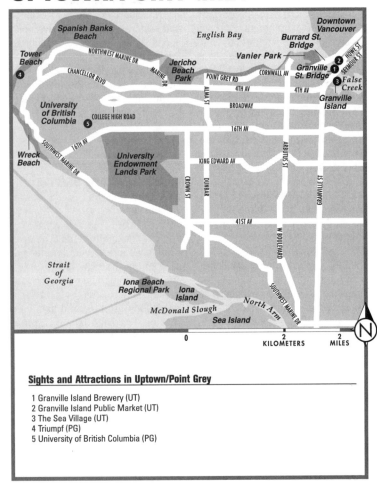

Sights and Attractions in Uptown/Point Grey

1 Granville Island Brewery (UT)
2 Granville Island Public Market (UT)
3 The Sea Village (UT)
4 Triumpf (PG)
5 University of British Columbia (PG)

brews and is found in every pub in town. Little wonder. It's a preservative-free Bavarian-style pilsner. If you've never been in a brewery and have always wondered how the golden stuff was made, you couldn't have a better opportunity to find out. The smells alone are worth the admission price. Hours vary seasonally—call ahead. $6

adults, $5 seniors and students. (Uptown)

GRANVILLE ISLAND PUBLIC MARKET
1669 Johnson St.
Vancouver
604/666-5784
The Granville Island Public Market is the heart and soul of Granville Island.

Oh, the delicious mix of smells! Anything and everything food-related from Vancouver's ethnic and mainstream communities is here in this 4,645-square-meter beehive of activity. Visitors and locals alike come to this indoor market to buy fresh produce, breads, meat, seafood, and fast foods. Others come just to look, walk, and people-watch among the hundreds of stalls. Benches and picnic tables are outside the market on the dock. Open daily 9–6. ᵗ (Uptown)

THE SEA VILLAGE
Dockside on the north side of the Emily Carr College of Art and Design
Vancouver

Chances are you'd miss this unusual community unless you were really looking for it. Tied up to the dock is an intricate community of small houseboats in a series of interlocked floating docks. This is West Coast living at its most picturesque. The houseboats are a rainbow of colors—blues, yellows, and reds against the comparative whiteness of the West End

high-rises across False Creek. On a windy day you can hear the docks creak as the boats strain against them, seagulls circle overhead, and residents come and go in their small boats—houseboat residents are the only people who live on Granville Island, and they do it in style. (Uptown)

POINT GREY

TRIUMPF
University of British Columbia
Westbrook Mall
Vancouver
604/222-7355

There aren't many places where you can tour an atomic research center that specializes in subatomic particles. Fortunately, you don't have to worry about anything blowing up. A visit here is as safe as a walk in the nearby park. A free 90-minute tour allows you to watch the world's largest cyclotron— a circular particle accelerator in which charged subatomic particles are accelerated spirally outward by an alternating electric field—in action. It's

The world's largest cyclotron at the Triumpf atomic research center

Triumpf

EAST VANCOUVER

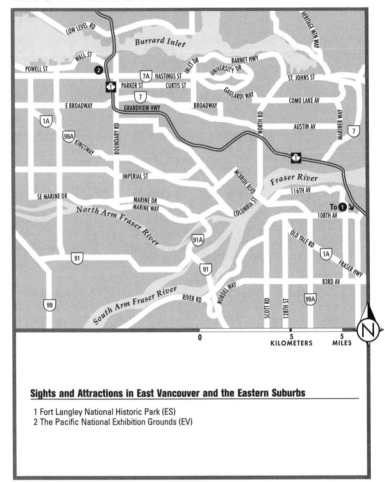

Sights and Attractions in East Vancouver and the Eastern Suburbs

1 Fort Langley National Historic Park (ES)
2 The Pacific National Exhibition Grounds (EV)

capable of generating millions of volts. The center is located south of 16th Avenue in the Westbrook Mall. Summer tours Mon–Fri twice daily; winter Mon–Fri twice weekly. Drop-in tours available. Call in advance for hours. Free. & (Point Grey)

UNIVERSITY OF BRITISH COLUMBIA

2075 Westbrook Mall
Vancouver
604/822-2211

It's a wonder that students get anything done on this UBC campus. The views of the mountains, Howe Sound, Vancouver Island, Gulf Island, the city, and the ocean must be terribly distracting to any student with an eye for beauty. The university is home to about 40,000 students, but it's much more than just a place of study. It's also a jumping-off point to the forests, beachfront, gardens, theaters, and remarkable architecture. Walking tours depart from the student union building (at the center of campus, behind the library) Sept–April Tue–Thu 9:30 and 12:30; call ahead for summer tour times. Free. ♿ (Point Grey)

EAST VANCOUVER

THE PACIFIC NATIONAL EXHIBI-TION GROUNDS
East Hastings St. at Renfrew St.
604/253-2311
The Pacific National Exhibition (PNE) is an agricultural fair that has been held yearly since 1910. But what was originally designed as an exhibition of farming has grown to be much more. Held over a couple of weeks at the end of August and early September (ending on Labor Day), the PNE is one of the largest agricultural fairs in North America. You'll see horse shows, craft shows, horticultural exhibits, a petting farm, and an international food fair, as well as musical entertainment. Government plans to move the exhibition and turn the grounds into a large neighborhood park are in the works.

The exhibition itself is only one element within the 114-acre PNE grounds. You'll also find Hastings Park, home to thoroughbred horse racing (See Chapter 10, Sports and Recreation) and Playland, a large amusement park that's open April 2 through Labor Day ($17.95 adults, $14.95 for anyone less than 48 inches tall). The PNE Grounds are also the home of the now-largely-vacant Pacific Coliseum, a 16,000 seat stadium where the Vancouver Canucks hockey team used to play. The stadium is now used primarily for conventions and exhibitions. ♿ (East Vancouver)

NORTH SHORE

CAPILANO SUSPENSION BRIDGE
3735 Capilano Rd.
North Vancouver
604/985-7474
Scary! This is one of Vancouver's oldest attractions—a swinging footbridge only five feet wide, suspended 70 meters above the Capilano Canyon. Originally built in 1889 by George Grant Mackay and two local Natives, it was designed to span the 450 feet between the two sides of Capilano Canyon and thereby provide a link between the two halves of Mackay's property. The current metal bridge is a vast improvement over the original, and today thousands of tourists can walk across the secure but shaky span. Anthropology and forestry tours are offered along the canyon's rims May through September. Summer daily 8–dusk; winter daily 9–5. $8.50. (North Shore)

GROUSE MOUNTAIN
6400 Nancy Greene Way
North Vancouver
604/984-0661
The most spectacular views of the city, English Bay, Mount Baker, and the Strait of Georgia are from the top of Grouse Mountain. This is one of Vancouver's most popular attractions year-round because of its skiing facilities, restaurants, hiking, and other family entertainment. Take the Lion's Gate Bridge to Capilano Drive; the road ends at the cable-car station, from which the aerial tramway—

Skyride—will whisk you to the 1,100-meter summit. You'll arrive next to a large building housing a gift shop, a theater, a full-service restaurant (the Grouse Nest), a cafeteria, and a pub. Walking paths and nature trails offer some of the best hiking on the West Coast, all within just a few minutes of downtown Vancouver. During the winter you can ski, and the Peak chair lift stays open in the summer. Hikers should check the mountain map and ask for a trail map at the Skyride—the really ambitious ones can climb to the top via the Grouse Grind. Round out the day with a visit to the multimedia Theater in the Sky for a high-definition video about British Columbia. During summer there are 25-kilometer mountain bike tours of the nearby trails and tandem paragliding from the top of the peak. Helicopter tours are also available. Limited ♿ accessibility. Open daily 9 a.m.–10 p.m. Skyride $16.50 adults (round trip). ♿ (North Shore)

LIGHTHOUSE PARK
Marine Dr. and Beacon Ln.

West Vancouver
604/925-7200
The main attraction of this rugged park on the North Shore is, well, the lighthouse. Atkinson Point was first charted and explored by Captain George Vancouver in 1792, and a crude lighthouse was constructed and manned beginning in 1875. Point Atkinson Lighthouse, built in 1912, is a working lighthouse, though it is open to the public occasionally. The trail to the lighthouse, about a 10-minute walk, is one of the North Shore's best. Featuring one of the area's last remaining stands of old-growth Douglas fir, as well as a host of eagles, the park is an ideal place to meander on any of the numerous trails, picnic, or get some fine photos of the surrounding ocean, islands, and English Bay. Park open daily dawn to midnight; lighthouse open for summer tours only. (See also Chapter 8, Parks, Gardens, and Recreation Areas; and Chapter 10, Sports and Recreation.) ♿ (North Shore)

The Grouse Grind

If you have a good set of lungs and thighs of steel, try hiking up—straight up—Grouse Mountain. It's a 2.9-kilometer walk from the trailhead at the end of Capilano Road (at the bottom of the Skyride) to the summit. If you're in great shape, it'll take about an hour. Otherwise, it will take from 90 minutes to two hours at a comfortable pace. Carry water, wear hiking boots, and be careful—winter avalanches are not uncommon. The hike up is free, but if you decide you'd rather take the Skyride back to the base, it will cost you five dollars.

NORTH SHORE

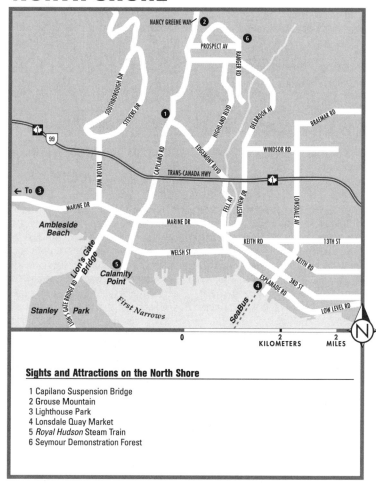

NANCY GREENE WAY ❷
❻
PROSPECT AV
RANGER RD
SOUTHBOROUGH DR
STEVENS DR
HIGHLAND BLVD
DELBROOK AV
BRAEMAR RD
❶
CAPILANO RD
EDGEMONT BLVD
WINDSOR RD
99
TAYLOR WAY
TRANS-CANADA HWY
← To ❸
MARINE DR
FELL AV
WESTVIEW DR
LONSDALE AV
Ambleside
Beach
MARINE DR
Lion's Gate Bridge
KEITH RD
13TH ST
WELSH ST
KEITH RD
❺
Calamity
Point
3RD ST
LION'S GATE BRIDGE RD
ESPLANADE RD
❹
First Narrows
SeaBus
LOW LEVEL RD
Stanley Park
N

0   2   2
       KILOMETERS   MILES

Sights and Attractions on the North Shore

1 Capilano Suspension Bridge
2 Grouse Mountain
3 Lighthouse Park
4 Lonsdale Quay Market
5 *Royal Hudson* Steam Train
6 Seymour Demonstration Forest

LONSDALE QUAY MARKET
123 Carrie Cates Court
North Vancouver
604/985-6261

In 1985, hoping to cash in on some of the offshore and local tourist dollars pouring into the area, the city of North Vancouver decided to follow Granville Island's lead and build a market of its own. The Seabus, the ferry service that crosses Burrard Inlet from the old Canadian Pacific Terminal, arrives at Lonsdale Quay, so the city chose the quay as the location for the market. The market's now a major part of the quay. Its glazed and galleried interior is a throwback to nineteenth-century industrial architecture. Getting to the market is half the fun—glide across the water on the Seabus. Once you get there, you can shop at the market or simply sit at one of the restaurants and gaze at the Vancouver skyline. Open daily 9–6. ᕕ (North Shore)

ROYAL HUDSON STEAM TRAIN
B.C. Rail Station
W. First Ave. between Pemberton Ave. and Philip Ave.
North Vancouver
604/984-5246

OK steam buffs, all aboard! The *Royal Hudson*, Engine 2860, is the last of the 65 steam trains that crisscrossed Canada a half-century ago. Now it takes passengers along Howe Sound to Squamish, combining a sense of British Columbian history with beautiful scenery. The restored coaches and gorgeous views transport passengers back to a time when British Columbia was little more than wilderness and rails. In fact, in the summer of 1939 King George VI and Queen Elizabeth made a royal tour of Canada in this train. The trip can also be combined with a boat trip on the M.V. *Britannia*, one of Canada's largest excursion vessels. Early June–mid-Sept, train departs at 10 a.m.; advance booking is advised for individuals and is required for groups of 20 or more; $46.50 adults 19–59, $40.50 seniors 60 and over, $40.50 children 12–18, $12.75 children 5–11; children under 5 free. (North Shore)

SEYMOUR DEMONSTRATION FOREST
Lillooet Rd. exit off Upper Levels Hwy.
North Vancouver
604/432-6286

It may look like a park, but it's really a part of the Seymour watershed, a series of lakes on Seymour Mountain that provide water to residents of the Lower Mainland. The primary purpose of the demonstration forest—backed by the provincial government and the British Columbia's forest industry—is to help the public understand forestry practices. Fourteen times larger than Stanley Park, this area includes 50 kilometers (30 miles) of paved and gravel roads, attracting hikers, cyclists, and in-line skaters. At the information center in the parking lot, staff members will point you to the best trails. You can also take a 90-minute guided walking tour that will take you through a forest of western red cedar, western hemlock, Douglas fir, amabilis fir, and Sitka spruce. The Forest Ecology Loop trail is one of the easier hikes in the park—great for families with young children. The 22-kilometer (14-mile) hike to the Seymour Dam is much more challenging. To get to the demonstration forest, take the Lillooet Road exit from Highway 1, go past Capilano College, through a cemetery, and up a gravel road to the forest entrance. Despite the

Visitors brave the Capilano Suspension Bridge, p. 109

Capilano Suspension Bridge

Gassy Jack Deighton

One of Vancouver's first non native residents was Jack Deighton, a saloon owner whose boisterous storytelling and drinking abilities earned him the nickname "Gassy Jack." Born in Hull, England, in 1830, he went to sea at the age of 14 and eventually landed on the West Coast.

After working a few odd jobs, Deighton opened the Globe Saloon in 1867 at what is now the intersection of Carrall and Water Streets in Gastown. When the business failed later that year, he and his wife canoed around Point Grey to Burrard Inlet, where he set up another saloon for the employees of a nearby sawmill. Thanks to the built-in clientele, his second business venture was successful. The town—eventually named Gastown in Jack's honor—pretty much grew up around his saloon.

Personal tragedy struck when Jack's wife died in 1870. It wasn't long, however, before he remarried, this time to his deceased wife's niece, a woman named Qwahalia. But Jack's years were numbered, too, and he only lived for another four years before dying from unknown causes at the age of 44. He wasn't around when Gastown, which became Vancouver, burned to the ground in 1886.

350,000 visitors who come here every year (most of whom are schoolchildren on field trips), this is one of Vancouver's best kept secrets. Open in summer only. Call for times. Free. (North Shore)

EASTERN SUBURBS

FORT LANGLEY NATIONAL HISTORIC PARK
Off Hwy. 1
Langley
604/513-4777

You'll find a bit of Disney in this restored Hudson's Bay Company post about one hour east of downtown Vancouver. It was here that British Columbia was declared a British Crown colony. The fur-trading post was built in 1827. The current Fort Langley has only one original building, the storehouse, but everything else has been built to original 1850s specs. Period-costumed entertainers/guides create the crafts of the original pioneers. To get there, take the main highway (Highway 1) and follow the signs at the Fort Langley

SOUTHERN SUBURBS

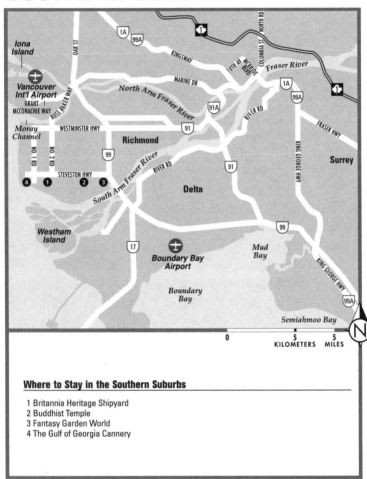

Where to Stay in the Southern Suburbs

1 Britannia Heritage Shipyard
2 Buddhist Temple
3 Fantasy Garden World
4 The Gulf of Georgia Cannery

turnoff. Mar–Oct daily 10–5; Nov–Feb open for pre-booked tours. $4 adults, $3 seniors, $2 children 6–12. (Eastern Suburbs)

SOUTHERN SUBURBS

BRITANNIA HERITAGE SHIPYARD
5180 Westwater Dr.

Richmond
604/718-1200

Dating from the 1890s, this is the oldest shipyard structure remaining on the Fraser River. The weathered buildings include two former boat works, a cannery house, a former dwelling of Japanese laborers, and a recreated Native dwelling dating from the nineteenth century, when

The Skyride takes visitors to Grouse Mountain's 1,100-meter summit, p. 109.

the Salish established fishing industries along the West coast. The shipyard also has special events that highlight old fishing skills (net setting and the making of various tools). A walk on these boardwalks really is a walk into the past. Open year round; call for hours. (Southern Suburbs)

BUDDHIST TEMPLE
9160 Steveston Hwy.
Richmond

TIP

The Gastown Merchants Association provides free 90-minute tours of Gastown from mid-June to the end of August. The tour begins at Gassy Jack's statue in Maple Leaf Square at two o'clock daily. It takes you around the area and provides fascinating historical information.

604/274-2822
This place has been called the most exquisite example of Chinese palatial architecture in North America. With golden porcelain tiles and flying dragons on the roof and marble lions at the foot of the stairway, the temple looks as though it belongs in the heart of China. Leave your shoes outside if you want to enjoy the incredibly ornate interior and the sweet smell of incense. The temple is about 20 minutes from Downtown. Open daily 10–5. Free, but donations accepted. ♿ (Southern Suburbs)

FANTASY GARDEN WORLD
10800 No. 5 Rd.
Richmond
604/277-7777
This may well be Canada's most infamous theme park. Once owned and operated by former British Columbia Premier William Vanderzalm, the property became a political liability when he sold it to Taiwanese business executives under questionable circumstances. It got more ink than any other theme park in Canadian

TRIVIA

Located 20 miles south of Downtown at the far southwestern tip of Richmond, Steveston is home to the largest fleet of commercial fishing vessels on Canada's west coast.

history and turned out to play a major role in the premier's eventual political demise. Despite its dark history, the park has remained a delightful place for adults and children alike. Millions of flowers fill the gorgeously landscaped terrain, a farm has small animals for children, and a European village allows visitors to sample foods from several countries and to experience English tea in the afternoon. You can easily spot this four-hectare spread from Highway 99 near the George Massey tunnel on the way to the U.S. border—just look for the giant windmill. Open daily 9–5. $3.50 adults, $2.50 seniors, $2 children, $7.50 family of four. ♿ (Southern Suburbs)

THE GULF OF GEORGIA CANNERY
12138 Fourth Ave.

Richmond
604/664-9009
The Gulf of Georgia Cannery stands in monument to the industry that once dominated Richmond. Built in 1894, the complex turned out canned food, fish oil, and fishmeal until 1979. Now a heritage site, the original buildings still stand, and are an integral part of the Steveston waterfront. Across from the complex, near the path to Garry Point Park, the Gulf of Georgia Cannery Display Centre displays artifacts from the cannery and offers a compelling view of its history. May–mid-Oct daily 10–5. $5 adults, $2.50 children under 17, $3.50 seniors, $12.50 families. (See also Chapter 6, Museums and Galleries.) (Southern Suburbs)

Vancouver Art Gallery

6

MUSEUMS AND GALLERIES

You won't see many paintings by Renoir, Degas, or Rembrandt in Vancouver art galleries and museums. While a few such works can be found if you look hard enough, most of Vancouver's art is a reflection of the city itself—young, vibrant, fresh, multicultural, and West Coast. Vancouver's art scene is rich and enthusiastic, and many of its artists have established laudable reputations in the international community. Among those who have attained artistic fame now or in the past are Jack Shadbolt, Emily Carr, Gordon Smith, Lawren Harris, Bill Reid, Toni Onley, and Fred Varley.

The Vancouver community places great importance on social movements and the city's cultural past, and many museums reflect that devotion. These comprehensive and minute historical museums reflect the complex nature of Vancouver settlement. Throughout the city and suburbs, Native Peoples, Asians, and Europeans are all represented in a variety of specialty and general museums and science centers. Where does science begin and art end? Or vice versa? After your tour of the city's museums, galleries, and indoor and outdoor public art, you may no longer have the answer.

ART MUSEUMS

CANADIAN CRAFT MUSEUM
639 Hornby St.
Vancouver
604/687-8266
How many ways can you fold cloth or mold glass? Everything you wanted to know about how to make objects from paper, cloth, and other craft basics is contained within the walls of this three-story building tucked away on Cathedral Place. This is Canada's first national museum devoted en-

Who Was Emily Carr?

You'll hear the name Emily Carr mentioned often when you're in Vancouver. An art school on Granville Island was named after her, and the Vancouver Art Gallery has devoted an entire wing to her work. She was, and still is, British Columbia's artistic heart. Born in 1871, Carr painted and drew the natural elements in British Columbia long before it was easy to get from here to there or anywhere. It was just water and trees.

Summers on Queen Charlotte Island brought her into contact with the subject matter—Native culture and coastal landscapes— that would bring her recognition later in life. Her work was influenced by Impressionism, Fauvism, and Cubism, but she portrayed nature in a powerful style all her own. Her paintings, such as Rushing Sea of Undergrowth *(1936, Vancouver Art Gallery), are characterized by intense colors and swirling spiral forms.*

Always dressed in a shapeless coat and high-laced shoes, with her hair held in place by a dark hairnet, she spent a lifetime having her "modern" art lambasted by the artistic establishment. Still, many artists followed her lead. In fact, she was as important to the British Columbian art movement as the Group of Seven was to the rest of the country.

When Carr wasn't painting, she bred sheepdogs and made pottery. Chronically poor, she painted on manila paper, using oils she thinned with gasoline. By the 1930s her work was finally recognized on an international scale, but even that didn't help her finances. While recovering from the first of her four heart attacks, she began writing about her life. At the age of 70 her first book about travels with the Natives of the Pacific Northwest, Klee Wyck, *was published. ("Klee Wyck" is the Indian name given to Carr by the First Nations people in Ucluelet, on Vancouver Island; it means "laughing one.") The book earned her a Governor General's Award. Three other books that followed,* The Book of Small, The House of All Sorts, *and* Growing Pains, *were chronicles of her own life.*

Carr died in 1945. Her birthplace in Victoria, at 207 Government Street, has since been restored for public viewing. Her works are on permanent display in both Vancouver and Victoria.

tirely to crafts. Located a couple of blocks north of the Vancouver Art Gallery, the museum includes local, national, and international craft artists. The permanent collection includes delicate glass, pottery, and jewelry, augmented by special exhibitions. The museum has a gift shop. Mon and Wed–Fri 10–5, Sat–Sun and holidays 10–6. $5 adults, $3 seniors, students, and children under 12. &. (Downtown)

EMILY CARR COLLEGE OF ART AND DESIGN
1399 Johnson St.
Vancouver
604/844-3811
The Emily Carr College of Art and Design, situated between the Granville Island Hotel and the market, welcomes visitors to its Scott Gallery, where student artwork is on display. Huge picture windows allow visitors to watch the budding artists at work. The college is one of the few Canadian art institutions that offer a bachelor degree. If you'll be in town for a while you can sign up for one of the visitor's art courses. Gallery open Mon–Sat 10–5. Free. &. (Uptown)

MUSEUM OF ANTHROPOLOGY
University of British Columbia
6393 NW Marine Dr.
Vancouver
604/822-3825
The magnificent Museum of Anthropology houses a dozen galleries that reflect indigenous cultures from around the world. In fact, the work here amounts to the best collection of Pacific Northwest Native art on the planet. Although the building complex is relatively new—built in 1976—the University of British Columbia has had an anthropology program and collection for 50 years and

is recognized as a world-class research facility.

In the Great Hall, light streams in from 14-meter-high windows to highlight weathered cedar totem poles. In the Masterpiece Gallery you'll find intricately carved pieces of argillite, ivory, gold, silver, bone, and wood, most of which date from the eighteenth century. The old merges with the new in Bill Reid's massive sculpture, *The Raven and the First Men.* The sculpture depicts how the raven fooled the first people into emerging from their clamshell. Other exhibit halls have work from European, South Pacific, and Vancouver artists. The museum also has an outdoor sculpture garden and two carved Haida houses. Hours vary (call ahead). $6 adults, $3.50 seniors and students (See also Chapter 7, Kids' Stuff.) &. (Point Grey)

VANCOUVER ART GALLERY
750 Hornby St.
Vancouver
604/662-4700
The Vancouver Art Gallery is about as Downtown as you can get. It occupies an entire block in the absolute center of the city, right next to the Hotel Vancouver. The neoclassical building was designed by British architect Francis Rattenbury, whose other credits include the parliament buildings and the Empress Hotel in Victoria.

The museum's permanent collection includes a wide variety of Canadian, British, and American works dating back to the sixteenth century, but it's known mostly for its works by Emily Carr, a British Columbian who painted West Coast Native Peoples and landscapes (see sidebar, this chapter). The exhibits in the Children's Gallery change frequently, and on the third Sunday of each month

MUST-SEE MUSEUMS & GALLERIES

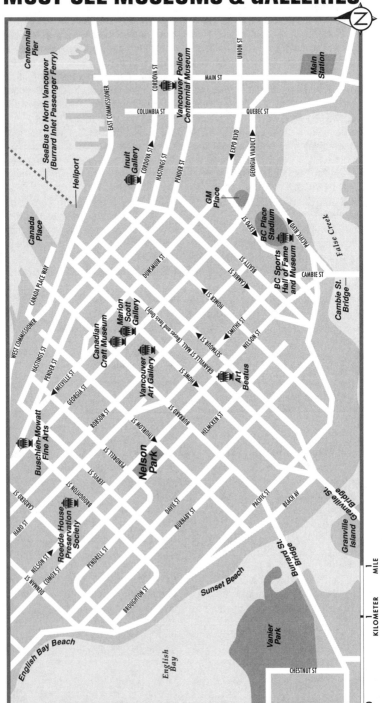

Centennial Pier

SeaBus to North Vancouver (Burrard Inlet Passenger Ferry)

Heliport

UNION ST

Main Station

CORDOVA ST

MAIN ST

Vancouver Police Centennial Museum

EAST COMMISSIONER

COLUMBIA ST

QUEBEC ST

Inuit Gallery

CORDOVA ST

HASTINGS ST

PENDER ST

EXPO BLVD

GEORGIA VIADUCT

Canada Place

GM Place

EXPO ST

BC Place Stadium

PACIFIC BLVD

False Creek

CANADA PLACE WAY

DUNSMUIR ST

BEATTY ST

BC Sports Hall of Fame and Museum

CAMBIE ST

Cambie St. Bridge

WEST COMMISSIONER

HASTINGS ST

PENDER ST

MELVILLE ST

GEORGIA ST

ROBSON ST

Marion Scott Gallery

Canadian Craft Museum

Vancouver Art Gallery

HOMER ST

CAMBIE ST

SMITHE ST

SEYMOUR ST

GRANVILLE ST MALL (Buses and Taxis Only)

HOWE ST

NELSON ST

Art Beatus

Buschlen-Mowatt Fine Arts

THURLOW ST

BURRARD ST

HELMCKEN ST

CARDERO ST

NICOLA ST

BROUGHTON ST

JERVIS ST

BUTE ST

Nelson Park

PENDRELL ST

DAVIE ST

BURNABY ST

PACIFIC ST

BEACH AV

Granville St. Bridge

Granville Island

NELSON ST

COMOX ST

DENMAN ST

Roedde House Preservation Society

BROUGHTON ST

Sunset Beach

Burrard St. Bridge

English Bay Beach

English Bay

Vanier Park

CHESTNUT ST

0   KILOMETER   1

0   MILE   1

the place is filled with kids enjoying art-making studios, interpretive performances, guided tours, and art demonstrations. You'll find a casual restaurant on the mezzanine floor. Call for special exhibit openings. $10 adults, $6 seniors and students, children 12 and under free. (See also Chapter 5, Sights and Attractions, and Chapter 7, Kids' Stuff.) ♿ (Downtown)

SCIENCE AND HISTORY MUSEUMS

BURNABY VILLAGE MUSEUM
6501 Deer Lake Ave.
Burnaby
604/293-6501
Getting married when you're in town? There's no better place to do so than here, where an entire turn-of-the-twentieth-century village was constructed from scratch to celebrate British Columbia's centenary in 1958. Get married in the church, then walk over to the ice-cream parlor for your reception. If you're not getting hitched, take a look at the 1890s dentist office—guaranteed, your jaw will tighten. Those hooked to the Internet will appreciate modern technology even more when they see what a professional printer had to go through in the old days. On the other hand, those who wish the technological revolution had never happened can relive their childhoods by taking a spin on the colorful 1912 carousel. In all, 30 buildings depict life between 1890 and 1925. Summer daily 9–9; call ahead for non summer hours. Free ♿ (Eastern Suburbs)

CANADIAN MUSEUM OF FLIGHT AND TRANSPORTATION
Langley Airport
5333 216th St.
Langley
604/532-0035
You'll want to take flight after seeing the vintage aircraft in this wonderful museum. The museum is in Langley Airport, a small-aircraft facility off Highway 1, about one hour from downtown Vancouver. The collection includes a Tiger Moth, a Sopwith Camel, and an Avro Canuck, among

A 1940 Harvard MKII at the Canadian Museum of Flight and Transportation

Dennis Cardy

TRIVIA

The Vancouver Art Gallery claims a ghost named Charlie as one of its permanent residents. He supposedly lives in the catacombs, where the holding cells of the former courthouse were located, and is said to be the spirit of William Charles Hopkinson, an immigration officer murdered there in 1914.

others. But the exhibit offers more than old hardware. The library has an extensive collection of books and pamphlets, the exhibits explain how planes fly, and a terrific gift shop sells aircraft memorabilia. Daily 10–4. $5 adults, $4 seniors, $12 families. ♿ (Southern Suburbs)

CITY OF VANCOUVER ARCHIVES
Vanier Park
1500 Chestnut St.
Vancouver
604/736-8561
From the outside this place looks like a cement bunker designed to survive an atomic blast. Inside, however, is quite a different story. In fact, it's downright tranquil. This quiet government office building contains wonderful old photos of the city and enough Vancouver-related literature to keep you burrowed in pages for a lifetime. If you're a tourist, you probably won't be interested in the papers, maps, newspaper clippings, and books. But the photos, most of which are displayed in binders, are worth seeing. Located just behind the Southam Observatory. Mon–Fri 9:30–5:30. Free. ♿ (Point Grey)

GEOLOGY MUSEUM
University of British Columbia
6339 Stores Rd.
Vancouver

604/822-2449
Virtually unknown to tourists, this is a gem in every sense of the word. Not only can you find displays of every Canadian stone and rock that glows and sparkles, but you can also check out a collection of 80-million-year-old lambeosaurus dinosaur bones. Want to know what's happened in the past 4 billion years or so? This is the place to find out. Mon–Fri 10–5. Free. ♿ (Point Grey)

GORDON SOUTHAM OBSERVATORY
Vanier Park
1100 Chestnut St.
Vancouver
604/738-2855
You can't miss this place—it's the small domed building right next to the Pacific Space Centre. The Gordon Southam Observatory houses a 50-centimeter reflector telescope, and on clear nights an astronomer will explain how it works and let you look through it to see the stars and galaxies. You can even take your own photos of the moon and listen to old NASA broadcasts. This hands-on approach to astronomy is a delight for children and adults alike. Winter Fri–Sun 12–5; summer 7 p.m.–11 p.m. when the sky is clear. Free. ♿ (Point Grey)

The Group of Seven

The Group of Seven, founded in 1920 as an organization of self-proclaimed modern artists, is to Canada and Canadians what the Impressionists are to France. You'll hear the name often and see the group's paintings at the Vancouver Art Gallery and elsewhere. The original members consisted of Franklin Carmichael, Lawren Harris, A. Y. Jackson, Franz Johnson, Arthur Lismer, J. E. H. Macdonald, and F. H. Varley, all of whom became friends in Toronto between 1911 and 1913. All except Harris, who was independently wealthy, made their living as commercial artists, and several of them even worked together in the same shop.

Tom Thomson, another commercial artist, was included in this circle of friends, but since he died in 1917 he never became an official member of the group. He was important to the other artists, however, and as an avid outdoorsman he piqued their interest in painting the rugged landscape of northern Ontario.

The Group of Seven was drawn together by a common sense of frustration with the conservative and imitative quality of most Canadian art. They were essentially Romantic, with mystical leanings, and constantly presented themselves as Canada's national school of painters, thereby angering the artistic establishment. Like the European symbolists and post-Impressionists from the late-nineteenth and early-twentieth centuries, the Group of Seven rebelled against the constraints of nineteenth-century naturalism and tried to establish a more equitable and independent relationship between art and nature.

THE GULF OF GEORGIA CANNERY NATIONAL HISTORIC SITE
12138 Fourth Ave.
Richmond
604/664-9009
As you'll quickly discover, there's more to catching salmon than pulling in a net. Built in 1894 in historic Steveston, this was once the biggest cannery on the West Coast, and it retains many of the smells and the harsh working character of those days. At one time, the cannery's 10,000-member workforce consisted

mostly of Japanese immigrants, attracted to the area by what seemed then to be an unending supply of salmon. The Cannery Store and Canning Line exhibit takes you down a 1930s-era salmon-canning production line, complete with accompanying noise and clatter. May–mid-Oct daily 10–5. $5 adults; $2.50 children under 17; $3.50 seniors; $12.50 families. & (Southern Suburbs)

HASTING MILLS STORE MUSEUM
1575 Alma St.
Vancouver
604/734-1212
Built in 1865, the Hasting Mills Store was Vancouver's first general store, meeting place, post office, and church, and—as the headquarters of the British Columbia and Vancouver Island Spar, Lumber, and Sawmill Company—the city's first employer. It was also one of the very few buildings that survived the fire of 1886. In 1930 the building was moved from its original location in Gastown to its present spot at the north foot of Alma Street in Point Grey. Inside the store you'll find notions, furniture, hardware, toiletries, and dry goods dating from Queen Victoria's time. June–mid-Sept daily 11–4; winter weekends 1–4. Admission by donation. & (Point Grey)

PACIFIC SPACE CENTRE
Vanier Park
1100 Chestnut St.
Vancouver
604/738-7827
Want to wallow in space and space gadgets? The Pacific Space Centre is a recent, natural outgrowth of the H. R. MacMillan Planetarium. Occupying the top floor of the planetarium, it has one of the finest stargazing programs in North America. It's not quite the Enterprise's "Holo-deck," but the Cosmic Interactive Exhibition Gallery will give you a good idea of what it might be like. The museum's state-of-the-art ground station Canada Multimedia Theatre allows astronaut wannabes to take a journey to Mars on British Columbia's first full-motion simulator. Tue.–Sun. 10–5. $12.50 adults, $9 ages 13–18, $8.50 ages

The Gulf of Georgia Cannery, built at the turn of the last century, p.123

A. Kirkby

5–10. (See also Chapter 7, Kids' Stuff.) ♿ (Point Grey)

ROEDDE HOUSE PRESERVATION SOCIETY
1415 Barclay St.
Vancouver
604/684-7040

You could throw quite a party at this place. This is Vancouver's first restored house-museum. Built in 1893, the house was once the residence of Vancouver's first bookbinder, Gustav Anton Roedde. It's also one of the very few residences built by architect Francis Mawson Rattenbury (designer of the Vancouver Art Gallery). Fully restored down to the wallpaper, the house is one of nine old residences in Barclay Heritage Square in the heart of the West End. You can rent the place, complete with an 1893 Steinway, for your own private party. Summer daily 10–5. Call ahead for admission fees and off-season hours. ♿ (Downtown)

SCIENCE WORLD
1455 Quebec St.
Vancouver
604/443-7440

On the east end of Burrard Inlet, south of Chinatown, Science World sits like a golf ball with an attitude. Check out exhibits such as Gravitram, where you can experiment with energy and the forces of gravity, and Search Gallery, which focuses on British Columbia's natural history. In the latter exhibit you'll find tree roots hanging from the ceiling, a crawl-through beaver lodge, and a see-through beehive. Another exhibit describes the study of physiognomy (how faces express feeling, deceive, encode identity, and record experience), and the Science Theatre includes laser-light and electricity shows.

The centerpiece and biggest draw, of course, is the 400-seat Omnimax Theatre, in which the audience is surrounded by huge images on the five-story, domed screen, and engulfed in wrap-around sound. The theater's shows cover a wide variety of subjects, including the vast and icy world of Antarctica, the explosive ring of Pacific Rim volcanoes, and the history of transportation. Mon–Fri 10–5, Sat–Sun and holidays 10–6; Omnimax Theatre open evenings. Admission for both Science World and Omnimax Theatre $14.50 adults, $10.25 seniors, students, and children; Science World admission only $11.25 adults, $7.50 seniors, students, and children; Omnimax admission only $9.75; children ages 3 and under free. (See also Chapter 7, Kids' Stuff.) ♿ (Uptown)

VANCOUVER HOLOCAUST EDUCATION CENTRE
Jewish Community Centre
50-950 W. 41st Ave.
Vancouver
604/264-0499

Since it opened in 1994, the education center has been an important part of Vancouver's cultural life. Its mandate is to combat prejudice and racism by educating the citizens of British Columbia, especially students and teachers, about the events and implications of the Holocaust. Local survivors of the Holocaust created this teaching museum, and many have recorded eye-

TRIVIA

The Science World dome has 391 lights and 766 triangles.

witness testimonials. The center's interdisciplinary programs have traditionally supported arts and film. Among the moving art exhibits are rubbings by Nomi Kaplan taken directly from the headstones of Jewish graveyards in Europe. Her presentation of the inscription at Treblinka honors those slaughtered in that infamous Polish camp, while making us confront the darkest side of human nature. Mon, Wed, Sun 9–5; Tue, Thu 9–9; Fri 9–3. Free. ♿ (Uptown)

VANCOUVER MARITIME MUSEUM
1905 Ogden Ave.
Vancouver
604/257-8300
The first thing you'll see at the Maritime Museum is at the entrance— a Kwakiutl totem pole that towers more than 30 meters into the sky. Then your eyes will fall on the wooden 1928 sailing ketch, the *St. Roch,* on display in its own permanent, glass building. The former Royal Canadian Mounted Police (RCMP) craft, the first sailing vessel to circumnavigate the Northwest Passage from west to east, was built in 1928 as a supply ship for the far-flung arctic RCMP detachments. In 1944, *St. Roch* traveled the more northerly route of the Northwest Passage. It was retired in 1948, and after spending four years in Halifax, Nova Scotia, it was brought to Vancouver as a museum ship. The craft was brought ashore in 1958, and the building was constructed around it in 1966. Inside the museum is a hands-on interactive area where kids can maneuver an underwater robot. Mon–Sat 10–5, Sun noon–5. $6 adults, $3 seniors and students, children under 5 free. (See also Chapter 7, Kids' Stuff.) ♿ (Point Grey)

VANCOUVER MUSEUM
1100 Chestnut St.
Vanier Park
Vancouver
604/736-4431
If you like odd-looking hats, you'll love the roof atop this place. It's shaped in the form of a traditional Coast Salish cone-hat. The Vancouver Museum is the place to see how the city grew from a wilderness on the edge of the ocean to a major North American city in just 100 years. Exhibits include a replica of a sawmill, elaborate dresses and other clothing, and thousands of individual items ranging from Native carvings to railway passenger cars. Located next to Vanier Park, the building also houses the H. R. MacMillan Planetarium. Open daily 10–5; Thurs until 9pm. $8 adults, $5.50 children under 12. (See also Chapter 7, Kids' Stuff.) ♿(Downtown)

Old Man *mask carved by Norman Tait on display in the Vancouver Museum's Orientation Gallery*

Vancouver Museum

The Marine Building

The Marine Building, at the corner of Hastings and Burrard Streets, is an art-deco masterpiece. The tallest building in the Commonwealth even a decade after it opened in 1931, it serves today as one of Vancouver's most venerable office towers. Inside and out are carvings and sculptures in terra-cotta, brass, stone, and marble. Relief panels near the outside base depict the history of transportation along the West Coast; a frieze featuring waves, sea horses, and marine fauna wraps around the building, and over the entranceway is a ship's prow sailing out of the sunset. In the lobby are green-and-blue-tiled walls, colored floor tiles, and a beamed ceiling lit by bulbs recessed within ships' prows.

OTHER MUSEUMS

BC GOLF MUSEUM
2545 Blanca St.
Vancouver
604/222-4653

Fore! Situated between the 16th green and the 17th tee at the University Golf Club on the eastern edge of UBC, the club's original 1931 clubhouse now houses Canada's only golf museum. The museum building contains six galleries depicting the evolution of the game, as well as an extensive golf library of more than 1,200 volumes covering instruction, history, biography, fiction, architecture, and current environmental concerns. Two halls display exhibitions of special interest and feature golf history and memorabilia from all over the Pacific Northwest. You can explore more than 100 volumes of clippings and photographs (one section is devoted to Ben Hogan's performance in the 1967 Masters) or investigate the history of a particular golf course or golfer in the public-archives area. The museum gift shop has calendars, Pringle sweaters, and prints. Oh, and bring your clubs—there's a small putting and chipping green just outside the museum's door. Tue–Sun 12–4. Free. ♿ (Point Grey)

BC MUSEUM OF MINING
Hwy. 99
Britannia Beach
604/688-8735 or 604/896-2322

If being underground doesn't bother you, then the former Britannia Copper Mine—now a national historic site—in Britannia Beach is a must-see. A guided underground tour on electric rail carts gives you an idea of what it was like drilling and retrieving ore in what was once one of the biggest copper mines in the world. You can also pan for gold. Just take Highway 99 toward Whistler. You'll arrive at the museum after a gorgeous drive along Howe Sound. Open daily 10–4:30, but times may vary according to the season, so call ahead. $9.50 adults, $7.50 seniors and students, children under 5 free. (North Shore)

BC SPORTS HALL OF FAME AND MUSEUM
BC Place Stadium, Gate A
777 Pacific Blvd., S.
Vancouver
604/687-5520

This museum contains the finest collection of sports memorabilia in the province. It highlights British Columbia's greatest athletes—including disabled athletes like Terry Fox and Rick Hanson—and offers a chance to experience certain sports for yourself. You can test your skills at climbing, throwing, or racing, or take a tour of the stadium. The exhibitions in 18 rooms cover 150 years of sporting history, from an 1860s Victoria picnic to the present. Sometimes current professional athletes come in for demonstrations. Daily 10–5. $6 adults, $4 seniors and students, children under 5 free; group tours $3.50 per person. & (Downtown)

GRANVILLE ISLAND SPORTFISHING MUSEUM AND MODEL SHIPS MUSEUM
1502 Duranleau St.
Vancouver
604/683-1939

If you've ever reeled in a 38.5-kilogram Chinook salmon you'll know what you're in for at the Granville Island Sportfishing Museum. If you haven't, well, take a seat in the museum's simulator and get ready for the battle of your life. This is your chance to see what it's like, and you had better have the arms, shoulders, stomach, and back to put up a good fight. Also in the museum is a full-scale model of an 84-kilogram halibut. The Model Ships

Museum houses detailed models of many ships, including the *Bismarck*. Tue–Sun 1–5:30. $3 adults, $1.50 seniors, students, and children; children under 6 free. & (Uptown)

VANCOUVER POLICE CENTENNIAL MUSEUM
240 E. Cordova St.
Vancouver
604/665-3346

This museum has enough material to keep a screenwriter busy for a lifetime. Housed in the old Coroner's Court Building near the main police station, it was created in 1986 for the centennial celebrations of the local constabulary. On display are wanted posters, a preserved larynx fractured by a fatal karate chop, and the old morgue and autopsy room where actor Errol Flynn ended up in 1959 after dying at a local hotel. There's also a crime-scene recreation of "Babes in the Woods," a 1953 murder that remains unsolved. Mon–Fri 9–3. $5 adults, $3 seniors and students. & (Downtown).

GALLERIES

ART BEATUS
888 Nelson St.
Vancouver
604/688-2623

Much of Vancouver's art scene is a throwback to when the city was very British and European. Until recently that focus resulted in many of the city's worthy minority artists not receiving the recognition they deserved. Today, however, things are different. This gallery, for instance, emphasizes contemporary Chinese arts from both Canada and Asia. You'll find a wide range of form and substance—traditional to contem-

Public Displays of Art in Vancouver

Public art in Vancouver is such a natural extension of the overall environment that it often goes unnoticed by locals. But if you open your eyes, you'll see intriguing pieces on display all over town.

This could well be called the totem pole capital of North America, with the towering structures visible throughout the city. You'll find clusters of them in Stanley Park, near Brockton Point, and behind the Museum of Anthropology at the University of British Columbia. Poles rise from the plaza in front of the CBC building at 700 Hamilton St., in front of the Maritime Museum in Vanier Park, in the Plaza of Nations on False Creek, and outside the Van Dusen Gardens at West 37th Avenue and Oak Street.

One of the more unusual public art pieces can be found at the entrance to Stanley Park: The Search, by Seward Johnson, is a bronze of a woman sitting on a park bench rummaging through her purse. In Robson Square, Inuit artist Etungat's bronze Bird of Spring seems to take elegant wing, while Robert Dow Reid's fiberglass Birds in Flight soar outside the building at 700 West Pender Street. In the lobby of Cathedral Place on West Georgia, across from the Hotel Vancouver, is Navigational Device, by local glass artist Robert Studor. It's a large fragment of fractured glass—found on Lyell Island in the Queen Charlotte Islands in northern British Columbia—held together by brass circles; you'll see hieroglyphics etched on the glass.

Sometimes the most intriguing public art requires a bit of exploration to find. In Continuity, for example, a work by Letha Keate depicting two cherubic children balancing on a log, is outside the Brock House, a senior citizen community center at 3975 Point Grey Road. Further west along the beach at Spanish Banks is Christel Fuoss-Moore's concrete nautical piece, Anchor.

porary—including paintings, small sculptures, and silk prints. You'll also find some of the best art deals in Vancouver. (Downtown)

BAU-XI GALLERY
3045 Granville St.
Vancouver
604/733-7011

Buschlen Mowatt Fine Arts

The Buschlen-Mowatt gallery focuses on international art.

The legendary artist Jack Shadbolt, who lived in British Columbia from 1912 until his death in 1999 at the age of 90, used Bau-Xi for his major exhibits. This gallery is the most important exhibition space for top Canadian artists. But you shouldn't expect anything too elaborate. The philosophy of Bau-Xi is to focus on the art, not the surroundings, so the paintings, prints, and watercolors—most of which are contemporary—are presented on plain walls. If you want to see the work of the latest leading contemporary artists, this is the place to look. (Uptown)

BUSCHLEN-MOWATT FINE ARTS
111-1445 W. Georgia St.
Vancouver
604/682-1234
This place is definitely upscale. No surprise, considering it's located in a fashionable office building next to Stanley Park and has a reputation as one of the city's finest galleries. The focus at Buschlen-Mowatt is on international artists—if you're inter-

ested in buying or viewing works by Picasso or Miro, this is your place. But you'll find the hottest names in contemporary art here as well—Bill Reid, for instance. Exhibits are consistently dramatic and fascinating. Daily. (Downtown)

CHINATOWN ART GALLERY
51 E. Pender St.
604/687-0729
All of the art here is imported from China. Several small shops are devoted to specific art disciplines, such as porcelain, woodwork, and silk screens. Most of the work on display here is inexpensive, and many items can't be found anywhere else. Though this Chinatown gallery is free, of course, you'll find plenty of opportunity to use your credit card. (Downtown)

CRAFT-HOUSE GALLERY
1386 Cartwright St.
Vancouver
604/687-7270
Located in The Loft, a building that houses several small art and artisan galleries across from the Granville Island Market, this popular crafts shop has just about everything and anything made from glass, clay, cloth, wood, paper, and delicate wiring. The artists are British Columbian, and the work is exquisite. Every month the gallery owners exhibit what they believe to be special—unusual designs, unique colors, or intriguing styles—in a small adjoining room. Tue–Sun 9–5, extended summer hours. (Uptown)

DIANE FERRIS GALLERY
1565 W. Seventh Ave.
Vancouver
604/737-2629
This is not a small gallery. Diane Ferris specializes in exhibiting the works

of artists who work on large canvases—like Alan Wood, for instance. Ferris favors cutting-edge locals as well as international artists such as Alberta-born Attila Richard Lukacs, who spent a decade living and working in Berlin before moving to New York. Lukacs is known predominantly for his continuing series of paintings of primates, male skinheads, and American military cadets. Tue–Sat 10–5:30. (Point Grey)

FEDERATION GALLERY
1241 Cartwright St.
Vancouver
604/681-8534
This gallery offers a wonderful collection of work by current members of the Federation of Canadian Artists, the country's premier artists' association. In keeping with the philosophy of its founder, Group of Seven artist Lawren Harris, the Federation Gallery is a casual place. Over the course of any given year you'll find just about every possible discipline exhibited here—from watercolors, to new and mixed media, to prints, to sculpture. Exhibitions change frequently. (Uptown)

GALLERY OF B.C. CERAMICS
1359 Cartwright St.
Vancouver
604/669-5645
Need a pot to put on your mantle? This is the place to find one. The Gallery of B.C. Ceramics is run by members of the Potters Guild of British Columbia who have been chosen by a jury of their peers to show their work. That means their work meets the gallery's standards for technical quality, innovation, and aesthetic appeal. Many of the items sold are functional, some are merely decorative, and others are simply gor-

geous. Look as hard and as long as you want—you won't find anything less than perfect. Daily 10:30–5:30, closed Mon in winter. (Uptown)

INUIT GALLERY
345 Water St.
Vancouver
604/688-7323
If an Inuit has carved an object from soapstone, chances are it's here or can be ordered. This place, set in the heart of Gastown, is North America's leading Inuit art gallery. The Inuit use soapstone because it's soft and doesn't chip. In addition to soapstone carvings, you'll find a wide range of masks, jewelry, and woodcarvings. One of the hottest sellers in the gallery is its show catalog, a veritable collector's item thanks to its fine reproductions. (Downtown)

KHOT-LA-CHA COAST SALISH HANDICRAFTS
270 Whonoak St.
Capilano Reserve
604/987-3339
Khot-La-Cha Coast Salish Handicrafts, located on the Capilano Reserve at the northern end of the Lion's Gate Bridge, is a fantastic source for woodcarvings and jewelry by local artists. Check out the store's Cowichan-style sweaters. These heavy wool cardigan sweaters are handmade by the local Squamish people. Real Cowichan sweaters are made by the Cowichan band on Vancouver Island and can be found on the island as well as throughout the Lower Mainland. The imitations you'll find here are just as good, however, and come at a much better price. (North Shore)

LEONA LATTIMER GALLERY
1590 W. Second Ave.

Vanier Park

The Vanier Park area in Point Grey is within easy walking distance of Downtown, located on the south shore of False Creek just west of Granville Island and on the eastern edge of Kitsilano. The park embraces a wide range of activities and places to explore, including the Pacific Space Centre and H. R. MacMillan Planetarium, the Vancouver Museum, the Gordon Southam Observatory, the Vancouver Maritime Museum and St. Roch, and the Vancouver Academy of Music. Additionally, it's the site of two major annual events—the Bard on the Beach Shakespeare Summer Festival and the International Children's Festival.

Vancouver
604/732-4556
Engraved gold and silver jewelry, prints, argillite carvings, masks, immaculate wood boxes, and button blankets are the specialties here. This gallery, located off the southern edge of Granville Island and ensconced in what looks like a Native longhouse, is an easy walk from Granville Islands. The masks, representing animals important to the First Nations people, are particularly fascinating. (Uptown)

MARION SCOTT GALLERY
481 Howe St.
Vancouver
604/685-1934
One of the oldest galleries in Vancouver, The Scott used to be an all-encompassing gallery that sold all Pacific Northwest Native art, but in recent years it has narrowed its focus to Inuit pieces. Today this gallery has one of the city's most complete collections of eastern Canadian Inuit prints, stone carvings, and jewelry. It's a good place to go if

you don't find what you need at the Inuit Gallery (see listing, above). (Downtown)

MORRIS AND HELEN BELKIN ART GALLERY
University of British Columbia
1825 Main Hall
Vancouver
604/822-2759
This contemporary space opened in 1995 as the new home of the UBC Fine Arts Gallery. The gallery's university mandate is to promote understanding and discussion of the fine arts and issues in art history, criticism, and curating. In addition to its temporary exhibitions, the gallery houses a 1,500-piece permanent collection. The collection, established primarily through donations, emphasizes contemporary Canadian art. The gallery is also the home of various archives, among them the Morris/Trasov Archives of the Seventies, the Peter Day Collection of Concrete Poetry, and the Kenneth Coutts-Smith Papers. Tue–Sat 10–

4:30. $2 adults, $1 seniors; students free. (Point Grey)

PRESENTATION HOUSE
333 Chesterfield Ave.
North Vancouver
604/986-1351

Photographers will love this place. Not only is it one of the longest-standing galleries in the Vancouver area, but it is still faithful to presenting contemporary Canadian photography as an art form. The wooden building, a former house, also has a small theater for lectures and small performances. The admission fee is based on a "pay-what-you-can" system, making the programs more accessible to the community, and most special events are free and open to everyone. Call ahead for hours. (North Shore)

RICHMOND ART GALLERY
180-7700 Minoru Gate
Richmond
604/231-6440

The Richmond Gallery, located in the Richmond Library/Cultural Centre, displays contemporary art by local and international artists in 5,000 square feet of exhibition space. The gallery is quite involved in community art and often hosts artist-run workshops and other programs suitable for children and adults alike. About 20 exhibits are staged here each year, including one especially for children. Another 20 exhibits are staged annually at the Richmond's auxiliary gallery at the nearby Gateway Theatre, which is part of the Cultural Centre. Exhibitions reflect a wide variety of media and styles. Programs and tours provide the public with opportunities to meet artists as well as to create their own art. Mon–Fri 9–9, Sat–Sun 10–5, closed holidays. Donations are appreciated. (Southern Suburbs)

ROBERT HELD ART GLASS
2130 Pine St.
Vancouver
604/737-0020

This has to be one of the most fascinating art experiences in the city. Held is a glassblower whose work is sold throughout Canada. Known as the "father" of the art glass movement in Canada, his creations of vases, perfume bottles, and paper weights are highly collectible works of art. Art glass begins with the metamorphoses of sand, soda ash, and lime, heated in a furnace to 2300 degrees Fahrenheit; the molten glass is gathered in a blowpipe, and the fluid mass is manipulated into the desired shape; color is added in the form of metal oxides; the piece is then placed in an annealer for cooling, and the final stage involves grinding. Held invites people into his cavernous studio to watch him and other artists design delicate vases, glasses, and a variety

Check out the UBC art gallery—it's full of innovative ideas by talented student artists. Another student gallery can be found at the Emily Carr College of Art and Design on Granville Island (see listing, this chapter).

of decorative pieces. The studio is just a couple blocks from Granville Island, west of the Granville Street-Bridge. Mon–Sat 10–5. (Uptown)

THREE VETS
2200 Yukon St.
Vancouver
604/872-5475
Three Vets is the name of the store, but put aside your first impression. This clothing and outdoor-equipment store hides one of the city's best-kept art secrets. At the back of the store, behind all of the hiking and camping gear, is a small storage room and gallery filled with Northwest Native art from about 300 artists. The curator, Jerry Wolfman, has been collecting these pieces—paintings, prints, bowls, jewelry, rattles, plaques—for nearly two decades, and has neatly stashed them all in this small space. Why here? In 1983, some members of the Squamish Nation came to Wolfman's store to buy camping gear, and they just happened to have some original wood carvings with them. A trade was made and soon word got out that these were some of the best examples of local Native carvings around. Since then, Wolfman has made a second career as a sales agent for a number of Native artists. Prices range from about $12 for a letter opener to about $7,500 for a ceremonial carved mask or a seven-foot totem pole. Wolfman now markets to major galleries in the United States, including the Smithsonian Institution in Washington. (Uptown)

WESTERN FRONT
303 E. Eighth Ave.
Vancouver
604/876-9343
The Western Front Society is an artist-run center dedicated to the production, exhibition, and promotion of contemporary electronic/media art. It's a leading-edge performance theater that merges electronic music and sound with film, slides, television, and now even the Internet. Founded in 1973 by eight artists who wanted to create a space for new art forms, the Western Front quickly became a gathering place for poets, dancers, musicians, and visual artists. It's housed in the turn-of-the-twentieth-century Knights of Pythias Hall, a two-and-a-half-story wooden building containing an exhibition space, a dance studio, a live performance venue, and a video production and recording studio. A popular interest in non-Western cultural traditions has helped the Western Front establish links with contemporary artists in East Asia, India, and Latin America. The center produces more than 100 events a year. Call for current exhibits, performances, and times. (Uptown)

Mits Naga

7

KIDS' STUFF

The thing about kids is that they come in older sizes. In Vancouver we call them adults. The truth is, many of Vancouver's attractions are just as appealing to adults as they are to kids. In fact, it's often not clear who enjoys certain activities—the so-called "kids'" activities—the most.

Thankfully, most of the city's more interesting attractions include programs for the younger set. Vancouver has much to offer children of all ages—from the petting zoo at Maplewood Children's Farm to the hands-on displays at Science World to shopping at the Kids Only Market at Granville Island. The Kids' Adventure Playground on Grouse Mountain is a must-see, as are several family attractions in Stanley Park, such as the Children's Farmyard Petting Zoo and the Miniature Railway. Kids and adults alike love the exhibits at the Pacific Space Centre and the BC Sports Hall of Fame and Museum. Whatever your mood, Vancouver is full of opportunities for families—whether you feel like heading for a trail in the nearby mountains, spending a day on the water, or making the best of a rainy day in a museum. Just be sure to ask about special admission prices for families; many attractions have such a plan, and a family of four can save quite a bit over a few days.

ANIMALS AND THE GREAT OUTDOORS

CHILDREN'S FARMYARD PETTING ZOO AND MINIATURE RAILWAY
Stanley Park
Vancouver
604/257-8530

If your kids show any reluctance at all about heading for the petting zoo (the original, traditional zoo closed some time ago), where they'll find peacocks, rabbits, and donkeys, point out that the miniature railway is nearby. A popular place for local school groups, the zoo includes kid-friendly explanations of animals and tips on what to do at every exhibit. Afterwards, take your children on the small steam engine to see more animals during a tour through the woods. The zoo/railway combination is one of Vancouver's most popular children's attractions, especially in the summer, so it does become crowded. Apr–Sept daily; Oct–Mar weekends only. Admission to zoo $2.50 ages 13 and over, $1.75 children 6–12; train is $5.95 ages 13 and over, $3.95 children 6–12; children under 6 free with paying adult. & (Downtown)

CLEVELAND DAM AND FISH HATCHERY
Capilano Canyon Regional Park
4500 Capilano Rd.
North Vancouver
604/666-1790
Solve the mystery of how and why the salmon leave and return every four years to reproduce and, in the process, end their lives. This federal-government display will show you the entire migration process. It's a spectacular—and sad—event. By the time the fish finish leaping up the ladders and into the holding tanks, they're ready to lay their eggs and die. Some of the fish are already beginning to change shape and color as they reach the end of their lifelong cycle. The story of life and death is presented very well in the nearby displays. To get there, take the first left after the suspension bridge and follow the road to the end. Open daily; call ahead for seasonal hours. Free. (See also Chapter 8, Parks, Gardens, and Recreation Areas.) &
(North Shore)

GREATER VANCOUVER ZOOLOGICAL CENTRE
5048 264th St.

Aldergrove
604/856-6825
This is as close to African wildlife as you can get in Vancouver—though it is a bit out of town. About 48 kilometers from downtown Vancouver, you'll find 124 different animal species roaming this 48.5-hectare land in the Lower Fraser Valley. Jaguar, buffalo, zebras, antelope, giraffes, and camel are just a few of the creatures you'll see, all exhibited in large, natural surroundings. Visitors can stroll the grounds along asphalt walkways, or take the Safari Express Train (an additional $1.50 per person) to see camels, hippos, white rhinos, and tigers up close. There's also an area where children can pet some of the small animals. Other attractions include hot-air balloon rides and a selection of eating areas. To get there, take the Trans-Canada to Aldergrove and follow the signs. Open daily 9–dusk. $10.50 adults, $7.50 children 5–15; children under 5 free with adult. (Eastern Suburbs)

KIDS' ADVENTURE PLAYGROUND
Grouse Mountain
6400 Nancy Greene Way
North Vancouver
Atop Grouse Mountain, behind the chalet next to the gondola station, is Kids' Adventure Playground, featuring logs, trees, ropes, and a kid-sized suspension bridge. You get to the mountain-top playground via a spectacular ride on a 100-passenger gondola, and on the way up you can take in the finest views of Vancouver, the Lower Mainland, the Strait of Georgia, Vancouver Island, and Washington State's mountains. Included in the price of the gondola ticket is a 30-minute video presentation, *Born to Fly*, which gives you a bird's-eye view of British Columbia. Just a short walk

Cow milking demonstration at Maplewood Children's Farm

Bill Staley

breeding kennel) to feed the fowl. Special events include the mid-summer Sheep Fair, the Farm Fair in mid-September, 101 Pumpkins Day in October, and the Country Christmas. Milking displays take place daily. Tue–Sun 10–4. $1.75 adults, $.90 seniors and children. & (North Shore)

RICHMOND NATURE PARK
11851 Westminster Hwy.
Richmond
604/273-7015
Come here for an educational (don't tell the kids) adventure. This 40-hectare park of peat moss and shrubs features boarded walkways (around a gorgeous pond) and natural trails through forest and wetlands. Keep your eyes open for the elusive coyote, and for owls, hawks, and other animals. Be sure to visit the Nature House, where you'll find games and live animals such as snakes, frogs, and salamanders. Be sure to bring wet-weather gear, especially rubber boots, if you plan to walk in the bog. To get there, drive south on Highway 99 and take the Shell Road exit, then turn left onto Westminster Highway. Open daily 9–4. Admission by donation. & (Southern Suburbs)

away from the playground is the venue for a twice-daily (in spring and summer) logger sports show, where competitors display traditional logging skills in springboard chopping, axe throwing, and power- and hand-saw speed contests. Open daily 9 a.m.–10 p.m. Skyride tickets $17 adults, $10.65 youth 13–18 years, $6 children 6–12 years. (North Shore)

MAPLEWOOD CHILDREN'S FARM
405 Seymour River Pl.
North Vancouver
604/929-5610
City kids will love this place. Maplewood has more than 200 farm animals (including cows, horses, pigs, ponies, sheep, donkeys, and chickens) on a two-hectare layout. It was originally one of several working farms in the area, but when they all went bankrupt, unable to compete with the farming operations in the Fraser Valley, the North Vancouver Parks Department took Maplewood over. Put junior on a pony or buy birdseed at the ticket booth (a former

VANCOUVER AQUARIUM
Stanley Park
Vancouver
604/659-3474
Children love coming to this magical place to see the killer whales, seals, and other sea mammals up close. The beluga and harbor seal pools can be viewed from both outside and inside the facility. The aquarium, which includes tropical fish, an octopus, and reptiles, also happens to be Canada's largest Marine Mammal Rescue and Rehabilitation Centre. Rescue techniques are explained at the Habitat

TRIVIA

Of the nearly 500,000 people who visit Science World each year, about 84,000 are school children on field trips.

Success Stories exhibit. At the outdoor Max Bell Marine Mammal Centre you can meet a variety of recuperating animals. Call for hours. $12.95 adults, $10.95 seniors, students, and ages 13–18, $8.55 ages 4–12, children under 3 free. (See also Chapter 5, Sights and Attractions.) (Downtown)

FUN AND EDUCATIONAL

BC MUSEUM OF MINING
Hwy. 99
Britannia Beach
604/688-8735 or 604/896-2332
Even when this old Noranda copper mine was in its heyday, there seem to have been lots of kids about this place—if the photos in the museum store are any indication—and children of today will love this subterranean adventure. You and your kids will be clothed in special raingear to protect you from the water that drips from the tunnel roofs; you'll be placed on an underground railway and taken through winding darkened tunnels to areas where mining used to take place. At its peak, in the 1950s, the mine produced 6.4 million kilograms of copper ore daily. It closed in the mid 1970s, when the ore petered out, and it's now a national historic site. Operational mining equipment that you'll see on your visit includes slushers, muckers, and drills (don't worry, all of this will be explained to you on the tour). Later,

you can explore the museum building, with its hundreds of photos and artifacts. What better way to see what mining is really like. To get there, take Highway 99 through West Vancouver, past Horseshoe Bay and on toward Whistler. It's about a 30-minute drive from Horseshoe Bay—and a spectacular drive along Howe Sound. Open daily 10–4:30, but times may vary according to the season, so call ahead. $9.50 adults, $7.50 seniors and students, children under 5 free. (See also Chapter 6, Museums and Galleries.) (North Shore)

BURNABY HERITAGE VILLAGE AND CAROUSEL
6501 Deer Lake Ave.
Burnaby
604/293-6500
This recreation of a Victorian-era village, built in 1958 on 3.6 hectares, is a great place for a family to spend a warm summer day. Walk or run along boardwalks, watch a blacksmith at work, talk to costumed townspeople, shop in a general store, or visit a vintage ice-cream parlor. You can even rent the church for a wedding or take a ride on the 1912 carousel. Christmastime, when the entire village is ablaze in colored lights, is magical. To get there, take the Trans-Canada (Highway 1) toward Burnaby and get off at the Sperling Avenue exit. Open daily 11–4:30; extended hours July–Aug and Dec. $6.20 adults, $4.35 seniors, students, and disabled, $3.75

children 6–12. (See also Chapter 6, Museums and Galleries.) (Eastern Suburbs)

MUSEUM OF ANTHROPOLOGY
University of British Columbia
6393 NW Marine Dr.
Vancouver
604/822-3825

"Anthropology" is an awfully big word. Fortunately, junior won't even need to pronounce it. In fact, he'll be speechless when he sees the museum's monumental totem poles towering into the sky. He can stand and ponder artist Bill Reid's massive sculpture, *The Raven and the First Men*, an awesome carving of a raven perched on a partially opened clamshell, inside of which are human figures trying to emerge; the sculpture illustrates the Haida legend of the beginning of mankind. For children, this museum is a magical place—especially outside on the bluffs, where they can visit a replica of a Haida longhouse. (The longhouse is used by First Nations students and is not open to the public, but from the outside you can appreciate the hybrid Native/Northwest Coast architecture.) This place is guaranteed to inspire your children to want to know more about the people who first inhabited the region. Then you can explain what "anthropology" means. Hours vary (call ahead). $6 adults, $3.50 seniors and students. (See also Chapter 6, Museums and Galleries.) (Point Grey)

PACIFIC SPACE CENTRE
Vanier Park
1100 Chestnut St.
Vancouver
604/738-7827

If your children have ever wanted to experience what it's like to fly in space, this is their chance. The center's full-motion flight simulator takes kids to Mars and back without ever leaving the ground. If the trip into orbit doesn't inspire your child to become an astronaut, then the chance to maneuver lunar robots certainly will. The center devotes a large section to Canada's contribution to the NASA space program. As it turns out, we're not just spectators. Tue–Sun 10–5. $12.50 adults, $9.50 seniors and children 11–18, $8.50 ages 5–10, $40 families. (See also Chapter 6, Museums and Galleries.) (Point Grey)

RUSSIAN SUBMARINE
810 Quayside Drive
Westminster Public Quay
New Westminster
604/520-1070

When's the last time you tested your claustrophobic threshold and toured a submarine? This old 91-meter Soviet Foxtrot U-512 Patrol-class sub was used during the Cold War as a training submarine for elite young Soviet naval candidates. It was first

International Space Station Model at the Pacific Space Centre

commissioned in 1974, then was decommissioned in 1993 and sold. It is the first of its kind to be docked in North America. Tours last about 45 minutes, with as many as 15 people taken into the sub at once. Afterward stop off at the New Westminster public market at the eastern end of the pier. Open daily 9:30–6:30. $7.50 adults, $5.35 children ages 14 and under, $20 families. (Eastern Suburbs)

SCIENCE WORLD
1455 Quebec St.

Vancouver
604/443-7440
Try losing your shadow sometime. Or walking through the lens of a camera, blowing square bubbles, creating music with a giant synthesizer, or watching a spectacular three-dimensional slide and laser show. And then try to answer your kid's pointed question: "How does that work?" The great thing about Science World is that you'll be able to answer that question after trying the many hands-on exhibits in this geodesic dome–

Top 10 Science World Exhibits
by Sandra Eix, Ph.D.; Raymond Nakamura, Ph.D.; and Rob Lunde of the Science World Education Committee

1. **Plasma Ball**—A glass ball filled with plasma gas. Put your hand on it and your electrical current produces mini-lightening.

2. **Walk-on Synthesizer**—Move your feet around a keyboard and make music.

3. **Gravitram**—Put Velcro items on a wall and watch a Ping-Pong ball move, unaided, between them.

4. **Giant Lever**—Lift enormous weights with a lever.

5. **Crawl-in Beaver Lodge**—An authentic beaver lodge transported from northern British Columbia and reassembled stick by stick.

6. **Beehive**—A working beehive. Kids can watch the bees make honey.

7. **Tower of Bobble**—An outdoor kinetic sculpture by New York artist George Rhodes.

8. **Cyclone Chamber**—Press a button and watch a cyclone be created—under controlled conditions, of course.

9. **Shadow Wall**—Stand in front of a darkened wall and a flash of light will leave your image on the wall.

10. **Puzzles**—A number of different hands-on puzzles that test your patience and resolve.

shaped building at the east end of False Creek. Be sure to attend a show at the Alcan Omnimax Theatre—it will take you into visual worlds you can experience no other way. Open Mon–Fri 10–5, Sat–Sun 10–6. Theater open 10:45, noon, 1:15, 2:30, and 3:45, plus 5:00 on Sat, Sun, and holidays. Science World/Omnimax Theatre combo ticket $14.50 adults, $10.25 seniors, students, and children 4–18; Science World admission alone $11.25 adults, $7.50 seniors, students, and children; Omnimax Theatre admission alone $9.75; children ages 3 and under free. (See also Chapter 6, Museums and Galleries.) (Uptown)

VANCOUVER ART GALLERY
750 Hornby St.
Vancouver
604/662-4700
Take your children through the adult gallery and you'll have a bored kid in the adult world. Walk into the Children's Gallery, on the other hand, and you'll have a tough time getting them out. The Children's Gallery is really a workshop area where hands-on pro-

jects in a variety of disciplines are demonstrated and taught by teachers who take kids through the creative process. For example, the Vancouver Art Gallery hosts free painting classes where the goal is to encourage self-confidence and creativity, as well as the foundation for a life-long appreciation of art. Short talks and concerts for the kids are also held every week. Open daily, hours vary; call ahead for a schedule. $10.00 adults, $6 seniors and students, children under 12 free; (See also Chapter 5, Sights and Attractions, and Chapter 6, Museums and Galleries.) (Downtown)

VANCOUVER MARITIME MUSEUM
Vanier Park
1905 Ogden Ave.
Vancouver
604/257-8300
The museum's Pirates Cove exhibit allows kids to dress up like pirates then do the pirate thing on their own. The exhibit is filled with pirate artifacts, including pieces of eight. But the past is just part of the overall ex-

Kids can crawl through an authentic beaver lodge at Science World.

Science World

perience at the Maritime Museum, which also has a high-tech area in the Children's Discovery Centre where you can maneuver an underwater robot in a large tank. Observation telescopes focus on real ships anchored out on English Bay. Mon–Sat 10–5, Sun noon–5. $6 adults, $3 seniors and students, children under 5 free. (See also Chapter 6, Museums and Galleries.) (Point Grey)

VANCOUVER MUSEUM
Vanier Park
1100 Chestnut St.
Vancouver
604/736-4431
The Vancouver Museum is housed on the main floor in the same building as the Pacific Space Centre (see listing, above). You can walk the decks of a nineteenth-century passenger ship, or even take a seat in an 1880 CPR passenger train. Kids who have never seen a neon sign will love the museum's collection, salvaged over the years from soon-to-be-demolished buildings. Open daily 10–5, closed Mon Sept–June. $8 adults, $5.50 children under 12. (See also Chapter 6, Museums and Galleries.) (Point Grey)

THEATER AND FESTIVALS

CN THEATRE
Canada Pl.
Vancouver
604/682-4629 (Information)
604/280-4444 (Tickets)
Hang onto your stomach for the mother of all rides. This five-story-tall wraparound screen will take you directly into the action, no matter what it is. Scream, gasp, and hang onto the person next to you; the experience is so real, you and your children will think you're actually there, whether

it's at the Grand Canyon, in outer space, atop a mountain, or aboard an airplane as it skims over the ground. Daily showings noon–9:15. $10.50 adults, $7 seniors and students, $6 children; lower prices for matinees. (Downtown)

GREEN THUMB THEATRE
1885 Venables St.
Vancouver
604/254-4055
This unique theater organization develops and produces original Canadian scripts for young audiences. Staging plays and skits that are serious—exploring contemporary topics such as racism, illiteracy, and abuse—the company presents over 60 performances to over 180,000 children and teenagers annually. Each year, Green Thumb visits every school district in British Columbia and also tours nationally and internationally. Visitors to Vancouver, however, should catch the company performing in the Vancouver East Cultural Centre, its home venue. ⓑ (East Vancouver)

VANCOUVER INTERNATIONAL CHILDREN'S FESTIVAL
Vanier Park
1100 Chestnut St.
Vancouver
604/708-5655
This is the premium event for children. More than 200 local, national, and international acts designed specifically for children are staged in late May and early June in huge, colorful tents on the Vanier Park grounds. In addition to the paid-admission shows, you can find an endless amount of free entertainment, from clowns, jugglers, and mimes to makeup artists that will gladly give your child a new look. A side event,

Children's Clothing

Several stores that cater specifically to mothers buying children's clothing are scattered throughout the city. Among them are Absolutely Diapers (2050 W. Fourth Ave., 604/737-0603), where you'll find a variety of cloth diapers, toys, stuffed animals, and other infant items; Angels on Bellevue (1463 Bellevue St., 604/926-8737), where European designs reign supreme; Isola Bella (5692 Yew St., 604/266-8808), another European clothing outlet for a wide range of ages; Peppermintree Children's Wear (4243 Dunbar St., 604/228-9815), where in addition to a play area you'll find shoes, clothing, and accessories for everyone from infants to teenagers; and Please Mum (2041 W. 41st Ave., 604/264-0366), where you'll find a Vancouver-only selection of all-cotton items.

known as X-Site, is a series of children's theatrical productions, poetry, and art. (It's held at the Vancouver East Cultural Centre, 1895 Venables St. Call 604/254-9578 for tickets and times.) Open daily for two weeks in late May/early June. (Dates change yearly.) Ticket prices vary. Call ahead. (Point Grey)

STORES KIDS LOVE

BC PLAYTHINGS
3070 Edgemont Blvd.
Edgemont Village
North Vancouver
604/986-4111
"Play" is the operative word here. Creative, educational toys make up the bulk of the available items. The store caters to those ages eight and under, but its puzzles and other games will appeal to kids as old as 12.

Construction sets, preschool and art supplies, puppets, and a wide selection of CDs and tapes of wonderful children's stories are just a few of the toys, tools, gadgets, and more for sale. Children are welcome and encouraged to touch the items, but they should be supervised. (North Shore)

KIDS ONLY MARKET
1496 Cartwright St.
Vancouver
604/684-0086
Where was this place when the rest of us were kids? You'll find anything and everything a child ever wanted in this renovated two-story building at the entrance to Granville Island. (The island is connected to the mainland by a short, almost unnoticeable causeway.) Within the building are some 24 individual stores selling books, toys, and arts and crafts. A two-story play area features a huge

slide and playrooms. Next to the building is an outdoor, supervised adventure playground. On weekends the market is absolute chaos—and absolutely fun. Every day you'll find clowns and actors entertaining the children. (Uptown)

VANCOUVER KIDSBOOKS
3083 W. Broadway
Vancouver
604/738-5335
This 5,000-square-foot store carries the biggest assortment of children's books in the city. Absolutely filled with CD ROMs, tapes, and books, the store also employs a very knowledgeable staff of 20, so customers are always given the individual attention they need. While there aren't regularly scheduled book readings, authors do frequently stop in to read their own works. When author Robert Munsch was a guest speaker, the store rented a movie theater on the next block to accommodate the 400 people who signed up to see him. Other authors who have spoken at the store include Phoebe Gilman, Janet Stevens, Tommie dePaolo, and George Littlechild. The store also has an impressive selection of Spanish- and French-language books. Open Mon–Wed, Sat 9:30–5; Thu and Fri 9:30–9. (Point Grey)

MORE FUN ACTIVITIES

BC SPORTS HALL OF FAME AND MUSEUM
BC Place Stadium, Gate A1
Vancouver
604/687-5520
Here's the best place to discover if Freddie or Suzy will make it as a world-class athlete. In the Participation Gallery they can run, throw, rope, or row to their heart's content. They can then move on to the Hall of Champions to learn about Terry Fox and Rick Hansen. Fox was the one-legged man who ran halfway across Canada before being forced to stop near Winnipeg when his cancer returned; Hansen rode his wheelchair around the world to prove that the physically challenged can also be great athletes. Open daily 1–5. $6 adults, $4 seniors and students; children under 5 free. (See also Chapter 6, Museums and Galleries.) (Downtown)

BONKERS INDOOR PLAYGROUND
322-5300 No. 3 Rd.
Richmond
604/278-7529
This innovative indoor playground/theater combination is a great place to come when it's raining. Children between the ages of 4 and 12 are welcome to indulge in this maze of educational and fun games and activities. Plastic tunnels, ladders, slides, and ball pits are all a big hit. Children are also invited to participate in onstage skits that range in style and content from nursery rhymes and stories to extemporaneous plays. Located at the Lansdowne Park Shopping Centre and very well supervised by adults, Bonkers is a perfect place to drop off your children while you shop. Bonkers is a chain of centers in western Canada. Open daily, varying hours. $6.55 (hourly) ages 4–13, $4.95 (hourly) ages 3 and under. (Southern Suburbs)

CANADIAN PACIFIC RAILWAY ROUNDHOUSE
Davie St. and Pacific Blvd.
Vancouver
604/713-1800
Scramble aboard the first passenger-

Pick up free copies of BC Parent and West Coast Families to get the latest information on Vancouver's children's activities.

train steam engine to make it across the Rocky Mountains and into what was then Vancouver way back in 1887. Engine number 374 is in the building's atrium, a space that used to be the old Canadian Pacific Railway turnabout during Expo '86 but is now part of the Yaletown Community Centre. There aren't many places where a youngster can actually board a train and sit in the cabin like a real engineer. Open daily. Free. (See also Chapter 5, Sights and Attractions.) ♿ (Downtown)

RICHMOND GO-KART TRACK
6631 Sidaway St.
Richmond
604/278-6184
'Round and 'round she goes, and with luck your kid will win by a nose on this curvy, 800-meter asphalt track. This isn't a circuit where cars crash into one another; rather, it simulates a Formula One race track—the cars even look like cut-down racing cars and can fit two people. Any child younger than 10 or shorter than 137 centimeters has to be a passenger while Mom or Dad does the driving. To get there, take High-way 99 south to the No. 4 Road turnoff (the first exit after you cross the Oak Street Bridge), then turn left on Westminster Highway and right on Sidaway. Open daily noon–dusk, closed rainy days. $10 per car for 15 minutes. (Southern Suburbs)

SEABUS
Foot of Lonsdale St. and the
CP Rail Station
Vancouver/North Vancouver
604/521-0400
Take a ship ride on the ocean—from Downtown to the North Shore. (It's cheaper than cruising to Alaska!) You'll likely see a cruise ship or two, not to mention the greatest view of the waterfront anywhere. The Seabus has been crossing Burrard Inlet between the CP Rail Station Downtown and the Lonsdale Quay in North Vancouver every 15 minutes of every day since 1977. It's a major commuter service and part of the greater Vancouver transit system. While no automobiles are carried on the 12-minute ride, you can bring your bike along for no extra charge. Open daily. $1.50. ♿ (Downtown, North Shore)

8

PARKS, GARDENS, AND RECREATION AREAS

Remember that Vancouver's physical surroundings define almost everything Vancouverites do—especially how we play. Vancouver is the answer to the outdoor enthusiast's prayers: everywhere you look, there's a reason to be active. The city is literally surrounded by beaches, and locals flock to these shores even during the rainy season, when they can walk out to the water's edge during low tide to look for shellfish. The mountains just across the harbor offer skiing in the winter and hiking in the summer. Small sailing boats skim the waters of English Bay year-round. Locals like to brag that they can ski in the morning, sail in the afternoon, and play tennis in the early evening. And don't forget that Vancouver borders on wilderness. Want to take a hike? Get going. Start walking north over the Coastal Mountains that make up the North Shore and the next civilization you'll encounter is somewhere in Asia.

Visually, the city itself is really a series of parks separated by cement. While the crown jewel is 1,000-acre Stanley Park, Vancouver proper has some 174 public gardens and parks and hundreds more in the surrounding neighborhoods and regions. When you add the thousands of home gardens that abound, the city is a floral masterpiece. In fact, because of its temperate coastal climate, Vancouver doesn't have a single season without vibrant color—bright orange and yellow leaves in fall, rich pine evergreens in winter, pink and white blooms in spring, and every color of the rainbow in summer, when everything flourishes.

The thickest known Western hemlock tree found anywhere from Oregon to Alaska is located behind Grouse Mountain at Pipeline Pass. It is 2.7 meters thick and may be more than 1,500 years old.

BELCARRA REGIONAL PARK
Along Hastings/Barnet Hwy. to Loco Rd.
Port Moody
604/432-6360

If you're staying on the east side of the city, this delightful park, located just west of Burnaby in a community called Port Moody, is within easy reach. An hour from Downtown, it has several advantages. First, it rests along Indian Arm on Burrard Inlet and is therefore protected from winds. That may be why Sasamat Lake, in the middle of the park, has one of the warmest beaches on the Lower Mainland. Well-marked trails wind along the ocean at White Pine Beach and the sheltered coves that make excellent sunning and picnic spots. You can watch crabbers and anglers waiting for a bite. Open daily dawn to dusk. (Eastern Suburbs)

BRACKENDALE
North of Squamish along Hwy. 99
Tours at Brackendale Gallery
Brackendale
604/898-3333

Brackendale is about an hour from Vancouver, but if you're in the city in January, it's worth the trip. Each winter thousands of migrating bald eagles congregate on the Squamish River to fatten up on salmon. In 1994 the Squamish River saw the highest concentration of bald eagles on earth—3,769. Brackendale is a small community north of Squamish at the head of Howe Sound. From Vancouver, take Highway 99 toward Whistler and through Squamish. Once in Brackendale, follow Government Street to the dike that holds back the Squamish River. Park and walk along the dike for a viewpoint. The best place for viewing is behind the Sunwolf Outdoor Centre in an area called Eagle Run. Call the Brackendale Gallery to book a photo tour. Open daily dawn to dusk. (North Shore)

CAPILANO CANYON REGIONAL PARK AND HATCHERY
4500 Capilano Rd.
North Vancouver
604/666-1790

Spanning both North and West Vancouver, the park embraces the wild and the urban. It's fairly common to see a black bear staring at you from across the river below the Cleveland Dam and the reservoir. Pleasant picnic areas surrounded by colorful flower gardens offer great views of the water as it roars down the dam's spillway. The best part about going to this park is watching the salmon swim into the hatchery. Be sure to check it out—a glass-fronted observation area permits you to watch the salmon that have battled their way up the river. Below the hatchery is wilderness. Summer daily 8–7; winter daily 8–4. Free. (See also Chapter 7, Kids' Stuff.) (North Shore)

Dr. Sun Yat-Sen Garden, modeled in the Ming Dynasty style

CENTRAL PARK
Kingsway and Imperial St.
Burnaby

Central Park is one of the oldest parks in the city. The 90-hectare land is a great place to enjoy a variety of activities, from pitch-and-putt golf to horseshoes, tennis, swimming, and lawn-bowling. This former naval reserve, once a source of ship masts for the Royal Navy, also has hiking and biking trails. It's named after New York's famous landmark, in tribute to the wife of Vancouver's second, New York–born mayor. Vancouver's professional soccer team, the 86ers, plays its games at Swangard Stadium at the entrance to the park. Open daily 24 hours. (Eastern Suburbs)

DR. SUN YAT-SEN GARDEN
578 Carrall St.
Vancouver
604/662-3207

Zen out in the heart of Chinatown. Look for the enormous red gateway that marks the entrance to the Chinese Cultural Centre and the Dr. Sun Yat-Sen Garden, the first authentic classical Chinese garden built outside of China. Built during Expo '86, this classic Ming Dynasty garden was created with the help of 52 artisans from Suzhou, China's foremost garden city. To fully appreciate the power of this garden, you have to work at it. Sit and watch; explore what's in your heart. The Taoist balance between yin and yang—light and shadow, smooth and rough, large and small—creates perfect harmony in pebbled patios, lattice windows, delicate shrubbery, placid jade pools, and craggy gray limestone. Rocks, wood, plants, and water are used with remarkable, deceptive simplicity. Eventually, the differences reveal themselves: large and small, dark and light, hard and soft, straight and winding, artificial and natural. Everything is in perfect symmetry. After the dazzle of Chinatown, the gardens offer a quieter, more reflective experience. Open daily 10–5. $2. (Downtown)

ENGLISH BAY BEACH
Along Pacific St. and Beach Ave.,

between Denman St. and Burrard St.
Vancouver

The flesh party begins early and ends late during the summer. In this strutting area of the West End, patrolling dudes and not-so-shy babes parade their wares. Plays used to be performed atop the English Bay beach house during the 1930s. Today other activities have taken over. During July or August the spectacular Symphony of Fire, an international fireworks show, takes place over four days. Every New Year's Day well-fortified swimmers brave the cold to jump into the water for the Polar Bear swim. A wonderful gingerbread bandstand is still used for summer concerts. Open daily 24 hours. (Downtown)

GEORGE C. REIFEL MIGRATORY BIRD SANCTUARY
5191 Robertson Rd.
Ladner
604/946-6980

If you'd like to see what birds do in the privacy of their nests, this marshland sanctuary is the place to do it. The 260-hectare George C. Reifel Migratory Bird Sanctuary is devoted to at least 250 different species of birds. The peak viewing

TRIVIA

The Vancouver area once had the tallest tree ever measured on the planet. Featured in the *Guinness Book of World Records*, the Douglas fir was 120 meters tall and was located in the Lynn Valley area. It eventually fell.

time is from October to April. The sanctuary hosts the Snow Goose Festival in November, when hundreds of the giant birds take a break from their arduous journey south. The birds are not to be fed, and domestic animals are not allowed on the grounds. To get there, take Highway 99 south and exit at Highway 17; turn right on Ladner Trunk Road and at 47A Avenue go right; this becomes River Road; follow River Road over a small bridge that leads to Westham Island, where the sactuary is located. Open daily 9–4. $7 includes parking. Call ahead. (Southern Suburbs)

KITSILANO BEACH
Along Cornwall Ave. between Arbutus St. and Trafalgar St.
Vancouver
604/731-0011 (Kitsilano Pool)

This is the summer bod-watch area for the Kitsilano neighborhood. It's also a great place to catch a spectacular view. Look west to see English Bay spill toward Vancouver Island; northward are the North Shore Mountains, the West End skyline, and countless sailboats. The Nanaimo-to-Vancouver bathtub race, held each year on Canada Day (July 1), ends here. Participants build a fiberglass shell that's shaped like a small boat; a bathtub is inserted into this shell, and the whole thing is propelled by an outboard engine across the Strait of Georgia. Upon arrival at the beach, contestants must race from their tubs (not always easy, due to the cramped conditions) and ring a bell on the shore. Kids will love the Kitsilano Pool, a heated saltwater pool fronting the Kitsilano Showboat, a local institution that has provided free seaside entertainment since 1935. Local amateur groups sing and

Vancouver's Beaches

Vancouver is literally surrounded by sand. Beaches line the shore from Stanley Park (Third, Second, English Bay, and Sunset Beaches) to both sides of Point Grey (Kitsilano, Jericho, Locarno, and Spanish Banks Beaches). Lifeguards patrol the city's 10 beaches and pools from Victoria Day (end of May) through Labor Day from 11:30 in the morning to 8:45 each evening. For a real adventure, walk over to Wreck Beach, on the southern shore of Point Grey just below UBC's sand bluffs and opposite the Marine Drive residences. This is Vancouver's unofficial nude beach. A bit of advice: Don't go to ogle. You'll stick out like a—well, you'll be obvious. For more information on Vancouver's beaches, call 604/738-8535 (summer only).

act three days a week, weather permitting, during the summer months. Open daily 24 hours. (Point Grey)

LIGHTHOUSE PARK
Marine Dr. and Beacon Ln.
West Vancouver
604/925-7200

Lighthouse Park, 12 kilometers south of Horseshoe Bay, is the most rugged of the North Shore's parks. More than 60 bird species have been spotted here. Because logging in the area ceased in 1881, when the region was set aside as a reserve, the Douglas firs are enormous, some as large as 61 meters tall and 2 meters in diameter. Numerous trails, some lengthy, meander through the park's dense forest, but the trail to the lighthouse is along a well-marked walkway and only takes about 10 minutes. The lighthouse, located high on the bluffs of the North Shore, has warned approaching ships of dangers since

1912. The park is only about 20 minutes from downtown Vancouver, across the Lion's Gate Bridge. Open daily dawn to midnight. Lighthouse open for summer tours only. (See also Chapter 5, Sights and Attractions; and Chapter 10, Sports and Recreation.) (North Shore)

LOCARNO AND JERICHO BEACHES
Along NW Marine Dr. between Trimble and Blanca Sts.
Vancouver

A beach is a beach is a beach. Right? Well, not always. At least not here. This strip of shoreline is absolutely stunning. Locals come to Locarno and Jericho Beaches, which run the entire length of the north end of Point Grey, to take photos to send to their relatives. Stand on the sand and you'll be rewarded with views of the North Shore Mountains, Howe Sound, Bowen Island, Stanley Park, the city

Thanks a lot, New York! In 1909 the citizens of New York presented Vancouver with a gift of eight pairs of gray squirrels for Stanley Park. Now the place is overrun with them.

skyline, cruise ships, and glorious sunsets. At low tide you feel you can you can walk right across the bay—it's a great place to search for shells and to play in the tidal pools. A dirt path runs along the shore's length, and grassy picnic areas are scattered between the road and the sand. Open daily 24 hours. (Point Grey)

LYNN CANYON PARK AND ECO-LOGICAL CENTRE
3663 Park Rd.
North Vancouver
604/987-5922

Lynn Canyon is a natural park surrounding a deep gorge cut into Seymour Mountain over the course of centuries by Lynn Creek. Located alongside Mount Seymour Provincial Park and the Mount Seymour Demonstration Forest, this is one of North Vancouver's most popular summer hiking and fun places. One of the reasons for its popularity is a 68-meter-long suspension bridge hovering 75 meters above the rushing waters of Lynn Creek. The suspension bridge and nearby Ecology Centre—an educational center that offers information about the interdependence of plants, animals, and people—is an ideal place to start a hike. Guided walks are available. If you go it on your own, be careful: every year there are deaths on this mountain because people wander off well-marked trails or jump into inviting—but treacherous—swirling wa-

ters; if you get caught here at night, you could stumble into one of several deep canyons. To get there, take Highway 1, Trans-Canada, east to Lynn Valley Road and turn left; a large sign at Peters Road points the way to the park entrance. Open daily 8 a.m–10 p.m. (North Shore)

MOUNT SEYMOUR PROVINCIAL PARK
Mount Seymour Pkwy. and Lillooet Rd.
North Vancouver
604/924-2200

This is one of Vancouver's most popular multi-sport mountains, with all kinds of enthusiasts taking turns on the slopes during the year. A few

Irises border Livingstone Lake at the VanDusen Botanical Garden. p. 155.

VanDusen Botanical Garden

Greenpeace

Vancouver has a long-established love-hate relationship with Greenpeace, the international ecological organization that had its origins in a Vancouver apartment in 1969 after the United States detonated a nuclear weapon in the Aleutians.

The group of people who gathered in that apartment—originally calling itself the Don't Make a Wave Committee—consisted of university law students, government employees, and Vietnam protesters; they spent most of that first evening debating ways to protest the planned nuclear test off Alaska's Amchitkca Island. As one of the men left for the evening, he raised his first two fingers in the traditional greeting of the 1960s peace movement. "Peace," he said. Another member of the group responded, "Make it a green peace." Thus the name of the organization.

Greenpeace now operates a fleet of protest vessels around the world, including tugs, fish boats, and river boats. Greenpeace organizations have been founded in 30 countries, and they boast a total membership of more than five million, plus a paid staff of 1,000. The organization's budget is now over $40 million a year.

Oddly, the region that once was proud to count itself as Greenpeace's founding place now often finds itself at loggerheads with the organization. While issues such as nuclear arms and whaling are still among Greenpeace's priorities, so too are problems like toxic pollution and the destruction of rain forests. It's the latter issue, and the highly visible European campaigns against the purchase of British Columbian lumber thought to be logged from old-growth forests, that sometimes pits Greenpeace against Vancouver-area forestry companies and small communities that depend on logging for their well-being.

hundred yards up the mountain is the entrance to the difficult Northlands Golf Club; the top of Seymour Mountain is one of three major ski hills just minutes from Downtown; and in summer the whole mountain is prime hiking turf. Even if you participate in none of these activities, you can drive up the 13-kilometer paved road to the top, where you'll find great views, picnic areas, and a snack bar. From Vancouver, take Highway 1 across the Second Narrows Bridge to Exit 22, Mount Seymour Parkway; at Lillooet Road, you'll see a large green sign on the left indicating the entrance to the park. Open daily 8 a.m–10 p.m. (North Shore)

NITOBE MEMORIAL GARDENS
NW Marine Dr. (UBC)
Vancouver
604/822-6038
This authentic Japanese teahouse and garden is just south of the Museum of Anthropology. Within minutes you'll find yourself in a landscape designed with harmony, balance, and tranquility in mind. Everything seems perfectly suited— fir and cedar trees contrast the classical arrangements of shrubs and small walking bridges. Walkways meander around pruned cherry, maple, and pine trees. The teahouse and garden are especially beautiful when

the cherry trees bloom in April or May and when the irises bloom in late June. Summer daily 10–dusk; winter Mon–Fri 10–2:30. $2.50 adults; $5.75 combination ticket for the Nitobe Memorial Gardens and UBC Botanical Gardens. (Point Grey)

PACIFIC SPIRIT REGIONAL PARK
4915 W. 16th Ave.
Between NW Marine Dr. and SW Marine Dr. at UBC
Vancouver
604/224-5739
No one in Vancouver refers to this place by its official name—to locals it's known as the "Endowment Lands." This vast piece of property at the end of Point Grey on the UBC lands was endowed to the university by the provincial government in 1911, and it has since become both a research area for UBC's forestry students and a recreational area for walkers, cyclists, and horseback riders. More than 55 kilometers of horse and walking paths wind throughout the forest's 800 hectares. You can enter the forest at several points— from the north above Locarno Beach, where you'll find wildflowers and ravines, and from the south just up from the Fraser River, where you can see the tallest trees and wildlife, including raccoons and coyotes. Open daily 24 hours. (Point Grey)

PARK AND TILFORD GARDENS
440-333 Brooksbank Ave.
North Vancouver
604/984-8200

The eight theme gardens here were created in 1968 on the grounds of a privately owned distillery. The Rose Garden alone has nearly 300 plants. Check out the Oriental Garden—it includes traditional bonsai trees and a tranquil pond. The former distillery buildings are now a shopping center and a film studio. Open daily 10–5. Free admission and parking. (North Shore)

QUEEN ELIZABETH PARK AND BLOEDEL FLORAL CONSERVATORY
Cambie St. at 33rd Ave.
Vancouver
604/257-8570

It may be on the large size for a jewel, but this is definitely one of the crown gems among Vancouver's parks. Located on the city's highest point (150 meters), it's a photographer's delight—not only does it offer dramatic vistas of the North Shore, the mountains, and the city skyline, but it's also a photo-worthy destination in itself. Flowers, oh so many flowers, as well as manicured bushes, tranquil ponds filled with ducks and other wild birds, and other wildlife delight the eyes. Check out the Henry Moore bronze sculpture, *Knife Edge—Two Pieces*, atop the water reservoire on the plaza. Inside the silver-domed Bloedel Conservatory is a simulated rain forest, featuring plants from Mexico, South America, and Africa; the conservatory also has a dry-desert environment. Park open daily 24 hours; conservatory open summer Mon–Fri 9–8 and Sat–Sun 10–9, otherwise daily (except Christmas) 10–5. $3.50 adults; discounts for families, seniors, students. (Uptown)

Top 10 Exhibits in the VanDusen Botanical Garden

by Margaret Johnson, Garden Director, and Nancy Wong, Director of Marketing for VanDusen Botanical Garden

1. Elizabethan Maze any time of year
2. Holly Collection in January and February
3. Magnolias in March and April
4. Rhododendron Walk and Azaleas in May
5. Laburnum Walk in late May and early June
6. Meconopsis Dell in the Sino-Himalayan Area in May
7. Perennial Garden in July and August
8. Fragrance and Herb Gardens in August
9. Autumn Colors in September and October
10. Festival of Lights in December

STANLEY PARK
Northwest edge of Downtown Vancouver

Stanley Park is a wonderful place to take the family, to go for a walk, or to simply relax. An 10.5-kilometer seawall promenade completely surrounds the park and provides spectacular views across Burrard Inlet, Georgia Strait, and English Bay. It's along this promenade that you'll find Vancouver's finest—the sandcastle builders, windsurfers, joggers, walkers, cyclists, in-line skaters, the weird, and the wonderful. You'll also pass the Tudor-style Vancouver Rowing Club, the Nine O'Clock Gun, Brockton Point, Lumberman's Arch, Prospect Point, Siwash Rock, and Second Beach. Other attractions are the Vancouver Aquarium, a miniature train, a zoo and petting zoo, totem poles, and the Lion's Gate suspension bridge, which spans Burrard Inlet. The park also has tennis courts and a pitch-and-putt golf course. (See also the sidebar in Chapter 5, Sights and Attractions.) (Downtown)

UBC BOTANICAL GARDENS
6840 SW Marine Dr.
Vancouver
604/822-9666

Plan an entire day around two neighbors. Virtually across the street from the UBC Football Stadium is the oldest and arguably the finest botanical garden in the entire country. Its five gardens—the Asian Garden, the BC Native Garden, the Alpine Garden, the Physick Garden, and the Food Garden—are spread over 70 acres (28 hectares). Each is an amazing collection of the best of its kind. Home farmers, for example, will love the Food Garden, which must be the best organized garden on the planet. A dozen raised beds and some 180

Stanley Park's totem poles

© John Elk

fruit trees are packed into just three-quarters of an acre; all crops are donated to the Salvation Army. Gardens open daily 10–dusk. $4.50 adults; discounts for seniors, students; $5.75 combination ticket for UBC Botanical Gardens and Nitobe Memorial Gardens. (Point Grey)

VANDUSEN BOTANICAL GARDEN
5251 Oak St.
Vancouver
604/878-9274

What do you do with a former golf course, anyway? Why not turn the grounds into gardens? This garden is named after W. J. VanDusen, former president of the Vancouver Foundation, a private philanthropic organization that funds arts and community projects in the city. In the 1970s the foundation teamed with the city and provincial governments to buy the land from the then–Shaughnessy Golf Club (which moved to a bigger piece of land in the city's Point Grey area) and transformed the 23-hectare site into a series of small gardens. Crisscrossing paths wander through 40 gardens, skirting lakes and ponds and passing bamboo and redwoods. Be sure to walk among Canada's largest collection of rhododendrons. The Sprinklers restaurant, near the entrance of the gardens, is one of the city's most popular eating establishments, serving up West Coast fare amidst the shrubbery. Garden open daily 10–dusk. $5.50 summer, $2.75 winter. Discounts for families, seniors, and children 6–18. (Uptown)

Pacific Centre

9

SHOPPING

Vancouverites love to shop. But in Vancouver shopping is not simply about buying things. It's also about style and about experiencing the wide variety of cultural realities that make up the Vancouver mosaic. Many "shoppers" walk the streets simply to watch people or enjoy the atmosphere. And this is a city that embraces a multitude of styles—from jeans to the latest fashions from Paris and Milan. In fact, the downtown area has attracted an international collection of well-known designers, such as Ralph Lauren, Dunhill, Chanel, Armani, Versace, and Cartier, among others.

Clothing isn't all you'll find Downtown. The Yaletown district, for example , is one of the city's leading areas for home furnishings. Walk the streets of Chinatown and you'll swear you're far removed form North America as you pass stores stocked with oriental goods. And in Gastown, the original Vancouver, the old warehouses and office buildings have been restored and refurbished and turned into shops, many selling Native art and crafts.

For a taste of contemporary Asia, prowl the five closely clustered shopping malls in Richmond that are under the general banner of Asia West—Aberdeen Centre, Fairchild Square, Parker Place, President Plaza, and Yaohan Centre. Vancouver's Chinatown is the old-style Chinese neighborhood; Asia West is the new—an area of high energy where old traditions are not lost among the bright lights and chrome and glass. The centers are an exotic tourist destination, accepted and frequented by the whole community.

Point Grey has several major shopping areas, the most important of which are Kerrisdale and Kitsilano. Kerrisdale is a three-block, upscale West Side neighborhood along 41st Avenue west of West Boulevard. Kitsilano is a much broader area. The largest concentraton of shops, restaurants, and boutiques lies along Fourth Avenue west of Burrard Street. Kitsilano also includes a several-block-long area along 10th Avenue near the entrance to UBC and along Broadway from MacDonald west to Alma.

These parallel streets are within a few minutes of each other by bus or car.

On Commercial Drive you can wander into stores with labels and accents from Italy... and the list goes on. So staple your wallet to your pocket, because there are more ways to spend your money in Vancouver than there are waves in English Bay during a windstorm.

SHOPPING DISTRICTS

DOWNTOWN

As you'd expect, Downtown is the city's primary shopping area. In terms of shopping, it's a mini United Nations. Chinatown specializes in items from Asia; Gastown is where you'll find exquisite Native art; the West End is where the latest fashion boutiques can be found; the downtown core near the Vancouver Art Gallery is home to the largest department stores; and Yaletown is where Vancouverites shop for furniture and household accents.

It may come as a surprise, however, that much of the shopping in the downtown area takes place underground. You can wander for hours through the underground corridors that link department stores and office buildings. The city's busiest shopping area is at Georgia and Granville Streets, where three department stores—The Bay, Eaton's, and Holt Renfrew—are connected by an underground mall with about 200 shops. Known as Pacific Centre Mall, it is easily reached via the department stores or through the office towers situated on the street corners.

Further along Georgia Street, beneath the Royal Bank and the Hyatt hotel at the corner of Burrard, you'll find a long passageway of stores, called the Royal Centre. There are boutiques that you won't find elsewhere. The Royal Centre also includes some small fast-food joints and a movie theater complex.

Still, you don't have to be a groundhog to enjoy downtown Vancouver's shopping thrills. Above ground, Granville Street, Robson Street, and the waterfront offer plenty of chances for you to separate yourself from your cash. On Burrard and Hornby Streets between Georgia and Robson, for example, you'll find international haute couture shops that cater to tourists and locals alike, with Chanel, Romeo Gigli, Celine, and Versace among the major outlets. A couple of blocks north of Georgia and Granville are two upscale shopping areas—Sinclair Centre and The Landing—with boutiques, restaurants, and services for those who prefer a more personal relationship with their salespeople.

BIG TOP HAT SHOP
73 Water St.
Vancouver
604/684-7373
Whoever said that hats were out of fashion has never been here. Ellen Anderson and Renata Crowe have collected what appears to be an endless variety of hats. Need a really weird one for a wacky party? How about a chapeau to define your personality? If you can't find what you need in their huge selection, don't worry. They can have one custom-made for you. (Downtown)

BIRKS
698 W. Hastings St.
Vancouver
604/669-3333
Birks is to Vancouver what Tiffany's is

to New York—the place where Vancouverites have always done their jewelry shopping, long before competition came to the city. Birks stores are found in every major Canadian city; this one is where brides have always registered their weddings. You'll find nothing but quality in this wide selection of crystals, rings, necklaces, and other expensive baubles. (Downtown)

CHINTZ AND COMPANY
950 Homer St.
Vancouver
604/689-2022
Of the many home-furnishings stores in Yaletown, Chintz and Company is probably the most fun. It has virtually everything under the sun in folk art and other design ideas. You'll find batik cushions, dishes, glassware, and all the little touches you would expect in a well-defined home. Ask someone to help you in designing your interior around your accessories. (Downtown)

COWS VANCOUVER
1301 Robson St.
Vancouver
604/682-2622
You probably thought that cows were only good for milk and beef. Well, you're in for a surprise or two as you wander among the memorabilia devoted to these four-legged creatures. You'll find cow T-shirts, children's clothing, and an endless line of bovine trinkets. And the ice-cream parlor serves homemade ice cream in freshly baked waffle cones. (Downtown)

DRIVER'S DEN
213 Carrall St.
Vancouver
604/687-2818

© John Elk

Gastown shops and the Gassy Jack statue

If your car is your castle, this place is for you. Everything in this store is car-oriented. Car buffs will revel in the smells of fabric and metal. (Yes, every gas jockey knows that metal has an odor!) You'll find models, hats, posters, neat stuff from the Indy 500, and much more—a veritable car-lover's dream. Don't miss the incredible vehicle in the back of the store. (Downtown)

EDDIE BAUER
Pacific Centre
777 Dunsmuir St.
Vancouver
604/683-4711
This Pacific Centre outlet is the place to shop if you want to look like an outdoorsperson without really getting soiled. The casual clothing, shoes, and high-quality accessories are the same here as in other Eddie Bauer retail outlets throughout North America. The store is tucked away in one of the upper levels of the center's newer wing. (Downtown)

The Bay (Hudson's Bay Company)

The Bay department stores date back to 1670, when the Hudson's Bay Company (HBC) was founded in London to make as much money as possible from the North American fur trade—and eventually anything profitable. For its first two centuries, HBC's chief interests were the fur trade, exploration, and settlement. The company ended up doing so well, in fact, that some of its executives formed their own firm, the North West Company, in Montreal. For the next several decades the North West Company competed vigorously with HBC, and in the process opened up large tracts of land to exploration throughout Canada and the American Northwest.

Eventually, HBC reabsorbed its competition and gained control over the fur trade in every region of Canada. Then, in 1868, the British Parliament made HBC turn over all of its assets to the newly formed government of Canada. After this, HBC's interests became more varied, and trading posts became consumer outlets. The company has a glorious and uniquely Canadian past and is now Canada's largest nonfood retailer, with stores across the entire country. In some small, isolated regions, it is often the only store for miles around.

GOLDEN AGE COLLECTIBLES
830 Granville St.
Vancouver
604/683-2819
Located in the heart of the Granville Mall, this place is a wonderful source of old movie posters, baseball cards, comic books, unique T-shirts, and other hard-to-find collectibles. Some are rare and expensive, others are just memorable but worth the price tag. (Downtown)

HILL'S INDIAN CRAFTS
165 Water St.
Vancouver
604/685-4249
This is one of many Gastown outlets that carry a wide selection of Native sculpture in soapstone and whalebone, as well as cedar carvings and ceremonial masks. It also has a collection of prints and metal art that you don't normally find in a specialty Native gallery/store. The Hill's three levels include one of the Lower Mainland's largest collections of Cowichan sweaters—those bulky, hand-knit, woolen sweaters made on Vancouver Island. (Downtown)

LEONE
Sinclair Centre
757 W. Hastings St.
Vancouver
604/683-1133

Not only does this upscale women's fashion store carry a wide range of notable labels in its collection (Versace, Armani, DKNY, among others), but it also also has its own line, A-Wear. Even if you don't buy anything, you must take a walk through this architectural jewel, a part of the Sinclair Centre, the original Vancouver Post Office building. Actually, Leones is a series of mini-stores, with rooms focusing on casual and formal wear. It carries a complete line of accessories for men and women. (Downtown)

MARQUIS WINE CELLARS
1034 Davie St.
Vancouver
604/684-0445

It wasn't too many years ago that the only place you could buy wine was at the local government-run liquor-board stores. Today you'll find a lot of small wine shops scattered around the city. This one's a little different because the owners are determined to educate local residents about wine. They carry an extensive selection of British Columbian wine as well as a wide range of international labels. Come in for one of their special wine tastings. (Downtown)

MARTHA STURDY DESIGNS
775 Burrard St.
Vancouver
604/685-7751

Sturdy's reputation was built on hand-blown glassware trimmed in gold leaf. Now she has taken it a step further and created cast-resin housewares and a line of limited-edition couches and chairs. No bargain hunt-

ing here, just high quality, creative work. (Downtown)

MURCHIE'S TEA AND COFFEE
970 Robson St.
Vancouver
604/669-0783

This Vancouver institution dates from 1894. You'll see small Murchie's outlets and products everywhere. Originally a teashop, it later expanded into coffee—long before Starbucks was even conceived. At this store you can choose from about 50 different tea varieties and about 40 coffee blends, including the house blend, Murchie's Best. Also offered is a large selection of gift boxes, samplers, clay teapots, bone china, and other kitchen items. (Downtown)

SALVATORE FERRAGAMO
918 Robson St.
Vancouver
604/669-4495

Located on the corner of Robson and Hornby Streets, directly across from the courthouse plaza, this is the Italian shoe store's first Canadian outlet. This world-class designer of men's and women's footwear offers quality service to boot. Pricey, yes. But in five years' time, when you're still wearing the same shoes, you'll think they were a bargain. The store also has a wide selection of accessories, including belts and purses. (Downtown)

THE UMBRELLA SHOP
534 W. Pender St.
Vancouver
604/669-9444

If you thought you knew umbrellas, you'll change your mind on a rainy day when you step into this mecca of bumbershoots. In business for 50-plus years, this is Vancouver's premier (and only) umbrella store. You'll find umbrellas in every shape and form imaginable. If you want something unusual, you can have it made for you on the premises. And if you need a repair, they'll do it. (Downtown)

VIRGIN MEGASTORE
788 Burrard St.
Vancouver
604/669-2289
Canada's first Virgin Megastore has the largest collection of music and entertainment items in the country, from tapes to CDs to all kinds of computer software. The three-level store's 140 private listening booths allow you to listen before you buy. Don't miss the laser/video viewing stations. This is the in place for the young set. (Downtown)

Chinatown

Chinatown is a special place simply for its originality. You can see things here that you won't see anywhere else in Canada. Many of the stores seem as though they have been around forever—in fact, some date back to the turn of the twentieth century. While Chinatown has become a diverse Asian mix, with Vietnamese, Taiwanese, Japanese, and Filipinos adding their cultural influences, it is still predominantly Chinese in character. Chinatown is bounded by Gore, Union, Taylor, and East Hastings Streets.

ARTLAND
111 E. Pender St.
Vancouver
604/688-0383
You'll find this place interesting even if you've never had a need for chops. What are chops, you ask? They're those small pieces of granite or marble that are usually used to mark a

painting or other work of art, but that can also be used on envelopes or letters. Words, slogans, and symbols are etched into the bottom of the chop, and a zodiac symbol—for your birth date—is carved into the top. Of course, there's also a wide selection of other Asian goods here. (Downtown)

ASIA IMPORTS
155 W. Hastings St.
Vancouver
604/687-4912
If you expect quality, you should also expect to pay for it. The goods here include handmade quilts, embroidered silk blouses, exotic kimonos, jade, ivory, and other expensive items. Ask for the Battenburg-style lace and cutwork. Insiders claim the selection here is the best in town. (Downtown)

CHINA ARTS AND CRAFTS IMPORTERS
895 E. Hastings St.
Vancouver
604/251-2554

Sign and streetlamp in Chinatown

© John Elk

Vancouver's Auction Houses

Here's a rundown on Vancouver's three long-time auctioneer houses:

- ***Love's*** *(1635 Broadway, 604/733-1157), in operation since 1912, has no real specialization. Items vary almost week to week. Auctions are held Wednesdays at noon and at seven o'clock. (Point Grey)*

- ***Maynard's*** *(415 W. Second Ave., 604/876-6787), founded in 1902, has a large merchandise area (selling everything from furniture to art to clothing) in addition to its regular auctions, held Wednesday evenings at seven o'clock. (Uptown)*

- ***Tyldesley's*** *(1050 Vernon Dr., 604/254-2111) features collectibles—jewelry, estate items, paintings, and porcelain—as well as a wide variety of office equipment and furnishings. Auctions take place on Tuesday evenings, with previews on Mondays. (Uptown)*

This huge store imports large quantities of art, including stone, wood, and jade carvings, as well as magnificent room dividers and furniture. Be sure to check out the hope chests, which sell at about one-half of what they cost at other places in Chinatown. If you don't want to carry anything that large out the door, try on a 14-inch vase or a set of tiny ceramic soup spoons for size. (Downtown)

HING WAH, LTD.
506 Main St.
Vancouver
604/683-3838

One of the biggest herbalist stores in Chinatown, Hing Wah is filled with ancient remedies and cures, from dried seahorses and lizards to ginseng and about 20 different health teas. You'll even find black seaweed, a food that when served to guests indicates you wish them a long life. If you're trying to find a cure for what ails you, you can describe your pain and have the herbalist grind up a personalized potion. (Downtown)

MING WO
23 E. Pender St.
Vancouver
604/683-7268

A Vancouver mainstay since 1919, this shop is legendary for its hard-to-find kitchen items. Its ongoing commitment to providing excellence at an affordable price has kept Vancouverites coming back for decades. Anything that you ever dreamed of having in your kitchen is here. Pots, ceramics, utensils, woks, wooden spoons . . . you name it. The store is always crowded, and it's absolutely filled with merchandise, so be careful not to knock anything off the shelves. Other outlets, stocked to meet the needs of the local clientele, are at 2066 W. Fourth Ave., 604/737-8106, and at 2707 Granville St., 604/737-7885. (Downtown)

TEN REN TEA AND GINSENG CO.
550 Main St.
Vancouver
604/684-1566
Come here for the finest selection of oriental teas in the city. Some of the teas cost as much as $68 a kilo ($150 a pound). Porcelain sets are also for sale. If the shop isn't busy and the owners feel up to it, they'll honor you with a Chinese tea ceremony. At the very least, you'll have the chance to taste a variety of brews. Be sure to pick up their informative and interesting pamphlet, *The Art of Tea Making.* (Downtown)

POINT GREY

Kerrisdale

Kerrisdale will transport you back to community storefront shopping. Located between the 1900 and 2400 blocks along West 41st Avenue, practically all your everyday needs can be met here. You'll find shoe shops, clothing stores, an Italian coffee shop, a kitchen store, several bagel places, a stationery store, bookstores, a camera shop, and a variety of excellent eateries.

ARITZIA
2125 W. 41st Ave.
Vancouver
604/266-6446
If you're a girl-on-the-go—one with, perhaps, a touch of attitude—you're exactly what this store wants. Located within the Hill's department store (see listing, below), Aritzia is designed to meet all the clothing needs of young women in their teens and 20s. You'll find designs by the French outfit Kookaï as well as a large selection made by Vancouver-area designers. You'll even find classic, retro-chic Hush Puppies shoes. Other outlets are at 1110 Robson St., 604/684-3251; Oakridge Centre, 604/261-2202; and 6551 No. 3 Rd. in Richmond, 604/244-1614. (Point Grey)

CHEAPSKATES
3644 W. 16th Ave.
Vancouver
604/222-1125
This used-sporting-goods company on Vancouver's West Side is a great place to find exceptional value on items like skates, skis, and other gear. You might have to search for what you want, but you can't argue with the prices. The store accepts trade-ins and will try to sell your used gear on consignment or for a set price. Other outlets are at 3496 Dunbar St., 604/734-1160, and 3208 Dunbar St., 604/739-1125. Each store sells something different, so call ahead

Don't walk past the gift shops in Vancouver's museums, art galleries, and special places. You can find some real treasures and art pieces at places like the Vancouver Aquarium, VanDusen Botanical Garden, Vancouver Art Gallery, and Capilano Suspension Bridge.

to find out if they have what you're looking for. (Point Grey)

FINN'S KERRISDALE
2159 W. 41st St.
Vancouver
604/266-8358

In a neighborhood that prides itself on continuity and conservative values, Finn's fits in very nicely. You'll find men's and women's clothes—the store is split virtually in half—that are subtle and well cut. On-site tailors are there for a quick turnaround on anything that needs altering. The store has a wide selection of sports coats, trousers, and sweaters for men and semiformal business wear for women. The store's second outlet, at 3031 Broadway, 604/732-3831, has a wider selection of casual wear. (Point Grey)

HILL'S OF KERRISDALE
2125 W. 41st St.
Vancouver
604/266-9177

This miniature department store offers something for everyone in the family while keeping a boutique-like atmosphere. The store is split into small sections, each with a specific specialty. Young women who want to make a fashion statement should shop in the Aritzia area, while Dad should find everything he needs at the front of the store. Jeans have their own boutique area, as do other clothing and jewelry items. (Point Grey)

KISA'S OF KERRISDALE CONSIGNMENT BOUTIQUE
2352 W. 41st St.
Vancouver
604/266-2885

Where best to find second-hand high-end clothing than in one of Vancouver's high-end districts? Walk down the stairs and you'll find a wide selection of consignment fashion, jewelry, handbags, and accessories, many of which are from Europe. This is a place where European consignments are encouraged and the store-owners often buy items outright for resale. Look around and you'll find little difference between many of the items here and those just put on a retailer's rack. (Point Grey)

MONALIZA'S
2283 W. 41st St.
Vancouver
604/266-4598

Is a Mona by any other spelling just as sweet? This lingerie shop was once called Vanity; after that store went out of business, locals wondered what would replace it. Well, the transition has been handled smoothly, with staff from the old store being transferred to this one. The store has a wide selection of cottons and products from Lejaby and Chantelle, plus a number of robes and gowns by Linda. (Point Grey)

S. LAMPMAN
2126 W. 41st St.
Vancouver
604/261-2750

If the clothing at Finn's is not your type, walk across 41st to Lampman for a more casual look. This small men's store has a wide variety of colorful and comfortable sweaters, trousers, shirts, and accessories. If you want to be ready for anything from the opera to a hip nightclub, this is the place to go. Designers include Calvin Klein, Lyle & Scott, and Alan Paine. Suits are also available but must be ordered. (Point Grey)

Kitsilano

Kitsilano was Vancouver's version of

Top 10 Biggest Shopping Malls

1. **Metrotown Centre** (Burnaby)—240 stores, 997,000 square feet

2. **Park Royal Shopping Centre** (West Vancouver)—250 stores, 990,000 square feet

3. **Pacific Centre** (Vancouver)—165 stores, 966,665 square feet

4. **Guilford Town Centre** (Surrey)—230 stores, 900,00 square feet

5. **Richmond Centre** (Richmond)—326 stores, 786,562 square feet

6. **Coquitlam Centre** (Coquitlam)—163 stores, 754,204 square feet

7. **Oakridge Centre** (Vancouver)—154 stores, 690,402 square feet

8. **Surrey Place Shopping Centre** (Surrey)—150 stores, 625,957 square feet

9. **Lansdowne Park** (Richmond)—140 stores, 620,000 square feet

10. **Eaton's Metrotown Centre** (Burnaby)—200 stores, 606,890 square feet

San Francisco's Haight-Ashbury. When the hippie era was over these stores were bought out, and little by little the old hippie-oriented shops gave way to more contemporary and upscale stores. Now Kitsilano consists of a series of diverse shopping neighborhoods selling everything from home furnishings to food. The hippie atmosphere may be gone, but the shops still attract a young crowd. They just have different tastes. The heart of the Kitsilano area is along Fourth Avenue between Burrard and Balsam. If you're walking west, stop at the Royal branch at Fourth and Balsam, cross the street, and walk back.

COAST MOUNTAIN SPORTS
2201 W. Fourth Ave.
Vancouver
604/731-6181
Come here for high-end camping, hiking, and other outdoors and travel goods like sleeping bags, water purifiers, freeze-dried foods, and satellite-tracking systems. This is the crème-de-la-crème store for the experienced mountaineer or hiker. Located in the heart of Kitsilano, near Burrard Street, it's known throughout the outdoors community for its quality goods. Be sure you examine the casual-clothing area for items that you can wear when you're not hiking. (Point Grey)

COTTONENTAL
2207 W. Fourth Ave.
Vancouver
604/733-6553

No, it's not a misspelling. Everything in this women's sportswear shop is made entirely of cotton. Much of it comes from Europe, where long-fiber Egyptian cotton is often used to great end. Among the names you'll find here are Calvin Klein and a Copenhagen line called Part Two. You'll also find a broad selection of Vancouver's Moratti line and a variety of women's undergarments. (Point Grey)

THE FLAG SHOP
1755 W. Fourth Ave.
Vancouver
604/736-8161

Looking for a flag . . . from anywhere? If these guys don't have it, they'll find it for you. You'll also find a huge number of pins, crests, and decals from virtually everywhere in the world, as well as a selection of colorful windsocks. (Point Grey)

MAGIC FLUTE
2203 W. Fourth Ave.
Vancouver
604/736-2727

If you're looking for a classical CD or tape, this is the place to find it. You'll also find information on live classical performances around town, as well as a large selection of books, videos, and CD ROMs. (Point Grey)

SECOND SUIT
2036 W. Fourth Ave.
Vancouver
604/732-0338

This is a combination consignment shop and factory outlet store and is popular not only among those looking for bargains but also with anyone looking for formal wear by Armani,

Hugo Boss, or Dior. The men's clothing here always seems to be in short supply—items are scooped up almost as quickly as they arrive. They have a much wider selection of women's attire and accessories, including suits, purses, jewelry, and cocktail dresses. (Point Grey)

THE URBAN BARN
1992 W. Fourth Ave.
Vancouver
604/731-9047

The Urban Barn sells Mexican and locally made furnishings and accessories, including lamps, bookshelves, glassware, and more. Many of the items are one of a kind. (Point Grey)

WEAR ELSE
2360 W. Fourth Ave.
Vancouver
604/732-3521

This upscale store has a different atmosphere from the company's clearinghouse (also see listing on p. 170). If you want, you can have a fashion consultant completely outfit you or simply coordinate what you already have with supplementary clothing or accessories. International and Canadian designers are well represented, and you'll find a good selection of casual clothing in the Wear Else Weekend department. (Point Grey)

WESTBEACH SNOWBOARD
1766 W. Fourth Ave.
Vancouver
604/731-6449

Boarders and non-boarders alike love this place. Westbeach Snowboard offers a wide selection of snowboards, skateboards, and, for anyone who just wants to dress in style, oversized flannel and fleece items. Teenagers aren't the only ones you'll find here. A lot of aging baby boomers with aching knees come here to make the transition from skis to boards. Still, on a busy day—especially Saturdays—the place is jumping with kids. (Point Grey)

UPTOWN

This vast area includes just about everything between Granville Island and the Fraser River east of and including Granville Street, East Broadway, upper Granville Street, and Oak Street. You'll find antiques shops and some of Vancouver's most sophisticated stores on Granville Street between 15th Avenue and Broadway. Interior-design stores, home-furnishings stores, and specialty shops are spread out between the Granville Street Bridge and 16th Avenue. Numerous fashion stores, shoe stores, and restaurants line Broadway between Cambie and Granville Streets.

BOBILO
2776 Granville St.
Vancouver
604/736-3458
The stone archway at the store's entrance is said to have come from a wrecked Mexican cathedral. Once inside you'll find extremely hip men's clothing from top contemporary designers like Claude Montana and Yohji Yamamoto, and a women's selection including clothing by Armani and Ferretti. You have to be adventurous to shop here—this is not mainstream clothing, and the styles aren't for the full-bodied. (Uptown)

CYCLONE TAYLOR SPORTING GOODS
6575 Oak St.
Vancouver

604/266-3316
Cyclone Taylor was a star player on the 1915 Vancouver Millionaires hockey team, the only team from Vancouver ever to win the Stanley Cup. Old Cyclone is dead now, but his son and grandson run the store. This is the place to go for in-line skates, ice skates, and related accessories. (Uptown)

EDWARD CHAPMAN'S LADIES SHOP
2596 Granville St.
Vancouver
604/732-3394
If you're conservative and you want a clean, classic line, try this place first. Edward Chapman's carries clothing from Germany and England, and although reputed to be a bit stodgy, is popular among women professionals. It's been satisfying discerning shoppers for nearly 100 years. (Uptown)

MOUNTAIN EQUIPMENT CO-OP
130 W. Broadway
Vancouver
604/872-7858
This is the biggest outdoor-goods store in the city. You'll find countless racks of everything you could possibly need for any outdoor excursion, from camping, biking, hiking, and kayaking to waterskiing, snow skiing, and climbing. A lifetime membership at this cooperative costs five dollars. As a member you'll receive large spring and fall mail-order catalog. Great quality and good prices explain why this store is always busy. If you want to test some of their gear, try renting for a day or two. (Uptown)

SPORTSMART DISCOUNT SUPERSTORE
2300 Cambie St.
Vancouver

Top 10 Jewelry Stores in Vancouver

As chosen by self-admitted Jewelry Princess Suzanne Fong, who represents DeBeers on the West Coast.

1. **Birks** *(698 W. Hastings St. 604/669-3333)—A Vancouver tradition. Has a little of everything.*
2. **Brinkhaus** *(Hotel Vancouver, 604/689-7055)—A long-time family business with very traditional pieces for the established society.*
3. **Bustopher's Goldsmiths** *(110-1058 Mainland St., 604/683-8243)—Funky little store with designer Andrew Costen working in a see-through workshop. Wonderful, whimsical pieces.*
4. **Cartier** *(408 Howe St., 604/683-6878)—Because it's Cartier.*
5. **Catbalue** *(1832 W. First Ave., 604/734-3259)—Designer Mary Ann Buis works in a beautiful personally designed store. Jewelry store downstairs, husband-architect on second floor, and their home on the third floor.*
6. **Creative Goldsmith** *(Park Royal Shopping Centre, West Vancouver, 604/926-7213)—Lovely little store in a big shopping center with great pieces for everyday wear.*
7. **Karl Stittgen** *(2203 Granville St., 604/737-0029)—The designer may be retired, but the store still carries his name and designs. He made gold leafs on rings famous.*
8. **Palladio** *(855 W. Hastings St., 604/685-3885)— Very upscale. Only sells flawless gems, so everything is quite expensive.*
9. **Tiffany's** *(633 Granville St., 604/681-3121)—In Holt Renfrew for the famous blue box.*
10. **Toni Cavelti** *(565 Georgia St., 604/681-3481)—Toni is where the tony people of Vancouver shop to say they own a piece of Cavelti.*

604/873-6737

This store has a policy that's hard to beat: If it can't beat other stores' prices on an item you've bought, you'll get your money back. There's a wonderful selection of sporting goods, including in-line skates, skis, snowboarding equipment, and clothing. Stay on top of the season, because items in the store literally change with the weather; don't expect to find golf clubs in February or skis in July. Other locations are at 1882 Marine Dr., 604/984-8494; 5381 No. 3 Rd., Richmond, 604/244-0317; and 599 Seymour St., 604/683-2433. (Uptown)

TAIGA WORKS
390 W. Eighth Ave.
Vancouver
604/875-6644

Taiga Works has a wide selection of locally manufactured items designed specifically for the local climate and conditions—especially the rain. High-quality tents, hiking gear, boots, and general sportswear draw customers from all over British Columbia. Be sure to ask for the Nordic down comforters that come with a 10-year guarantee. (Uptown)

THREE VETS
2200 Yukon St.
Vancouver
604/872-5475

Three Vets is well known for good-quality, entry-level camping, fishing, and hiking equipment at moderate prices. It's a great place to get started. Alpen Mountain Wear factory items are offered here at a discount. The store also has a decent collection of Native art for sale in the back (see Chapter 6, Museums and Galleries).(Uptown)

TILLEY ENDURABLES
2401 Granville St.
Vancouver
604/732-4287

Going on a safari? Want to look like you're ready to board a camel? This is a great place to find casual, elegant clothing suitable for anything from a casual day on the town to a rugged trip through the jungle. Shoppers are drawn to this retailer of fine clothing for its sense of style. You'll find cotton shorts, shirts, safari hats and jackets, and windbreakers. (Uptown)

TURNABOUT COLLECTIONS
3121 Granville St.
Vancouver
604/732-8115

You'll get good fashion for your dollar at this well-established clothing store. There are two outlets, each catering to a distinct clientele. The Granville Street outlet primarily carries designer labels for women. Typical labels include Armani, Liz Claiborne, and Byblos. The second store, at 3060 West Broadway, 604/731-7762, is funky and casual, and it caters to both men and women. (Uptown)

WEAR ELSE CLEARANCE CENTRE
78 E. Second Ave.
Vancouver
604/879-6162

It's hard to find better deals on big-name labels. This is the clearinghouse for anything that doesn't sell at the six Wear Else outlets (also see listing on p. 167) around the city. Those items—all quality controlled—end up here at discounts of up to 80 percent. Don't worry about marauding crowds and hysterical shoppers. It's open seven days a week and, while usually busy, has enough items to keep everyone content. (Uptown)

Granville Island

So much is said about Granville Island's theater, market, restaurants, and waterfront activities, that it's easy to forget its most appealing attraction—art. First and foremost, the island is an artistic haven— you'll find everything art-related here. If, for some reason, you're having trouble finding what you need, head for the Net Loft, the low-slung building across from the Granville Island Public Market. The Loft houses numerous small shops selling everything from silk paintings to one-of-a-kind jewelry, and it will certainly have what you're looking for.

BERMAN'S
1244 Cartwright St.
Vancouver
604/684-8332
Berman's is a fascinating store and a great place to watch artisans at work. Glass is the name of the game here. You'll find architectural leaded glass; blast-etched, kiln-fired, and slab (epoxy) glass; glass furniture; and glass sculpture. (Uptown)

MAIWA HANDPRINTS
1666 Johnston St.
Vancouver
604/669-3939
This store, located in the Net Loft, sells high-quality fiber art and handcrafted textiles from artisans around the world. You'll find a complete selection of tools, dyes, fabrics, fabric paints, textiles books, and other related products. In addition, the store offers workshops that cover the many aspects of the surface-and-textile design process. Ask a salesperson about them. (Uptown)

NANCY LORD
1666 Johnston St.
Vancouver
604/731-9190
This closet-sized space in the Net Loft creates and sells high-quality men's and women's clothing. Made-to-order garments are shipped directly to your hotel or home, whichever you prefer. All fabrics come from Switzerland, France, and Italy. The leather and suede are A-quality Italian lamb in natural-dye colors. (Uptown)

THE OCEAN FLOOR
1525 Duranleau St.
Vancouver
604/681-5014
In this intimate shop right across from The Keg restaurant, you'll find anything and everything nautical, including seashells, ship models, stuffed toys, lamps, chimes, coral, fine jewelry, and boat ornaments. Nothing in the store is on anyone's endangered species list. It's a fun place to let your imagination run wild. (Uptown)

RUDDICK'S FLY SHOP
1654 Duranleau St.
Vancouver
604/681-3747
Enter this place with visions of a large trout on the end of your fishing line. Bar none, this is one of the finest fly-fishing shops in the country. In it you'll find Orvis rods, clothing, plenty of fishing information, and a variety of accessories for wading and surviving in cold water. You'll also find the shop's own homemade flies. If you're new to the area and looking for that perfect fishing hole, they're willing to point you in the right direction. They even organize expeditions to

some of British Columbia's better fishing areas. (Uptown)

NOTABLE BOOKSTORES AND NEWSSTANDS

CHAPTERS
Robson and Howe Sts.
Vancouver
604/682-4066
Chapters was created in 1995 by the merger of Coles and SmithBooks. It's now Canada's largest book retailer and the third largest retailer in North America, with more than 20 superstores in Canada. You'll find a wide selection of just about everything, including computer software, as well as a coffee bar and floor attendants. Other Vancouver outlets—at Granville and Broadway (604/731-7822), Metrotown Centre (604/431-0463), and elsewhere—have essentially the same stock. (Downtown)

GRANVILLE BOOK COMPANY
850 Granville St.
Vancouver
604/687-2213
If you're a sci-fi fan, this is the place for you. Just a few doors north of the Orpheum on the Granville Mall, this bookstore stocks the newest best-sellers and has one of the city's finest collections of new and established science-fiction authors. It also has a surprisingly broad spectrum of music and theater books as well as many hard-to-find English-language magazines. (Downtown)

LITTLE SISTERS BOOK AND ART EMPORIUM
1238 Davie St.
Vancouver
604/669-1753
This is the only gay-and-lesbian bookstore in western Canada. But you don't have to be gay to shop here—everyone can relate to the T-shirts, calendars, sex toys, and greeting cards that are meant to garner a laugh no matter what your sexual orientation. In a neat move, the store has set aside a separate children's playroom to keep tots oc-

Buddy's Farm at the Granville Island Public Market

Andee Lanthier

Taking a salmon back home isn't a big deal. Most places that sell fish will also pack it in an easy-to-carry, travel-worthy package.

cupied while their parents shop. (Downtown)

UBC BOOKSTORE
6200 University Blvd.
Vancouver
604/822-2665
In addition to its 100,000 academic titles, this huge campus bookstore—the largest in western Canada—sells an enormous range of fiction, art and photo supplies, and British Columbian pottery, as well as the mandatory UBC-logo sweatshirts, coffee mugs, and hundreds of other items. It even has an on-site computer store. The students and sales personnel at this sprawling store know their books and can suggest alternatives if what you want isn't available. (Point Grey)

VANCOUVER BOOK WAREHOUSE
1150 Robson St.
Vancouver
604/685-5711
This bookstore has the largest number of remainders and bankruptcy stock in British Columbia, as well as a decent selection of current releases at reduced prices. Most of the titles are discounted by at least 50 percent, and, in the case of remainders, they are sometimes sold at 10 percent of their marked cost. If you're looking for a coffee-table book or cookbook published within the past 10 years, you're likely to find it here or at the city's other Book Warehouse

outlets: 632 W. Broadway, 604/872-5711; The Bay, 674 Granville St., 604/681-2183; or 2288 W. Fourth Ave., 604/733-5721. (Downtown)

WANDERLUST
1929 W. Fourth Ave.
Vancouver
604/739-2182
This traveler's bookstore includes thousands of books about Canada, the United States, and all kinds of foreign lands. But books aren't all you'll find here. Sharing space on the shelves are water purifiers, safety whistles, backpacks, and language tapes. It's a one-stop store for the discerning traveler, with books and accessories presented logically and neatly. It's simply amazing how much this place can hold. (Point Grey)

MARKETS

The Granville Island Public Market, built in the mid-1970s, ushered in a new concept for Vancouverites: European-style shopping with a distinctive sense of character. Today the Lower Mainland's half-dozen markets are more than just good places to buy fresh fruits and vegetables. You'll also find small stores selling a variety of locally and regionally made jewelry, crafts, wines, and other goods and services. In sum, markets—and the va-

riety of smells and humanity they produce and attract—have become integral parts of nearly every Vancouver neighborhood.

GRANVILLE ISLAND PUBLIC MARKET
1689 Johnson St.
Vancouver
604/666-6655
The Granville Island Public Market is the granddaddy of them all: it was the first market built in the city, and, even today, it's the biggest, the most varied, and—most people would agree—the best Vancouver has to offer. The 4,600-square-meter facility is right on the waterfront, next to a couple of restaurants, and is surrounded by arts and crafts stores, food kiosks, vendors, and, just off the docks, the boats of the harbor. If the season allows, try to find a table on the upper-level eating area—you'll be rewarded with a spectacular view of False Creek. (Downtown)

LONSDALE QUAY MARKET
123 Carrie Cates Court
North Vancouver
604/985-6261
Part of the Lonsdale Quay complex, which also contains the Seabus terminal and the Lonsdale Quay Hotel, this market carries everything from clothing to carrots, and there's an outside plaza where you can get a terrific view of Burrard Inlet and the downtown area. Take the Seabus across the harbor, get off at the terminal, and turn to the right. If you have children, be sure to find Kids Alley, a large section that's devoted to children's shops and a play area. To get away from the food, head for the second floor, where you'll find fashion stores and assorted gift shops. (North Shore)

ROBSON STREET MARKET
1610 Robson St.
Vancouver
604/682-2733
The weird, the wacky, and the absolutely wonderful do their daily shopping here. Just sit, watch, and take notes. In short order you'll find enough idiosyncratic behavior to write a textbook on the subject. Head for the second floor, where artisan-vendors sell their wares around a cluster of cafés. On one wall is a bright, 43-meter-long mural depicting life in the West End. (Downtown)

VANCOUVER FLEA MARKET
703 Terminal Ave.
Vancouver
604/685-0666
Talk about cleaning out the garage. There are nearly 350 stalls—selling everything from CDs to lawnmowers—in this largest of Vancouver's flea markets. Sure, you'll find an inordinate number of T-shirts, cheap linens, and household tools, but if you get there early and plan to be out in an hour, you also might discover a great deal. There's always one item out of someone else's junk that you'll consider a treasure. $1 admission. (East Vancouver)

WESTMINSTER QUAY
810 Quayside
New Westminster
604/520-3881
If you're staying Downtown, you can spend a full day at this place. Take the SkyTrain from Downtown for a 30-minute view of the city. The train drops you off within a block of the market. It's not as large as the Granville Island Market, nor as fashionable as the Lonsdale Quay, but this glass-walled structure does house a large and interesting variety

of retail outlets, artisans, and produce vendors. The highlight: the hunger-inducing smells from the Farm Cottage Baking Company's oven. (Eastern Suburbs)

MAJOR DEPARTMENT STORES

ARMY & NAVY DEPARTMENT

STORE
27 W. Hastings St.
Vancouver
604/682-6644

You won't hear people bragging about shopping here, even though they do—and often. Decidedly downmarket, A&N is where you shop if you're looking for necessary everyday items that you don't need to impress anyone with. Spend some time

---

Vancouver's Chocolate Shops

Vancouver may not have an international reputation as one of the world's biggest chocolate destinations, but the truth is that many of the city's residents are chocoholics. There isn't a neighborhood in which you won't find at least one chocolate outlet. Look for these exceptional stores:

- ***Bernard Callebaut Chocolates*** *(2698 Granville St., 604/736-5890) makes what aficionados claim is the finest chocolate in the world.*
- ***Chocolate Arts*** *(2037 W. Fourth Ave., 604/739-0475) uses art by Haida artist Robert Davidson to create chocolate medallions with Haida designs. Check out the liqueur-laced truffles.*
- ***Daniel Le Chocolat Belge*** *(1105 Robson St., 604/688-9624) has been around Vancouver since 1987, when Belge provided his recipes for visiting heads of state at the Commonwealth Conference. The "gift gallery" has an abundance of exclusive items.*
- ***Olde World Fudge*** *(Granville Island Public Market, 604/687-7355) offers the chance to watch the goodies being made just before you eat them.*
- ***Purdy's*** *(Pacific Centre and elsewhere, 604/681-7814) is a Vancouver institution. Long before there was any other chocolate store, there was Purdy's. Try their ice cream.*

in this store on the edge of Gastown and you'll likely find bargains galore in the various departments. The store's semiannual designer shoe sales are two of Vancouver's most riotous events, turning staid and proper shoppers into aggressive mobs. (Downtown)

THE BAY (HUDSON'S BAY COMPANY)
674 Granville St.
Vancouver
604/681-6211
This is more than just another department store; more than any other Canadian institution, this company is responsible for much of the exploration that led to Canada's status as a nation. You can still buy a Hudson's Bay woolen blanket here, but first you should compare it to the offerings at the other ministores in the Bay complex, like Hilfiger and Polo. There are Bay outlets in most suburban shopping malls. (Downtown)

EATON'S
701 Granville St.
Vancouver
604/685-7112
Located diagonally across the street from The Bay, Eaton's is housed in the Pacific Centre office complex. You can't miss the huge, white-tiled edifice that Vancouverites have nicknamed "The Mausoleum." The chain, Canada's second oldest, went bankrupt in late 1999, but many of its outlets were purchased by Sears Canada. The downtown store will keep the Eaton's brand name as will major stores in Toronto and in other large Canadian cities. The new Eaton's is expected to re-open in late spring 2000. (Downtown)

HOLT RENFREW & CO.
633 Granville St.

Local Seafood

Since Vancouver is a seafood town, you'd better understand the lingo—especially if you're buying salmon to take home. A salmon is not just a salmon. Each has it own taste and degree of firmness. Spring salmon (also called Chinook or king salmon) is the tastiest, the firmest, and the most expensive. Pink salmon is the smallest of the species, light in color and the least expensive. Chum is mild, delicate fish that in its canned form is sometimes called keta. To some tastes, Coho is the crème de la crème, with its full flavor and firm flesh. Sockeye is also a top prize for its fighting abilities and rich flavor. If you're not a fan of salmon, Vancouver's got plenty of other delightful fresh seafood from which to choose: rock cod, ling cod, halibut, shark, mussels, oysters, shrimp, and scallops.

Vancouver
604/681-3121

It took a while for this boutique department store to shake its image of being an Eastern Canadian transplant. Selling clothing more suited for the bitter-cold winters of Quebec and Ontario didn't help them make the transition. But after a couple of decades located in the Pacific Centre directly across the street from the Bay, all that's behind them, and today the store is as West Coast as any. Upscale, it prides itself on selling the highest-quality goods in town. (Downtown)

MAJOR SHOPPING MALLS

ABERDEEN CENTRE
4151 Hazelbridge Way
Richmond
604/273-1234

Oddly, this Richmond mall is one of western Canada's most popular tourist destinations. The center is home to a diverse range of stores, Japanese and Chinese restaurants, a bowling alley, a movie house showing Chinese films, a variety of fashion boutiques, and a fortune-teller's outfit. (Southern Suburbs)

ARBUTUS VILLAGE SQUARE
SHOPPING CENTRE
4255 Arbutus St.
Vancouver
604/732-4255

If it looks somewhat old fashioned, that's because this was one of Vancouver's first experiments with shopping malls; even after a major renovation, it retains a small-town feel. Serving the upper-middle-class clientele of Point Grey, it has a series of boutiques, a bookstore, food outlets, a grocery store, and a liquor store. In essence, it tries to provide a village atmosphere for neighborhood shoppers. (Point Grey)

BRENTWOOD MALL
261-4567 Lougheed Hwy.
Burnaby
604/298-7314

One of the eastern suburb's largest shopping malls, Brentwood Mall features about 110 shops and services, including large outlets for Eaton's and Zellers. It's an especially handy shopping area for anyone staying at a Burnaby hotel. It has a large market area called Kins Farm Market, and you might want to check out the Old Dutch Bakery and Gar-Long Meats and Seafood for picnic items or food for your room. If you're encumbered by clothing and carry items, use the mall's free coat and parcel check. The mall also offers free stroller and wheelchair loans as well as gift-wrapping. (Eastern Suburbs)

CITY SQUARE
1-555 W. 12th Ave.
Vancouver
604/876-5102

City Square, located across the street from Vancouver City Hall, was originally two school buildings from the 1920s. They were sold in the 1980s and converted into a stone, steel, and glass shopping mall. Major tenants include Safeway, Fitness World, and a number of small shops and boutiques. (Uptown)

COQUITLAM CENTRE
2929 Barnet Hwy.
Coquitlam
604/464-1414

Located on the eastern edge of greater Vancouver at the foot of Westwood Plateau, Coquitlam Centre has more than 250 stores and serves as a focal point in a community dominated by upscale, middle-class, and young families. One of the wonderful aspects of this shopping center that embraces a combination of small stores and large department store outlets is its wonderful collection of art, especially its sculptures (27 of them can be seen around the center). Opened in 1979, the center won the Governor General's Award for Excellence in Architecture, and it was enhanced by a complete renovation in 1989. Its openness and art displays are an unusual departure from the typical shopping-mall experience. (Eastern Suburbs)

FAIRCHILD SQUARE
4400 Hazelbridge Way
Richmond
604/273-1234
Fairchild Square consists of eight distinctive, two-story buildings surrounding a central courtyard. In addition to its commercial retail space, the square is also home to dental, medical, legal, and hair-styling businesses. This is the most neighborhood-oriented of Vancouver's malls. Individual stores have their own business hours. (Southern Suburbs)

GRANVILLE MALL
From Smithe St. to the waterfront
Vancouver
This was once Vancouver's major entertainment strip, an area of bright neon signs, theaters, and nightclubs.

Then, in the 1970s, it was turned into a pedestrian-dominated mall, and today motorized traffic between West Hastings and Nelson Streets is limited to buses. After dark it's both exciting and a bit seedy, attracting a wild mix of the young, panhandlers, and concertgoers. During the day, however, the mall is essentially a conduit for walkers and shoppers going into Eaton's, The Bay, the Granville Book Company near The Orpheum, and the Pacific Centre. (Downtown)

THE LANDING
375 Water St.
Vancouver
604/687-1144
This mall, at the entrance to Gastown, is in a restored and renovated warehouse dating back to 1905. You can get to the shopping plaza through the Steamworks restaurant (see Chapter 4, Where to Eat) or through an elegant entrance off Water Street. Inside the multilevel shopping and dining area are designer boutiques like Polo, Ralph Lauren, and Fleet Street. (Downtown)

LANSDOWNE PARK SHOPPING CENTRE
5300 No. 3 Rd.
Richmond
604/270-1344
Just 10 minutes from the airport, this sprawling mall's 140 outlets include many specialty shops and department stores, such as Eaton's and Toys 'R'

Us. Bonkers Indoor Playground, located next to the Toys 'R' Us, is a convenient place to leave your children while you shop. (Southern Suburbs)

METROTOWN
4800 Kingsway
Burnaby
604/438-2444
The mother of all shopping malls, the three-block complex includes more than 450 shops, every one of the city's major department stores, 12 theaters, a recreation center, 75 restaurants, a residential tower, and a hotel. The four parts of the shopping complex are Metrotown Centre, Eaton Centre, Holiday Inn, and Station Centre. The new Metropolis is a stadium-style theater with 10 screens. The mall is just 15 minutes from Downtown via the SkyTrain. (Eastern Suburbs)

OAKRIDGE CENTRE
Cambie St. and 41st St.
Vancouver
604/261-2511
Serving the high-end clientele of Oakridge, Shaughnessy, and Point Grey, Oakridge Centre is a bright collection of about 150 boutiques, jewelry stores, and restaurants. Outlets include The Bay, Zellers, and French and British clothing designers. Free parking. (Uptown)

PACIFIC CENTRE SHOPPING MALL
W. Georgia St.
Vancouver
604/688-7236
If you're Downtown at any of the central hotels, this will probably be the first shopping mall you'll encounter. About 165 businesses can be found in this three-block underground complex, including men's and women's fashion stores, jewelry stores, restaurants, and even a hotel

(the Four Seasons). The north end of the complex is the newest section, where you'll find a three-story waterfall, a glass rotunda, and a lighted atrium that makes the place cheery and bright even on a rainy day. Take a break from the shopping and have lunch at the atrium in the Four Seasons, just above the mall. If you take the SkyTrain in from the suburbs, get off at the Granville station under The Bay. (Downtown)

PARKER PLACE
4380 No. 3 Rd.
Richmond
604/273-0276
With more than 130 shops and services, this is the largest Asian shopping center in western Canada. Parker Place is the most consumer-focused of Asia West's five centers, with electronic stores, European fashion boutiques, and oriental grocers, among other businesses. The Asian food courts are complemented by a large water fountain and overhead skylights. (Southern Suburbs)

PARK ROYAL SHOPPING CENTRE
2002 Park Royal S.
West Vancouver
604/925-9547
Park Royal Shopping Centre, a massive, 250-store complex that spreads out on both sides of Marine Drive at the foot of the Lion's Gate Bridge, includes a public market, a Disney outlet, and the usual department stores (The Bay, Eaton's). The center also has a driving range, movie theaters, bowling lanes, and a concierge desk. (North Shore)

PRESIDENT PLAZA
8181 Cambie St.
Richmond
604/270-8677

This plaza is attached to the four-star Radisson President Hotel. (See Chapter 3, Where to Stay.) Inside, the exotic T & T Asian supermarket is an excellent source of fresh meat, fish, and poultry, and it carries a wide variety of ginseng and other Chinese teas. (Southern Suburbs)

RICHMOND CENTRE
6551 No. 3 Rd.
Richmond
604/273-4828
The Richmond Centre is home to a number of department stores (The Bay, Sears, and Zellers) and an international mix of merchants like Benetton, The Gap, Esprit, Biana Nygard, and Jacob. It also has a Famous Players cinema complex. (Southern Suburbs)

ROYAL CENTRE MALL
1055 W. Georgia St.
Vancouver
604/689-1711
Located directly beneath the Royal Bank of Canada and adjacent to the Hyatt hotel, the Royal Centre provides some unique shopping opportunities. For example, it houses Dack's Shoes, a Canadian manufacturer that has produced quality men's footwear for a nearly a century. Keep walking south along the corridors and you'll find yourself beneath the Bentall Centre, a group of office towers on Burrard Street. (Downtown)

SINCLAIR CENTRE
757 W. Hastings St.
Vancouver
604/666-4438
This old Canada Post Office building, built in 1909, was the site of a riot in 1938 when unemployed protesters clashed with the local constabulary. Today the only protests you'll hear in the building are from shoppers shelling out their money for upscale fashion items in Leone and other fashion stores. Dorothy Grant's, located on the street level of the multistoried building, is a good place to find coats, caps, vests, and accessories with a distinctive Haida flavor. (Downtown)

YAOHAN CENTRE
3700 No. 3 Rd.
Richmond
604/231-0601
A block north from the President Plaza in Richmond, this Japanese supermarket is one of the largest in North America featuring a wide range of Japanese products and seafood at reasonable prices. After you've toured—and eaten—at the massive food fair with its Japanese, Chinese, Taiwanese, Korean, and Malaysian cuisine, take the escalator to the second level. There you'll find fashion boutiques and specialty shops. (Southern Suburbs)

FACTORY OUTLET CENTERS

Though some of the following stores are located in shopping malls, you'll find that most of the Lower Mainland's factory outlets are attached to the places where the goods are made. Labels, therefore, will often only be that company's. The costs are greatly reduced depending on what kind of designations the goods have—wholesale (50-percent off), factory cost (75-percent reduction), or factory clear-out (up to 90-percent off). Keep in mind that some of the sizes may be off, and keep your eyes open for other potential flaws.

DANIER LEATHER
3003 Grandview Hwy.

Vancouver
604/432-6137

The leather and suede produced by this company are stylish and magnificently crafted in the Italian tradition. The store is easy to navigate, with separate areas for men's and women's clothing. The sizes and color ranges are often broken, but the value is enormous for the quality that's there. This large store is the clearance center for Danier Leather outlets throughout Canada. (East Vancouver)

JANA & CO. IMPORTS
1190 Homer St.
Vancouver
604/688-3657

Sweaters, anyone? You'll find more than just sweaters at Jana & Co., but sweaters are the main reason most women shop here. Jana & Co. designs its own line then has the clothing made in Asia. You'll find a wide selection of end-of-the-lines, one-of-a-kinds, samples, and returns. The "factory bargains" are upstairs. The receptionist will send you to the browsing salesroom. (Downtown)

JANTZEN FACTORY OUTLET
196 Kingsway
Vancouver
604/876-3344

You'll find a wide selection of sportswear at this on-site factory outlet—everything from sweaters to swimwear. Look carefully for flaws since a lot of the items come from irregular lines. Ask about the seasonal sales that cut the wholesale prices by a further 25 to 60 percent. (East Vancouver)

JILL HAMPTON LADIES CLOTHING
Royal Centre Mall
1055 W. Georgia St.
Vancouver

604/681-2611

Jill Hampton, located on the top floor of the Royal Centre, contains an enormous selection of items in sizes ranging from 4 to 18. It's the official factory outlet for Aero Garments and features Seasons Sportswear, Petite Network, and other clothing lines. Be sure to ask about the periodic sales at the factory itself, located on Vancouver's east side. The sales are held once every three or four months. (Downtown)

PORTEGAZ
1009 E. Cordova St.
Vancouver
604/254-4731

This is one of the most varied factory outlets in the Lower Mainland, with dresses, blouses, pants, skirts, ensembles, and fabrics,—such as silk ($7 to $10 per meter), linen, and cotton in assorted colors—going for up to $70 off list price. Two important elements make this place unique—the terrific selection and the attentive staff. While you might find better prices at some other outlets, the items here are nicely detailed with few flaws. If you're looking for something specific, call ahead because stock changes week to week. (Downtown)

TURNSTYLES
280 Nelson St.
Vancouver
604/684-6274

This agent's clearance center has a wide selection of designer lines, including Tabi, Coastlines, Mister Leonard, Lauren Jeffries, Paris Star Holiday and Cruise Wear, and others. Most of the items, handled by the Nash Agency, are samples and are displayed daily as well as during sales. You might also want to check out the attractive and marked-down lines of costume jewelry. (Downtown)

©John Elk

10

SPORTS AND RECREATION

Vancouver is a physical city. If we're not running, skiing, golfing, cycling, or playing tennis, then there's a good chance the weather is bad. And, in that case, we're probably watching hockey, football, or a road race. But the truth is that we don't particularly like to sit. The rule of thumb in this city is that if the weather if good, spectator sports are out of luck. The spectators will be scarce. Vancouver's surroundings make it quite difficult to avoid physical activity. On a clear winter's evening, if you look toward the North Shore Mountains, you'll see three well-lit summits. To the right is Mount Seymour, in the middle is Grouse Mountain, and to the left is Cypress Bowl. If you like snow and if skiing or snowshoeing is your sport, these three peaks seldom fail to deliver. On the other hand, Vancouver isn't so bad when it comes to warm-weather activities, either. You'll see countless sailboats in English Bay, hikers, walkers, runners, cyclists, and equestrians. In addition, nearly 20 new golf courses have opened in the region over the past decade, making this one of the most golf-friendly cities in Canada.

However, if you do prefer the spectator's chair, you won't be disappointed. Vancouver is home to many professional teams and events. You'll find the NHL's Canucks, the NBA's Grizzlies, and the Canadian Football League's BC Lions. The PGA's Air Canada Championship is held here, as is the Molson Indy car race. Vancouver also has plenty of professional soccer, lacrosse, baseball, and horse racing.

All of these activities beg for your participation—whether physically or from the comfort of a box seat. Athletics are a major part of life here in Vancouver. If you're not active now or if you've never been a sports fan, your stay in Vancouver may change that.

PROFESSIONAL SPORTS

Auto Racing

THE MOLSON INDY
Vancouver
604/684-4639

Those aren't giant mosquitoes you're hearing over Labor Day weekend. It's the sound of Indy cars racing around the city's downtown course. The Molson Indy is Canada's largest spectator event and is run on the streets around the east end of False Creek and the Science Centre. There are three practice days, then the race itself. More than 350,000 people are attracted to the race site around BC Place Stadium. ♿ (Downtown)

Baseball

VANCOUVER CANADIANS
Nat Bailey Stadium
4601 Ontario Sts.
Vancouver
604/872-5232

This is the greatest five-dollar entertainment package in the city. The Vancouver Canadians were in the Triple A Pacific Coast League since 1978 and

BC Place Stadium

OK, so there's a lot of football played here. It is, after all, the home of the CFL's BC Lions football team. But there is more to this place than just jock business. It opened in 1983 as the world's largest air-supported dome. With 60,000 seats it also hosts major concerts, trade shows, and other large gatherings. It was in this enormous building that Queen Elizabeth II invited the world to Expo '86.

Some of the province's largest trade and consumer shows, like the Pacific International Auto Show, the BC Home and Garden Show, the Spring and Fall Gift Shows, the Gold Show, the Ski Show, the Vancouver International RV Show, the Boat Show, and more take place under the dome each year. Parking in the stadium lots ranges from $7 to $10 during events. In other nearby parking lots, the rates vary from as little as three to six dollars.

The dome consists of an outer fabric membrane and an inner fabric liner. This shell is in turn attached to a two-way steel-cable net system and anchored to a huge concrete base ring. There's enough concrete in the stadium to build a sidewalk from Vancouver to Tacoma, Washington.

Canadian Football League (CFL) Rules

- *Twelve players per side (the NFL has 11).*
- *Three downs (the NFL has four).*
- *No "man in motion" rule. Backs are allowed to move at will.*
- *No fair catches on a punt. A 10-yard zone between the tackler and the punt receiver must be maintained until after the catch.*
- *A single point is awarded to the kicking team on a punt or field goal into the end zone that isn't run out.*
- *Fields are 20 yards longer and 10 yards wider than those in the NFL.*

have provided Vancouverites with superb baseball for years. Located next to Queen Elizabeth Park, Nat Bailey Stadium (named after a restaurant entrepreneur) treats spectators to one of the prettiest views in baseball. It also brings back memories for anyone who enjoyed the game years ago: The field is made of real grass, and the scoreboard is manual. Alas, the Canadians are moving to Sacramento, California, in the summer of 2000 and are being replaced with a Single A team. But the location is the same, and the sound of wood on horsehide will be just as real. ♿ (East Vancouver)

Basketball

VANCOUVER GRIZZLIES
GM Place Stadium
800 Griffiths Way
Vancouver
604/280-4400
The Grizzlies, the NBA's 29th franchise, played their first game in GM Stadium on October 14, 1996. They have yet to make the NBA playoffs, and the only real record they hold is that for consecutive losses (23 in the 1995–1996 season). But the truth is that the team has had the city behind it every step of the way during its short history, and its fans are among the most enthusiastic in the league. Like most other expansion franchises, the Grizzlies are still trying to make their mark. They'll get there—eventually. ♿ (Downtown)

Football

THE BC LIONS
BC Place Stadium
777 Pacific Blvd. S.
Vancouver
604/583-7747
The Canadian Football League's BC Lions play in the domed, 60,000-seat BC Place Stadium across from GM Place. The Lions have been a cornerstone of the CFL since they joined the league in 1954. Quarterbacks Doug Flutie and Joe Kapp, as well as running back Willie Fleming are among the finest athletes to have played on the team. The Canadian football season runs from June to November and

ends with the Grey Cup (our Super Bowl), which the BC Lions won in 1964, 1985, and 1994. Canadians like to think that CFL games—with bigger fields, fewer downs, and more passing—are much more exciting than those of the NFL. ♿ (Downtown)

Golf

PGA AIR CANADA CHAMPIONSHIP
Northview Golf and Country Club
6857 168th St.
Surrey
604/899-4641
This used to be the Greater Vancouver Open until the airline took over full sponsorship. It's held on Labor Day weekend on the Northview Golf and Country Club's Arnold Palmer–designed course in Surrey, about 45 minutes from Downtown. The tournament purse for 1999 increased to $2.5 million (U.S.) from 1998's $2 million. In 2000 the purse will be $2.8 million, in 2001, $3.1 million, and in 2002, $3.4 million. Some of the best players on the tour play in this tournament; past win-

ners have included Brandel Chamblee, Mark Calcavecchia, and Guy Boros. A variety of full-tournament and daily ticket options are available. ♿ (Southern Suburbs)

Hockey

THE VANCOUVER CANUCKS
GM Place Stadium
800 Griffiths Way
Vancouver
604/280-4400
One goalpost. That's right, one lousy goalpost is all that kept Vancouver from tying the New York Rangers with less than a minute to go in the seventh game of the 1994 Stanley Cup finals. Unfortunately, that near miss has been the highlight of this franchise's history, and the Canucks continue to break our collective heart season after season. ♿ (Downtown)

Horse Racing

CLOVERDALE RACEWAY
6050 176th St.

Hastings Park Racecourse, p. 188

Ralph Bauer Photo

Amateur Sports

Vancouver has a long tradition of being involved in a variety of individual and team amateur sports. Certainly, the climate and the terrain encourage involvement in individual endeavors like cycling, jogging and running, skiing, mountain climbing, kayaking, canoeing, mountain biking, and even walking. The fact is that the city is surrounded by wilderness and regional parks that encourage unorganized participation. But there's also a long tradition of organized team sports—such as baseball, hockey, tennis, and golf—especially at the youth level, where every Lower Mainland community has active participation.

The first amateur sporting event in what is now greater Vancouver took place in New Westminster in 1859—a track and field meet that included a foot race, hurdles, high jumps, and shot put. The first team event, however, didn't take place until 1886, when a rugby team from Vancouver beat one from New Westminster on a muddy field on Cambie Street close to the current BC Place Stadium location.

It was from these first small activities that the amateur sports scene in Vancouver developed. Vancouver is now home to 88 amateur associations—one for almost every sport from archery to wrestling. All fall under the umbrella of Sport BC, the agency representing all of the province's amateur organizations. Located at 1367 West Broadway (Uptown), Sport BC is a central clearinghouse for all information about sport organizations, and their automated information line (604/737-3000) provides information on almost every sport.

Softball is the most popular of team activities—there are 3,000 registered teams and 45,000 players in the Lower Mainland. Soccer, however, is a close second, with 37,000 registered players. Hockey accounts for 25,000 registered players and another 10,000 unregistered players participating in loosely organized leagues around the Lower Mainland.

Sprinter Percy Williams was the first athlete from the Lower Mainland to make a really big international impact when he was a double gold-medallist in the 1928 Amsterdam Olympic games, winning the 100-and-200 meter events. In 1930, a women's team won the World Basketball Championship at the women's World Games in Prague, beating France 18–14 in the final. And in 1972, Karen Magnussen of North Vancouver won the 1972 World Figure Skating Championship in Prague.

But at least in terms of world record holders, sprinter Harry Jerome of North Vancouver was the finest sprinter the country ever produced. For four years in the 1960s, he held world records in both the 100-yard and 100-meter sprints (9.1 and 10.0 seconds respectively). Gold medallist at the 1966 Commonwealth Games and the 1967 Pan-American Games, he was also the bronze medallist at the 1964 Tokyo Olympics.

Swimmer Elaine Tanner garnered four gold medals and three silver medals at the 1966 Commonwealth Games, setting a games record that still stands. At the 1968 Olympics, she won two silvers.

But the event that still stands out in local legend, and the one that sport historians and publications around the world still refer to is renowned largely because a local photographer happened to be in the right place at the right time. It was at the 1954 Commonwealth Games in the now-razed Empire Stadium in East Vancouver that Dr. Roger Bannister of England and John Landy of Australia—who had individually run the world's first sub-four-minute miles—ran their famous duel. Bannister won, but both completed the race in under four minutes—the first time that two runners had ever accomplished this in the same race. And a photographer caught Landy looking over his shoulder near the finish line to see where Bannister was, just as the British athlete was passing him on the other side.

Sport BC or any of the following numbers can provide information on your favorite amateur sports.

Archery: 604/980-6848

Athletics: 604/688-6266

Badminton: 604/737-3030

Baseball: 604/737-3031

Basketball: 604/737-3032

Baton twirling: 604/241-1205

Blind sports: 604/737-3035

Bodybuilding: 604/748-7576

Bowling (indoors): 604/522-2990

Bowling (lawn): 604/224-4407

Boxing: 604/291-7921

Curling: 604/737-3040

Cycling: 604/737-3034

Deaf sports: 604/737-3041

Disabled sports: 604/737-3039

Equestrian: 604/576-2722

Field hockey (men): 604/737-3045

Field hockey (women):
604/737-3046

Figure skating: 604/737-3047

Golf: 604/294-1818

Gymnastics: 604/737-3049

Hang gliding: 604/980-9566

Judo: 604/737-3050

Lacrosse: 604/421-9755

Outward Bound: 604/737-3093

Parks and Recreation:
604/257-8492

Rugby: 604/737-3065

Sailing: 604/737-3113

Skiing (alpine): 604/737-3070

Skiing (cross-country):
604/545-9600

Skiing (disabled): 604/737-3042

Soccer: 604/299-6401

Squash: 604/737-3084

Swimming: 604/734-7946

Tennis: 604/737-3086

Wheelchair sports: 604/737-3090

Surrey
604/579-9141
If pacing and trotters are more to your liking, head south into Cloverdale for the October-through-April harness-racing season. (Southern Suburbs)

HASTINGS PARK RACECOURSE
Exhibition Park
Vancouver
604/254-1631
The Thoroughbreds run between April and October at Hastings and Renfrew at the Pacific National Exhi-

bition grounds. With the North Shore mountains as a background, you can't find a more scenic place to bet your hard-earned cash. The biggest race event here is the BC Derby, held on Labor Day. ♿ (East Vancouver)

Soccer

VANCOUVER 86ERS
Swangard Stadium
Boundary Rd. and Kingsway
Burnaby
604/930-2255
Soccer has been big in Vancouver

Beaches

Vancouver's sandy beaches offer a variety of views and activities. They are well patrolled by lifeguards during the summer season and are maintained by the Vancouver Parks Board. Among the favorites are English Bay (the site of the annual Polar Bear Swim on January 1), Sunset Beach, Kits Beach, Jericho Beach (the closest to downtown), Locarno Beach, and Spanish Banks. Kits and Locarno beaches have organized volleyball. All the beaches have concession stands.

ever since the days of the Vancouver Whitecaps and the now-defunct North American Soccer League of the '70s and '80s. With such a diverse ethnic population, it's no surprise that the city is a soccer hotbed. The Vancouver 86ers are British Columbia's top professional soccer team and play in the A League of the United Soccer League (USL), North America's second division of professional soccer and the highest level currently played in Canada. The 86ers are also one of Vancouver's most successful professional teams of the past decade. They have won four league championships and one North American championship. The professional soccer season starts in May and ends in September, and all 86ers games are played at Swangard Stadium (which seats about 5,000), on the Vancouver/Burnaby border at Central Park. (Eastern Suburbs)

RECREATION

Bird-Watching

GEORGE C. REIFEL MIGRATORY BIRD SANCTUARY

5191 Robertson Rd.
Ladner
604/946-6980
Watch 'em fly. Bird lovers from all over the world come to this place to see rare and common feathered creatures as they migrate between the seasons. Every now and then, a bird that should be hundreds of miles east or west gets lost and finds its way here, thus creating all kinds of local and international flurry. During the November Snow Goose Festival, a month-long event that features educational programs, lectures, and tours focusing on the snow goose, thousands of the giant white birds brighten up the sky on their migration. (For more information, see Chapter 8, Parks, Gardens, and Recreation Areas.) (Southern Suburbs)

Fishing

BAYSHORE YACHT CHARTERS
1601 W. Georgia St. at Cardero St.
604/682-3377
Located next to the Bayshore Inn, the company offers more than just a fishing adventure. The company has complete charter and catering services for fishing weekends, breakfast

Bicycling

There's no end to great bicycling routes in Vancouver. This city is practically custom-made for cyclists. The most popular route is the 10.5-kilometer Stanley Park Seawall, which offers spectacular views of the city and the North Shore Mountains. Mountain bikers enjoy riding the packed-dirt paths in the interior of the park. There are plenty of places near the park from which you can rent bikes—the most popular is Spokes Bicycle Rental and Espresso Bar (1798 W. Georgia St., 604/688-5141).

By far the most spectacular ride in Vancouver is a five-kilometer seaside route linking the Stanley Park Seawall with a number of waterfront paths. The route skirts Vanier Park and then follows the beaches along Point Grey Road to the University of British Columbia, providing magnificent views of the North Shore Mountains, the Strait of Georgia, and Vancouver along the way. You can pick up maps at several information kiosks or at any Tourism Vancouver outlet (604/683-2000).

You might also try the Steveston section of the 36-kilometer Richmond cycling loop that rims the community. The city of Richmond maintains the cycling loop, which consists of paved cycling paths along major roadways, hard-pack dirt paths along the seawall, and marked side roads through some of the city's most scenic areas. Park your car at the River Road RV park on the west side of the Dunsmuir Bridge and cycle along the flat seawall path to Steveston.

South of Southwest Marine Drive, east of the Point Grey Golf and Country Club, the Southlands area is a great place to ride. Paved roads with very little traffic meander among the small ranches and estates. The only things you have to watch out for are horses.

Contact Sport BC Cycling at 604/737-3034 for information about bicycling clubs.

Sport BC

Sport BC is the organization that keeps track of all of the province's organized sports activities. If you're looking for information about a sport in Vancouver—even ones not listed here—call the specific sporting office or the central switchboard at 604/737-3000.

board meetings, dinner cruises, company fishing derbies, office parties, and wedding receptions. The fishing charters last five hours and include bait and tackle for groups of 4 to 100. Fishing licenses are available. (Downtown)

GRANVILLE ISLAND CHARTER CENTRE
1808 Boatlift Ln.
Granville Island
604/683-1447
As its name suggests, it's located on Granville Island and offers half- and full-day guided fishing, cruising, and scuba trips from the island. With ad-

vance notice, you can also book multiday trips. Cellular phones are standard equipment. Each trip includes a guide, fuel, fishing tackle, bait, and cleaning and bagging of your day's catch. (Uptown)

SEWELL'S MARINA
Horseshoe Bay
604/921-3474
Howe Sound is a popular place for salmon fishing, and Sewell's Marina, with its 60-plus rental and charter boats, is a great place to get started. Charter a boat for a half or full day—you'll be shipped to wherever the fish are biting. Even if you don't catch

Bird lovers can see bald eagles just outside of Vancouver.

D. Leighton

"Fore" is rapidly becoming Vancouver's citywide anthem. Golf generates $215 million a year, and about $1.5 million in golf-related money is donated to area charities annually.

anything, the view is gorgeous. (North Shore)

Golf Courses

Fees for these courses vary widely; call ahead of time.

BURNABY MOUNTAIN GOLF COURSE
7600 Halifax St.
Burnaby
604/280-7355
This well-maintained municipal course, located not far from Simon Fraser University, is a great course for the entire family—there's a strong junior golf program and teaching facilities that encourage families to play together. That's not to say the course doesn't pose any challenges. You'll find many water hazards, doglegs, sloping lies, and small, two-tiered greens. You can always expect this popular course to be busy. Driving range; yardage 6,431; par 71; reservations 48 hours. (Eastern Suburbs)

FRASERVIEW GOLF COURSE
7800 Vivian St.
Burnaby
604/280-1818
This long-time Vancouver favorite underwent a complete redesign in 1997 and immediately became one of the finest layouts in the Lower Mainland. Its tree-lined layout overlooks the Fraser River (though you see it at only a couple of holes). The

par 3s will test your club selection. Driving range; yardage 6,700/6,296/5,890/5,152; par 72; reservations 48 hours. (East Vancouver)

FURRY CREEK GOLF AND COUNTRY CLUB
Hwy. 99
Lion's Bay
604/922-9576
You'll need two things—a lot of golf balls and a camera. You want target golf? This is the place. Opened in 1993, the entire course is built on the side of a mountain that overlooks Howe Sound. The setting is absolutely spectacular, with islands, ocean, and boats keeping you from focusing on your next shot. On the 10th hole you hit off a high bluff onto what seems to be a six-inch-wide fairway between water and woods. Afterwards you'll definitely want to linger in the magnificent stone clubhouse lounge that overlooks the 18th green and the sound. To get there, take Highway 99 toward Whistler. The course is on the northernmost side of Lion's Bay. No driving range; yardage 6,001/5,861/5,442; par 72/72/71; reservations 24 hours. (North Shore)

GLENEAGLES GOLF COURSE
6190 Marine Dr.
West Vancouver
604/921-7353
This wonderful nine-hole course is a Vancouver treasure. Near the ferry terminal at Horseshoe Bay but well

Buying Tickets

Call any of Vancouver's variety of ticket brokers and services for tickets to the sporting event of your choice.

- ***One Stop Ticket Shop***, *604/689-5500—they claim they'll get you the best prices.*
- ***Pacific Northwest Ticket Service***, *604/683-3515—for local events, the Super Bowl, the Masters, the Indy, the Kentucky Derby, and the World Series.*
- ***Showtime Tickets & Tours***, *604/688-5000—a broker that'll find you the ticket you need. They buy, sell, trade, and consign.*
- ***Ticketmaster***, *604/280-4444—the biggest broker in town, offering tickets (with a surcharge of about one dollar) for just about everything.*

removed from any traffic or noise, it has terrific ocean views and rolling, tree-lined fairways. And they don't call the ninth fairway "cardiac hill" for nothing. No driving range; yardage 5,183/5,131; par 70/73; no reservations. (North Shore)

GREENACRES GOLF COURSE
5040 No. 6 Rd.
Richmond
604/273-1121
Greenacres, located right next to the Mayfair Lakes Golf and Country Club (see listing, below), is about as different from its neighbor as one could imagine. It's in a parklike setting with mature trees everywhere along the flat, tight fairways. Most of the crown-shaped greens are small, and there are nine water hazards. Driving range nearby; yardage 6,022/5,787; par 71/73; reservations 48 hours. (Southern Suburbs)

LANGARA GOLF COURSE
6706 Alberta St.
Vancouver
604/280-1818
Don't be fooled by the shortness of this course. The course architects made up for it by creating undulating greens that will drive you nuts. If you hit your three-wood 220 yards, chances are you won't need to take your driver out of the bag. Just make sure your short game is up to par. No driving range; yardage 6,085/5,503/4,648; par 71; reservations 5 days. (Uptown)

MAYFAIR LAKES GOLF AND COUNTRY CLUB
5460 No. 7 Rd.
Richmond
604/276-0505
Site of the Canadian PGA Tour's Pacific Open, this demanding course may be flat, but it has 14 water areas ready to eat slices and hooks. The

links-style course is tight because of the water but has few trees. In late afternoon, a westerly wind makes the back nine extremely difficult. This is a semiprivate course and members have playing privileges before noon on weekends. To get there from Vancouver, take the Knight Street Bridge south; turn left on Westminster Highway, and drive about three kilometers (two miles); follow the signs to No. 7 Road and turn left. The entrance to the golf club is a few hundred yards ahead on the right. Driving range yardage 6,641/6,247/5,277 par: 71/71/72; reservations 48 hours. (Southern Suburbs)

MCCLEERY GOLF CENTRE
7188 MacDonald St.
Vancouver
604/280-1818

One of three Vancouver-area public courses to be redesigned since 1996, the McCleery Golf Centre rests along the Fraser River and is between two of the finest private courses in town, the Point Grey and Marine Drive Country Clubs. For a course that's below sea level, the drainage is quite good. Driving range; yardage 6,265/5,767/5,010; par 71; reservations 5 days. (Point Grey)

TRIVIA

Vancouver has more than 180 free public tennis courts. In addition there are six semi private clubs that offer indoor and outdoor pay-for-play facilities.

MORGAN CREEK
3500 Morgan Creek Way
Surrey
604/531-4653

This relatively new championship course is designed to enhance and preserve environmentally sensitive areas. So if you lose a ball in one of these areas, just kiss it goodbye. Fortunately, you shouldn't shank too many of your drives—this could well be the most user-friendly course on the Lower Mainland. There are wide, inviting fairways, tabletop-smooth greens, brilliant white sand traps, and a superb clubhouse. Near the U.S./-Canadian border. Driving range; yardage 6,786/6,244/5,665; par: 72; reservations 5 days. (Southern Suburbs)

NORTHLANDS GOLF COURSE
Anne MacDonald Way off Mount Seymour Rd.
North Vancouver
604/280-1111

This is, without doubt, the toughest course on the Lower Mainland. Designed by Les Furber, it opened as a full 18-hole course in 1997. Carved out of old-growth forest at the foot of Mount Seymour, the course features mountain terrain with large and generally level greens. The signature hole is the par-5 fourth, with a waterfall along the approach to the green. If you can manage the first hole, a tight par 4 with a lake on the left and forest on the right, you'll do just fine. A cart is recommended. Take your first left once you enter the Mount Seymour Provincial Park. No driving range; yardage 6,504/6,105/5,086; par: 71; reservations 3 days. (North Shore)

NORTHVIEW GOLF CLUB
6857 168th St.

Surrey
604/576-4653
This site of the PGA Air Canada Championship has two Arnold Palmer–designed courses. Pros play the Ridge Course, which presents a meandering, tight, tree-lined challenge over the first nine and a more open layout with scattered water hazards over the back nine. The Canal Course is more user-friendly—its fairways are wider, with no trees. Driving range on-site; Ridge Course yardage 6,900/6,475/6,001/5,231; par: 72. Canal Course yardage 7,101/6,646/6,085/5,314; par 72. Reservations: 1 week. (Southern Suburbs)

PEACE PORTAL GOLF COURSE
16900 Fourth Ave.
Surrey
604/538-4818
Built in 1928, this course may be old-fashioned, but it's wonderful just the same. You'll find majestic trees on rolling terrain where golfers of all abilities can enjoy every yard of play. Ravines add to the challenge. Near

the U.S. -Canadian border at Blaine. Driving range nearby; yardage 6,363/6,103/5,621; par 72; reservations 1 week. (Southern Suburbs)

QUEEN ELIZABETH PARK
Pitch and Putt Course
Cambie St. at 33rd Ave.
Vancouver
604/874-8336
This neat little pitch-and-putt course offers some of the best views of the city. Holes average about 110 yards in length. This is a great place to go after a quick stop at the Bloedel Conservatory. (See Chapter 8, Parks, Gardens, and Recreation Areas.) If you need clubs, you can rent them at the facility. Used balls are also available. First-come, first-served, and you can do it all for about $10. (Uptown)

RIVERWAY PUBLIC GOLF COURSE
9001 Riverway Pl.
Burnaby
604/433-3205
A desert course in the middle of a rain

Ski-Equipment Rentals

- *Carlton Cycle and Outdoor Recreation*, 3201 Kingsway, 604/438-6371 (East Vancouver)
- *Cypress Mountain Sports, 518-2002 Park Royal S.*, 604/878-9229 (North Shore)
- *Destination Ski Rentals*, 105-1550 Marine Dr., 604/984-4394 (North Shore)
- *Outa-Line Inline Sports* (snowboards only), 1231 Pacific Blvd., 604/899-2257 (Downtown)
- *Sigge's* (cross-country specialists), 2077 W. Fourth Ave., 604/731-8818 (Point Grey)

Furry Creek Golf and Country Club

Furry Creek Golf and Country Club, p.192

forest? That's exactly what you'll find here. This course looks like it should be in Palm Springs, and yet it's built on a peat bog. The gently undulating terrain includes natural streams, three small lakes, deep roughs, and sand bunkers, and the fairways are built up on all sides. Driving range; yardage 7,010; par: 72; reservations 48 hours. (Eastern Suburbs)

UNIVERSITY GOLF CLUB
5185 University Blvd.
Vancouver
604/224-1818
This challenging well-treed course is absolutely gorgeous, but if you tend to hook your shots off the tee, you're in for a long round. Located at the eastern end of the University of British Columbia. Driving range; yardage 6,584/6,147/5,643; par 72; reservations 1 week. (Point Grey)

Hiking

HOWE SOUND CREST TRAIL
North Vancouver/West Vancouver
604/924-2200 (trail conditions)

If you're a well-conditioned hiker, the 30-kilometer (18.6-mile) trail will take you across the North Shore Mountains and into Deep Cove just north of the ferry terminal. You'll have to do some planning for this trip, dropping one car off at the finishing point before you start the trail. If you're staying in Vancouver, start at Cypress Bowl. The trail has been well marked by an association of hiking clubs. Bring along an article of warm clothing, as the weather can change quickly. (North Shore)

LIGHTHOUSE PARK
Marine Dr. and Beacon Ln.
West Vancouver
604/925-7200
Set in a postcard environment, Lighthouse Park is located on the bluffs above Point Atkinson, where you'll find some of the last of the old-growth Douglas fir trees on the Lower Mainland. For a really great experience, hike the trails and then picnic next to the old lighthouse. You'll see plenty of eagles' nests and even the occasional white-headed bird itself. The red and white lighthouse sets off the atmosphere perfectly. None of the trails are difficult. Follow Marine Drive until you come to the Lighthouse Park turnoff. (See also Chapter 5, Sights and Attractions; and Chapter 8, Parks, Gardens, and Recreation Areas.) (North Shore)

Hot-Air Ballooning

FANTASY BALLOON CHARTERS
Langley Airport
Unit 209
Surrey
604/530-1974
Pop the champagne, gear up the fire, and take a hot-air balloon flight over the Fraser Valley. The balloons fly in

early morning or in the evening, when the air is less turbulent. Most of the balloons carry three to eight passengers; one can carry up to 12. While the flight itself is about one hour, allow three or four for the whole event, including instruction. $185 individual, $175 couples, $150 groups (minimum 6 people). (Southern Suburbs)

Ice-Skating

Even though Vancouver weather is mild and wet during the winter, ice-skating is a popular pastime. The climate virtually demands, however, that all rinks be indoors. Some rinks are open year-round for general skating, figure skating, and hockey.

KERRISDALE CYCLONE TAYLOR ARENA
5670 East Blvd.
Vancouver
604/257-8121
Cyclone Taylor was a member of the Vancouver Millionaires hockey team, winner of the 1915 Stanley Cup. This place is right next to a McDonald's and Point Grey High School, so you can expect to see a lot of teens here. It's open October through April for hockey and general skating, but call ahead because hours and days can vary. This arena is located in the heart of Point Grey's Kerrisdale neighborhood; you'll find terrific shopping along 41st Avenue when you've finished skating. When the ice comes off in summer, the facility is converted to an in-line skating arena. $2.75. Rentals available. (Point Grey)

KITSILANO COMMUNITY CENTRE
2690 Larch St.
Vancouver
604/257-6983

Like the Kerrisdale rink, Kitsilano's is next to a high school, Kitsilano Senior Secondary, and is part of a huge recreational complex that features indoor fitness facilities and a huge network of fields for football, soccer, and baseball. You can skate year-round here; general skating, figure skating, hockey, and skating lessons are scheduled on different days, so call for information. (Point Grey)

ROBSON SQUARE
Courthouse Complex
Vancouver
This covered outdoor rink is open daily November through March. However, you won't be able to get a full head of steam on this "polite"-sized rink designed for office workers who want to get a little exercise and fresh air. Finish your skating session with lunch or dinner at one of the restaurants that rim the rink. No rentals, but skating is free. (Downtown)

Kite Flying

VANIER PARK
Vancouver
Even if you don't do it yourself, you can watch some spectacular kite flying behind the museum complex as locals take their high-performance kites to battle. If you want to try your hand at it, Kites Horizons Aerosports (102-1807 Burrard St., 604/738-5867) and Kites on Clouds (131 Water St., 604/669-5677) can help you get started. (Point Grey)

Skiing

CYPRESS BOWL
West Vancouver
604/926-5612
604/419-7669 (snow conditions)
604/922-0825 (cross-country)

The newest of the North Shore Mountains' ski centers, Cypress Bowl is best suited for advanced skiers. You'll have 23 runs from which to choose, the longest being 13,200 feet (4,023 meters). If you're a downhill skier and want to give your joints a workout, take the Top Gun run around and over the moguls beneath the Sky Chair. Cross-country enthusiasts will find a good mix of hilly and flat terrain. More than 20 kilometers of groomed cross-country trails radiate out from historic Hollyburn Lodge. Unfortunately, you won't be able to get away from it all because this is a popular place. To get here, take the Cypress Bowl turnoff on the Upper Levels Highway and follow the signs. (North Shore)

GROUSE MOUNTAIN
North Vancouver
604/984-0661
604/986-6262 (snow conditions)
The base of this ski area is only 15 minutes from Downtown. A family hill offering facilities and instruction for skiing, snowboarding, snowshoeing, and backpacking, runs range from the gentle slopes of "the Cut" to the moguls and advanced runs of "the Peak." Because this is Vancouver's closest ski area, it's very busy. Like the other two North Shore hills, it has night skiing on well-lit runs. Take the Lion's Gate Bridge to Capilano

Drive, turn left, and drive to the end. (North Shore)

MANNING PARK RESORT
Manning Park
250/840-8822
You'll have to drive to get here, but the trip is worth it. Manning Park Resort is situated along Highway 3, an hour past Hope, and is considered by many to have the best cross-country skiing in southwest British Columbia. This is where you can really get away from it all. You'll find flat, groomed areas as well as steep backcountry hills. Sigge's Sports Villa (604/731-8818) in Kitsilano organizes day trips that include ski rentals, transportation, and lessons. (North Shore)

MOUNT SEYMOUR PROVINCIAL PARK
North Vancouver
604/986-2261
604/718-7771 (snow report)
Located 30 minutes northeast of downtown Vancouver, this park is a terrific and inexpensive place to experience a variety of winter sports, including tobogganing. The park encompasses Mount Elsay, Mount Bishop, and Mount Seymour, and its two distinct peaks both groomed for skiing. The park is especially appealing to snowboarders because of its varied terrain, and it's also a local favorite among cross-country skiers,

Best Places To Run

by Jay Parker, veteran marathon runner who can be seen almost every morning running on the streets of Vancouver's Point Grey

1. *From Brockton Oval in Stanley Park to the Anchor at the western end of Spanish Banks Beach in Point Grey. This is one of the longest continuous runs along the waterfront in Vancouver, and it'll take about three hours for the average jogger to complete. At about 20 kilometers (12 miles), it will test endurance, but a jogger can take it in sections—around Stanley Park, over the Burrard Street Bridge, and along the Point Grey waterfront. There are plenty of water fountains along the way.*

2. *Brockton Oval to Science World. This route takes you around the western end of Stanley Park, alongside the beach at Sunset Beach, and along the north side of the former site of Expo'86. It'll take about two hours round-trip.*

3. *Jericho Tennis Club to the Chan Centre and back. This route, which begins at the east end of Jericho Beach, takes you past Jericho, Locarno, and Spanish Banks beaches, offering stunning views of the North Shore Mountains and Howe Sound. The real test is going up the hill that leads onto the University of BC campus and the Chan Centre.*

4. *Pacific Spirit Park trails. This maze of dirt paths makes up one of one of the most pleasant jogging areas in Vancouver. And because the 56 different paths are well marked by signs and maps, it's almost impossible to get lost. Be prepared to share the paths with horses and small wildlife.*

5. *Stanley Park Seawall. This is still Vancouver's most popular jogging, walking, and running area. It's an asphalt path atop the seawall and an easy jog, at 10.5 kilometers (6 miles). If you need to cut it short at any time, simply cut across the interior of the park. You'll have great views of the North Shore Mountains, English Bay, and the downtown high-rises.*

especially after a fresh snowfall. Be sure to stay on the trails; the mountain can be a bit confusing if you hit unmarked territory. To get there, take the Second Narrows Bridge and get off at the Seymour Parkway exit. Turn left off the parkway at the well-marked exit. The roads can get bad— make certain you have good tires or chains. (North Shore)

WHISTLER RESORT
Whistler
604/687-7507
604/664-5614 (snow report/ special programs)
This is la crème de la crème of North American skiing. The village of Whistler sits at the base of two magnificent mountains—2,284-meter Blackcomb and 2,182-meter Whistler. The two peaks are home to the largest vertical drops on the continent, and they hold more than 200 official downhill trails (one is five miles long) of varying degrees of difficulty. All trails can be accessed via high-speed chair lifts. Those who prefer to get their turns in the backcountry can go heli-skiing (call the resort at 604/664-5625) on nearby glaciers and undeveloped peaks. Cross-country skiers won't be disappointed either; many groomed trails head into the trees from the village. (North Shore Day Trip)

Swimming

KITSILANO POOL
Next to Kitsilano Beach
Vancouver
604/731-0011
If you don't want your child swimming in the ocean, this is the next best alternative: a huge outdoor saltwater pool adjacent to the beach. It's heated to a comfortable 26 degrees Celsius (79 degrees Fahrenheit) and

has a graduated depth. Late May– Labor Day. $3.80 adults, $2 children 13–18, $1 children under 12, and $7 families. (Point Grey)

SPLASHDOWN WATERPARK
4799 Nu Lelum Way
Tsawwassen
604/943-2251
This 2.8-hectare park features 11 waterslides and is great for kids and adults alike. You'll find a full range of fun activities, from volleyball to basketball to just enjoying the sun. To get there, take Highway 17 toward the ferry terminal to 52nd Street; take a right and then a left onto Nu Lelum Way. Late May–Labor Day, 10–8. $18 adults, $12 children under 12, $7 park only. (Southern Suburbs)

UBC AQUATIC CENTRE
UBC campus next to the Student Union Building
Vancouver
604/822-4521
You don't have to be a student to use this first-rate facility. The Aquatic Centre was built for the Commonwealth Games in 1954 but has had several major face lifts since then. The public can use the facilities—including the sauna, Olympic-sized pool, whirlpool, steam room, exercise room, and toddler pool—in the evenings. Call ahead for times. $3.50 adults, $2.75 children 13–17, $2.00 children 3–12, $2.00 seniors. (Point Grey)

VANCOUVER AQUATIC CENTRE
1050 Beach St.
Vancouver
604/665-3424
Located on the north side of the entrance to False Creek and across the inlet from Vanier Park, this city-run facility features an Olympic-sized indoor pool, sauna, whirlpool, and

children's pool. It's a popular place throughout the year. Open Mon–Fri 6:30 a.m.–8 p.m., Sat–Sun 8 a.m.–9 p.m. in summer. Call for winter hours. $3.80. (Downtown)

Tennis

The best public tennis courts in town are directly behind the posh Vancouver Lawn Tennis and Badminton Club. The four courts are in immaculate condition at all times and are free to the public. The city also maintains tennis facilities at most community centers. The best one is at Stanley Park and includes 21 courts, 17 of which are by the Beach Street entrance. Courts are available on both a first-come, first-served basis and by reservation (604/878-8600) for a small fee. There are four other courts by Lost Lagoon at the foot of Robson Street.

Kitsilano Beach has 10 courts near the ocean and a nearby concession stand. Queen Elizabeth Park, at 33rd Avenue and Cambia Street, includes 12 courts built atop the city's water reservoir. If you don't mind wind, try the four courts at Jericho Beach Park just behind the Jericho Sailing Centre.

Indoor tennis is available during the winter for a fee at Burnaby Tennis Club (3890 Kensington, 604/291-0916); People's Courts (1650 Foster, Coquitlam, 604/878-8600); and University of BC Tennis Centre, near the ice-skating rinks (604/822-2505).

Walking/Running

For information on local running and walking clubs call Sport BC, 604/737-3000.

AMBLESIDE PARK
South of Marine Dr. at 13th Ave.

West Vancouver
Located along the North Shore, opposite English Bay from Point Grey, the paved walkway in Ambleside Park follows the railway tracks just below the high-rises. The path offers great views of the cruise ships in the harbor, English Bay, Stanley Park, and Downtown. Begin at the eastern end where the Capilano River enters English Bay. (North Shore)

KITS BEACH/VANIER PARK
Cornwall St. at Arbutus St.
Vancouver
Welcome to Vancouver's version of Muscle Beach. Follow the dirt and paved pathways around the beach (ogling at scantily clad men and women is allowed), through Vanier Park, past the museum complexes, and along Burrard Street Bridge. If you're in good shape, take the pathway beneath the bridge to the Granville Island side, where you can continue along False Creek all the way to the Science Centre. The whole trip is about 10 kilometers long. (Point Grey)

LOST LAGOON
Stanley Park
Vancouver
If you don't want to join the rush of humanity walking the seawall around Stanley Park, try shaking out your legs in a 1.6-kilometer stroll around Lost Lagoon at the park's entrance. You can feed the ducks and the swans and watch the fountain in the middle of the lagoon spray the gaggle of geese. (Downtown)

PACIFIC SPIRIT REGIONAL PARK
Between SW Marine Dr., Jericho Beach, Blenheim St., and 16th Ave.
Vancouver
The forested area that surrounds

UBC is one of the best walking and jogging areas in the city. There are 50 kilometers of paths that go through the park from the Fraser River across Point Grey to English Bay. The best running areas are off 16th Avenue and east through the forest. The visitors center on the north side of 16th Avenue west of Cleveland Trail can give you a map. (Point Grey)

SEAWALL
Stanley Park
Vancouver
Don't lose your footing as you read the plaques set at half-kilometer intervals along this 10.5-kilometer seawall. A popular route for runners and walkers, the path is also a hot spot for cyclists. It'll take you a couple of hours if you don't stop to gaze at the downtown skyline and the North Shore Mountains. It's easily accessible from downtown hotels simply by following the waterfront. (Downtown)

Windsurfing

Sometimes it seems as though there are hundreds of people on tiny sailboards darting about English Bay on a windy day. If you've never tried windsurfing before, consider joining them. A good place to learn is the Windsure Windsurfing School (1300 Discovery, 604/224-0615) at the Jericho Sailing Centre at Jericho Beach. The school offers a six-hour course that guarantees results. Pacific Boarder (1793 W. Fourth Ave., 604/734-7245) in Kitsilano, and Northshore Ski & Board (1625 Lonsdale, 604/987-7245) sell and rent wetsuits and boards.

Debra Sears

11

PERFORMING ARTS

Vancouver's love affair with the arts began when the city was just a few months old, when Keefer Hall was built as a combination skating rink and theater. Later, a little over a century ago, the city built an opera house and soon afterwards began to attract the luminaries of the time—Sarah Bernhardt, Mark Twain, and Henry Irving. Today, with 32 professional theatrical groups, two major theater festivals, and more than 21 venues, mainstream and experimental programming both get their fair share of exposure in what has become one of the world's top cities for the performing arts.

In music and dance the city's list of professional and amateur organizations has exploded during the past 15 years. Classical, jazz, and world music are now popular throughout the city. Performers from Asia and Europe arrive and perform in sold-out concerts at the city's largest venues without so much as a single ad in the newspaper. They rely solely on word-of-mouth and a few posters. Vancouver has become a popular destination for the world's major modern-dance choreographers, and as a result it has evolved into a hotbed of experimental concepts.

Other modes of performance art have seen similar success in recent years. The city is now the second-largest movie-making center in North America behind Hollywood, and it is host to a major annual film festival. The number of choirs in the greater Vancouver area—nearly 140—is staggering. And, while the Vancouver Symphony and Vancouver Opera continue to be the biggest and financially best-off institutions in Vancouver's performing-arts scene, the city also happens to be blessed with literally hundreds of small, lesser-known, spin-off ensembles. In short, if you've come to this city for a performance, you won't be disappointed.

THEATER

ARTS CLUB THEATRES
1585 Johnston St.
Vancouver
604/687-1644

Generally speaking, this is the most populist of Vancouver's theater companies, presenting a wide selection of drama, comedies, and revues guaranteed to bring in audiences. It's the largest regional theater company in western Canada, with a wide range of productions, and it has been a Vancouver institution since its formation in 1964. It made its first major impact 25 years ago with a stunning production of *Jacques Brel is Alive and Well and Living in Paris*.

Although the company had a somewhat tenuous beginning in a renovated former gospel hall on Seymour Street, it now has three theaters, all of which are in constant use. Two of the theaters are next to one another on Granville Island: the contemporary, 480-seat Main Stage; and the New Revue Stage, where productions like cabaret and local revue comedies are often staged. Both are just down the dock from the Granville Island Public Market. The third Arts Club stage recently opened at the newly renovated Stanley Theatre (see listing, below) on lower Granville Street. (Uptown)

BARD ON THE BEACH
Vanier Park
1100 Chestnut St.
Vancouver
604/733-1910 (summer)
604/325-5955 (year-round)

What a view! OK, so that might seem a philistine's approach to theater, but you just can't ignore the surroundings. In addition to the two Shakespearean plays that are staged all summer long (past performances have included *Macbeth*, *Measure for Measure*, and *A Midsummer Night's Dream*), you'll be treated to sunsets, mountains, and distant views of the city's high-rises. Spread a blanket on the grass and enjoy a picnic before the performance. And bring a cushion—the benches in the performance tent are quite hard. Staged on the south side of the entrance to Vanier Park, opposite the West End. (Point Grey)

THEATRE UNDER THE STARS
Stanley Park
Vancouver
604/687-0174

If there's anything in theater that resembles a Vancouver institution, this is it. Casts are enthusiastic, and the under-the-stars atmosphere makes for an enchanting evening of theater unlike anything else you'll see in town. And while the musical productions are not of top-professional qual-

---

T i P

One of the most ignored downtown parking lots is beneath the Law Courts building and one block from The Orpheum, site of the Vancouver Symphony and other major concerts. It's usually half full while others nearby are packed.

Filmdom's Gateway to the World

If you should stumble onto a street with a lot of cameras, lighting, mobile dressing rooms, and a few faces you think are familiar, congratulations. You've wandered into Hollywood North. In recent years Vancouver has become a major film and TV production center, second only to Los Angeles. Why Vancouver? Because the city has mountains and ocean, unique neighborhoods, and even a desert within within a four-hour drive. Because it's a city of multiple personalities, Vancouver has been China, Africa, Hong Kong, Vietnam, France, Seattle, Detroit, and even Beverly Hills.

ity, it doesn't matter; they are, nonetheless, well done, and you'll walk away having experienced something special. Remember to bring a sweater or light jacket. Held in the Malkin Bowl across from the Vancouver Rowing Club. (Downtown)

VANCOUVER FRINGE FESTIVAL
1163 Commercial Dr.
Vancouver
604/257-0350

Imagine this: 500 performances in 11 days. Sound busy? Well, it is. The Fringe Festival is held both indoors and outdoors, dawn to midnight, over two weeks in September in the Commercial Drive area. Here you'll find exceptionally wonderful and exceptionally bad theater performances mixed with a heavy dose of innovation and the never-tried-before. Some 100 companies are accepted on a first-come, first-served basis, and the resulting content varies from one-woman performances to gripping drama with a cast of dozens. There are no auditions and no standards to meet. (East Vancouver)

VANCOUVER INTERNATIONAL CHILDREN'S FESTIVAL
Vanier Park
1100 Chestnut St.
Vancouver
604/708-5655

Don't be fooled by the name. This event isn't just for children—just check out all the adult faces. Frankly, everybody's enthralled as they wander from tent to tent, taking in all the clowns and activities. This spring festival, held in late May and early June, attracts more than 200 local, national, and international acts. You can attend paid-admission shows or take advantage of an endless amount of free entertainment, including clowns, jugglers, mimes, and makeup artists. Make the event a family affair by planning a picnic at water's edge or by visiting the nearby Pacific Space Centre and the Vancouver Museum. Ticket prices vary. Call ahead. (See also Chapter 7, Kids' Stuff.) (Point Grey)

VANCOUVER PLAYHOUSE THEATRE COMPANY

Hamilton at Dunsmuir Sts.
Vancouver
604/873-3311
Employing many of the country's best actors and directors, this company blends the classical with the contemporary. It's the most established of the city's major companies and is the resident company of the Playhouse Theatre. The group typically performs plays by Shakespeare, Tennessee Williams, and Tom Stoppard, among others. (Downtown)

VANCOUVER THEATRESPORTS LEAGUE
Stanley Theatre
2780 Granville St.
Vancouver
604/738-7013
If you want irreverence, this is the place to go. You'll be treated to everything from murder to politics to talk shows to religion. When a subject is put into the hands of this 30-member improvisational group, you can guarantee they will stomp all over it. Each performance is different; the group satirizes everything that's hot in today's pop culture. One of the highlights of the performance is when three-member teams try to outdo each other for the night's improv "championship." (Uptown)

TRIVIA

Yvonne DeCarlo, the movie temptress of the 1950s and '60s (and the original Lily on TV's The Munsters), was once an usherette at the Orpheum Theatre.

MUSIC AND OPERA

CHINESE CULTURAL SOCIETY
Dr. Sun Yat-Sen Garden
578 Carrall St.
Vancouver
604/662-3207
The Chinese Cultural Society in Chinatown is the site of two quite different series offering Asian arts, Chinese Opera, and traditional music and dance. Chinese Opera is a formalized, colorful art form staged by local and international companies during the winter. In the summer the society presents Enchanted Evenings, during which the gardens are bathed in soft light from traditional lanterns while musicians and dancers perform and tell stories to children. (Downtown)

COASTAL JAZZ AND BLUES SOCIETY
435 W. Hastings St.
Vancouver
604/682-0706
Jazz, with a long tradition of smoky rooms and cool, soothing sounds, is nothing new to Vancouver. In fact, you can find many venues—including the Vancouver East Cultural Centre and the Western Front—that cater solely to this brand of music. Much of the Vancouver jazz movement's success over the past 15 years has been due to the Coastal Jazz and Blues Society, which presents traditional, alternative, and avant-garde jazz at venues around the city. Performers have included Miles Davis, Sun Ra, Shirley Horn, Ornette Coleman, Dizzy Gillespie, Diana Krall, Sonny Rollins, Cecil Taylor, and Wynton Marsalis. The society has a small budget and isn't able to mount advertising campaigns, so the best way to find out who's playing where

Buying Tickets

Vancouver has a variety of ticket brokers and services. And for sporting events, scalpers are always outside the stadiums waiting for someone willing to pay a premium. Sometimes, when an event is not sold out, scalpers are willing to sell at a loss just to rid themselves of the ducats. (It's only illegal if they try to sell on the venue property.)

- ***One Stop Ticket Shop***, *604/689-5500, says it'll get you the best prices for the city's sporting events, concerts, and theater.*

- ***Pacific Northwest Ticket Service***, *604/683-3515, not only has local events on their schedule but also can get tickets for the Super Bowl, Masters, Indy, Seattle sporting events, the Kentucky Derby, and the World Series.*

- ***Showtime Tickets & Tours***, *604/688-5000, is a broker that'll find you the ticket you need. They buy, sell, trade, and consign.*

- ***Ticketmaster***, *604/280-4444, is the biggest broker in town, offering tickets—with a surcharge of about one dollar—for just about everything.*

is by picking up their newsletter at any music store or public library. The society is also responsible in great part for the DuMaurier Jazz Festival, held for 10 days in late June. (various venues)

EARLY MUSIC VANCOUVER
604/732-1610
Early Music Vancouver (its formal name is Vancouver Early Music Society) is the Lower Mainland's leading presenter of period music. Besides staging 10 major concert series during its October–May season, the society also offers workshops and concerts during a joint summer program with the University of British Co-

lumbia. The society's collection of 20 replicas of old instruments—built by Vancouver craftspeople—is among the finest in the country. The society also sponsors the Vancouver Early Music Festival, which features teachers from the workshops and musicians from Canada, the United States, and Europe. (various venues)

FRIENDS OF CHAMBER MUSIC
Vancouver Playhouse
Hamilton at Dunsmuir Sts.
Vancouver
604/437-5747
This venerable organization brings in the world's finest chamber-music groups for a 10-concert season each

Vancouver International Jazz Festival, p. 205

October through April. The Beaux Arts Trio, Emerson Quartet, Tokyo String Quartet, and other international standard ensembles are regular visitors to Vancouver simply because this organization accepts nothing less than the very best. (Downtown)

MUSIC IN THE MORNING
Vancouver Academy of Music
1270 Chestnut St.
Vancouver
604/873-4612

Like your music with a cup of coffee? Well, you'll love this series, especially since it'll free up your evenings for even more activity. About 10 years ago, the society's founder and artistic director, June Goldsmith, decided that what the city needed was a musical series for those who worked at night or who simply didn't like going out in the evening. Today, the series, held September through June, has become one of Vancouver's biggest success stories. Coffee and cookies in the lobby of the Koerner Recital Hall—in the Vancouver Academy of Music— precede morning performances by

local, national, and international musicians. The music is mostly chamber music, with the occasional piano soloist. The intimate setting encourages a unique rapport between artists and audience. Music in the Morning also presents a learning series called Composers and Coffee, in which local and international music experts discuss various topics and encourage audience dialogue. (Point Grey)

PHOENIX CHAMBER CHOIR
604/273-1000

The Phoenix Choir, formed in 1983 by conductor Cortland Hultberg, is among the newest and best of Vancouver's major choirs. It took first place in the Contemporary and Chamber Choir categories of the CBC Choral Competitions in 1984 and 1994, and in 1989 it took the coveted BBC award for best overall performance. Since 1984 it has won a total of seven awards in these two competitions. In addition to presenting three concerts in Vancouver every year, the choir maintains an active broadcasting and recording schedule. (various venues)

Vancouver writer W. P. Kinsella shot to fame with his book *Shoeless Joe*. It was adapted for the big screen as *Field of Dreams*, starring Kevin Costner.

UZUME TAIKO
604/683-8240
North America's first professional taiko drumming ensemble, formed in 1988, is guaranteed to get your blood moving. Taiko is a traditional form of Japanese drumming. This band takes taiko and adds to it, fusing three drummers, a flautist, a cellist, and African and Latin percussionists. Uzume has developed a dynamic mix of old and new, bringing a vibrant, contemporary sensibility to an ancient art. (various venues)

VANCOUVER BACH CHOIR
5730 Seaview Rd.
West Vancouver
604/921-8012
The largest and oldest of the Vancouver-area choirs is the 130-member Vancouver Bach Choir, formed in 1930 by Herbert Mason. Its repertoire is grand and includes performances of major works by Bach, Beethoven, Britten, and Mahler with the Vancouver Symphony. Led by Bruce Pullan, the choir is heard nationwide on the CBC. (various venues)

VANCOUVER CANTATA SINGERS
604/921-8588
The Vancouver Cantata Singers, an award-winning 40-member ensemble led by conductor and artistic director James Fankhauser, performs a wide range of music during its regular season from September to May. The repertoire leans to the Baroque and early-Classical periods. The ensemble also commissions new works by Canadian composers Glenn Buhr, Stephen Chatman, Jean Coulthard, and Brian Cherney. (various venues)

VANCOUVER CHAMBER CHOIR
604/738-6822
The Vancouver Chamber Choir, led by its founder, conductor, and music director, Jon Washburn, was formed in 1971 as one of Canada's two professional choirs. The group saw success almost immediately, and in 1973 it became the first Canadian choir to win a first-place award in the prestigious BBC "Let the Peoples Sing" competition. The choir has become a major international force, touring the world both independently and for Canada's Ministry of External Affairs. Its Vancouver season (September–May) emphasizes short pieces and Canadian works. (various venues)

VANCOUVER NEW MUSIC SOCIETY
604/606-6440
Cutting-edge music—electronic, acoustical, or theatrical—is the reason for this company's existence. One of Canada's most respected contemporary music organizations, the society presents composers and music guaranteed to generate both controversy and an enthusiastic response. Works presented by the organization are by composers from

around the world, and many are either North American or international premieres. While many of the concerts are held at the Vancouver Cultural Centre, you can also expect them at universities and in churches. (various venues)

VANCOUVER OPERA
Queen Elizabeth Theatre
Hamilton St. at W. Georgia St.
Vancouver
604/682-2871
Wipe away the cobwebs, please. Opera in this town is often innovative and controversial without straying from the core of Italian classics that keep traditionalists coming back.

Vancouver Opera has grown from a one-opera-per-season organization, when it was founded in 1960, into a multimillion-dollar company. It has also become one of the hippest places in the city to be.

While the likes of Marilyn Horne, Dame Joan Sutherland, Placido Domingo, and other internationally recognized singers are no longer main-stage regulars, as they were before appearance fees went through the ceiling, the company still has strong lineups for their four or five productions (28 performances) each year. A few of the classics: Stravinsky's The *Rake's Progress*, Handel's *Alcina*, and Bizet's *Pearl*

Top 10 Operas Performed by the Vancouver Opera since 1960
by Doug Tuck, Information Officer of the Vancouver Opera

1. **Carmen**—Bizet's torrid story of love and murder (and VO's first production)
2. **La Boheme**—Puccini's lyrical opera about tragic betrayal
3. **Tosca**—Verdi's exploration in political deceit
4. **Madama Butterfly**—Puccini's great love story set in nineteenth-century Japan
5. **Rigoletto**—Puccini's musical adaptation of Victor Hugo's play, *Le Roi s'Amuse.*
6. **Marriage of Figaro**—Mozart's boy-chases-girl-chases-boy comic opera
7. **Barber of Seville**—Rossini's comic opera in which class differences are overcome by love
8. **Faust**—Gounod's lyrical, dramatic opera about a man who makes a pact with the devil
9. **The Magic Flute**—Mozart's lighthearted comic opera
10. **Lucia di Lammermoor**—Donizetti's operatic platform for coloratura sopranos

The Vancouver Symphony plays both contemporary and traditional music.

Fishers. The company also stages a recital series—in conjunction with other music organizations like the Vancouver Recital Society—which brings in such international operatic stars as Kathleen Battle, Dmitri Hvorostovsky, Ben Heppner, and Samuel Ramey. (Downtown)

VANCOUVER RECITAL SOCIETY
Vancouver Playhouse
Hamilton and Dunsmuir Sts.
Vancouver
604/602-0363
While most organizations depend on big names and reputations to draw audiences, this one has become a success by following a different path. If you want to know the names of the future superstars, just check out these performers. Founder and music director Leila Getz travels the world to find the best international talents before they become unaffordable. In addition, there are one or two special concerts during the year featuring big-name performers. In recent seasons the organization has gone into joint sponsorships of major concerts with the Vancouver Opera and other organizations. Getz is also in charge of the International Chamber Music Festival in August. (Downtown)

VANCOUVER SYMPHONY ORCHESTRA
Orpheum Theatre
Smithe St. at Granville St.
Vancouver
604/665-3050
Remember that haunting musical theme from Oliver Stone's great war film, *Platoon*? Well, the music that drove the film's pathos and drama

TRIVIA

Some feature films made in Vancouver: *Wrongfully Accused, Snow Falling on Cedars, Eaters of the Dead, Jumanji, Legends of the Fall,* and *Carnal Knowledge.*

T i P

For a daily listing of what's going on in Vancouver's arts scene, call the Arts Hotline at the Vancouver Cultural Alliance, 604/684-2787, or check out their Web site at www.culturenet.ca/vca.

was American composer Samuel Barber's *Adagio for Strings*. And the film score was played by the Vancouver Symphony Orchestra (VSO). It's not the first time the VSO has played for major films. It has also played the soundtracks for *The Changeling* and for the TV film *Baby M*, among others. Platoon won an Oscar for best soundtrack; *The Changeling* won one for best sound. The 76-member orchestra stages 11 different concert series through a regular season of about 40 weeks. Music ranges from traditional concert fare to contemporary and children's concerts. In addition to its Orpheum concerts, the VSO plays in unlikely venues like the top of Whistler Mountain, Grouse Mountain, and on Granville Island during the summer. (Downtown)

DANCE

BALLET BRITISH COLUMBIA
Queen Elizabeth Theatre
Hamilton St. at W. Georgia St.
Vancouver
604/732-5003
Even with only five programs and three special performances a season, this company has established itself as one of the Pacific Northwest's leaders. It's both an umbrella organization that brings in such renowned companies as the National Ballet of Canada, and a performance organization that mounts exciting and courageous productions. Both classical and contemporary dance is presented between September and June as part of its Dance Alive series. (Downtown)

DANCING ON THE EDGE FESTIVAL
Firehall Arts Centre
280 E. Cordova St.
Vancouver
604/689-0926
This is North America's largest annual festival of independent choreographers. Some 70 performances, conceived by choreographers from around the world, are staged during two weeks in July. The most interesting aspect of this dance orgy is the array of venues in which the perfor-

TRIVIA

A few of the television series filmed in Vancouver: *The X-Files, Stargate, The Commish, Strange Luck, M.A.N.T.I.S., MacGyver, The Outer Limits, Poltergeist, The Sentinel, Highlander, The Marshall, Reboot, Police Academy, 21 Jump Street,* and *Millennium.*

Vancouver Literature

Vancouver is one of North America's literary hot spots. More than 1,500 authors live in the province, and more than 250 book titles are published here every year. It's no coincidence that British Columbians, led by the citizens of Vancouver, read more books per capita than anyone else in the country.

The city's major literary event is the Vancouver International Writers and Readers Festival (604/681-6330). The festival, held on Granville Island, draws about 12,000 people over five days in October and presents Canadian and international writers who both read their works and interact with the audience. During the remainder of the year, festival organizers sponsor an authors series at various venues across the city. In the past the series has presented Gloria Steinem, Michael Ondaatje, Margaret Atwood, and Jeffrey Archer, among others.

There are regular readings by authors and poets at a variety of bookstores, at the main public library, and at several cafés. Call the Arts Hotline (604/684-ARTS) for readings schedules and other literary information.

mances are held: everywhere from the Firehall Arts Centre to beaches and street corners. (Downtown)

KAREN JAMIESON DANCE
Firehall Arts Centre
280 E. Cordova St.
Vancouver
604/685-5699
If Vancouver has anything that resembles a dance institution, it's Jamieson's dance company. This dancer and choreographer has been one of the leading fresh lights in Vancouver-area contemporary dance for 20 years. She creates original dance

that connects music and theater with movement and culture, implementing Asian, European, and indigenous dance techniques. (Downtown)

KOKORO DANCE
Firehall Arts Centre
280 E. Cordova St.
Vancouver
604/662-7441
It doesn't do this innovative company justice merely to say that it specializes in ethnic dance. It's much more than that, fusing a Japanese modern dance form called butoh with Western dance techniques. The results

Most choirs perform in a variety of locations. Call the Arts Hotline at 604/684-ARTS for choir-office phone numbers and performance venues.

are performances that incorporate live music, strong visuals, and physically demanding dance. While many of the performances take place at The Firehall, the company sometimes appears at the Vancouver East Cultural Centre at 1895 Venables Street. (Downtown)

CONCERT VENUES

BC PLACE STADIUM
777 Pacific Blvd. S.
Vancouver
604/661-7373
This 60,000-seat stadium is the home of the BC Lions football team as well as a variety of major conventions, concerts, and just about anything else that can make use of the vast floor space, private suites, and facilities. Big-time rock groups, such as the Rolling Stones, have performed here, as has tenor Luciano Pavarotti, various touring opera productions, and the "Three Tenors"—all with surprisingly good sound. (Downtown)

TRIVIA

The Vancouver area has 18 professional dance companies and 40 independent choreographers.

CHAN CENTRE FOR THE PERFORMING ARTS
6265 Crescent Rd.
Vancouver
604/822-9197
This $24-million performance hall was built in 1997 on the bluffs overlooking Howe Sound. It houses a 1,400-seat concert hall, a 200-seat studio theater, and a 150-seat cinema. Its great advantage is its newness and the fact that it has the best sight lines in the city. Its disadvantage is its remoteness; it's on the UBC campus and not easy to get to via public transit. It's currently in use by a number of choirs, small ensemble groups, and recital groups. (Point Grey)

FORD CENTRE FOR THE PERFORMING ARTS
777 Homer St.
Vancouver
604/602-0616
As you read this the fate of one of Vancouver's newest (1995) theaters is up in the air. Owned by the Livent entertainment group, it is one of the bankrupt company's major assets. No matter who eventually gains ownership, however, the Moshe Safdie–designed 1,824-seat theater will continue to be a major venue for theatrical and musical events. Safdie is the same architect who designed the controversial library right across the street. The most striking features of the theater are the grand

Vancouver's Audience-Friendly Theaters and Concert Halls

by Max Wyman, dance and music critic, author, and Canada Council member

- *Vancouver East Cultural Centre* (1895 Venables St., 604/254-9578)—*A converted church, this intimate performance space on the residential East Side has been a popular home to small-scale chamber music ensembles, dance troupes, pop and folk musicians, and community performance groups since 1974. (EV)*

- *The Orpheum Theatre* (Smithe St. at Seymour St., 604/665-3050)—*Originally part of the Pantages vaudeville circuit, this grand 2,788-seat theater has been lovingly restored to its original elegant, Moorish-flavored glory. (DV)*

- *Arts Club Theatres* (1585 Johnston St., 604/687-1644)—*On Granville Island, the 480-seat Main Stage and the 225-seat New Revue Stage offer a lively and consistently popular season of straight theater, musical comedy, and revue. (UV)*

- *Chan Centre for the Performing Arts* (6265 Crescent Rd., 604/822-9197)—*This 1,400-seat concert hall (with small theater attached) on the UBC campus is spectacular. (PG)*

- *Firehall Arts Centre* (280 E. Cordova St., 604/689-0926)—*This converted fire station on the fringe of Vancouver's historic Gastown quarter provides an intimate, 100-plus-seat venue for a lively program of dance, music, and alternative entertainment. (EV)*

- *Ford Centre for the Performing Arts* (777 Homer St., 604/602-0616)—*Built by Toronto-based Livent as a roadhouse for the organization's mega-musicals, this three-level, Moshe Safdie–designed theater accommodates about 1,800. (DV)*

multistory staircase, the mirrored walls, and the surprisingly comfortable and intimate auditorium. (Downtown)

GATEWAY THEATRE
6500 Gilbert Rd.
Richmond
604/270-1812

Vancouver author Douglas Coupland coined the term "Generation X," thereby giving a whole generation an identity.

In the heart of Richmond's Minoru Park area, this contemporary theater complex has two production spaces, an art gallery, and a photo gallery. Glass-walled lobbies provide outstanding views of the North Shore Mountains. Unlike most of the city's theaters, Gateway Theatre leads a unique double life. Half the time it's home to professional live theater—musicals, comedies, drama, classics, and mystery thrillers; the other half is spent hosting community performing-arts groups and others as they present a wide array of events including dance, Cantonese opera, concerts, and drama. The complex is often used by the Greater Vancouver Operatic Society and Ballet British Columbia. (Southern Suburbs)

GENERAL MOTORS PLACE STADIUM
800 Griffiths Way
Vancouver
604/899-7889
This is the venue for really big rock groups. While it's the home court for the Vancouver Grizzlies of the NBA and the Vancouver Canucks of the NHL, for most of the fall, winter, and spring, a variety of trade shows and rock concerts are held here. The 20,000-seat complex was designed as a hockey and basketball venue, so there are terrific sight lines to the floor. But this place also has amazing acoustics. Fully wired with fiber-optic technology, the sound is enhanced by acoustic panels that evenly spread out the sound. (Downtown)

MALKIN BOWL
Stanley Park
Vancouver
604/687-0174
Built in 1934, this is Canada's original permanent outdoor-theater facility. While it was originally built for musical events, in 1940 it became the venue for Theatre Under the Stars (TUTS), which has been staging productions of popular Broadway shows here every summer since. It's a great place to spend a warm summer evening. (Downtown)

ORPHEUM THEATRE
Smithe St. at Granville St.
Vancouver
604/665-3050
Located on the Granville Mall in the heart of downtown, the 2,800-seat theater is one of the finest concert halls in the country. Originally built as a vaudeville theater in the 1920s, the theater narrowly escaped being torn down and turned into a movie house in the early 1970s. The Orpheum is the primary venue for large-scale classical music, although the occasional pop artist plays there. It's the home of the Vancouver Symphony, and the city's large choirs have their major concerts here. In addition, The Orpheum is the theater of choice for many internationally renowned instrumental and vocal soloists—such

as pianists Murray Perahia, Vladimir Ashkenazy, soprano Jessye Norman, among others. (Downtown)

QUEEN ELIZABETH THEATRE AND PLAYHOUSE
Hamilton St. at W. Georgia St.
Vancouver
604/665-3050

Built in the mid-1950s, the 2,931-seat theater and 668-seat playhouse remain at the core of Vancouver's entertainment life even though new venues have been built throughout the city. The theater is home to the Vancouver Opera and Ballet British Columbia, and it is the venue of choice for many touring soloists, multicultural shows, and rock groups, even though it doesn't have the best acoustics in town. What it does have is a mammoth backstage—the largest in Canada. The intimate Playhouse is attached to

The Orpheum—Saving a Gem from the Wrecking Ball

It's hard to believe now, but in the early 1970s Vancouver's premium theater space was scheduled for the wrecking ball. When it opened in 1927 as one in the chain of Orpheum theaters across North America, it featured conservative Spanish Renaissance design; a basic color scheme of antique ivory and gold; black and gold arabesques; and ornamental colonnades. Glittering chandeliers illuminated the hall. But it was below the stage that the most impressive item was housed—an electric elevator that lifted three huge Wurlitzer organs. One of those organs is still played once a year.

When the Famous Players movie theater chain announced in 1973 that the Orpheum would be sacrificed for a multiplex movie palace, city hall was besieged by a letter-writing campaign to preserve the building as a concert hall. Fortunately, the campaign prevailed. The city bought the theater for about $4 million and then spent an equal amount bringing it up to standard for its 1977 opening.

The Orpheum is now the city's most prestigious hall, home of the Vancouver Symphony, and an official national historic site. Located on the Granville Mall, one block south of Eaton's, The Orpheum is one of the finest concert halls in the country.

the theater and is home to the Play-house Theatre Company, the Friends of Chamber Music, and the Vancouver Recital Society. (Downtown)

STANLEY THEATRE
Arts Club
2780 Granville St.
Vancouver
604/687-1644

Back to the ol' soft shoe, folks. Originally designed as a vaudeville theater in 1930 and later converted to a movie house, The Stanley was re-opened in November 1998 and is now the newest theater space in the city. The Stanley has got everything going for it, including the original interior architecture and the still-intact exterior neon. (Uptown)

VANCOUVER EAST CULTURAL CENTRE (VECC)
1895 Venables St.
Vancouver
604/254-9578

There is no better place in the city to have an intimate concert or theatrical experience than in this 350-seat facility, built in 1914 as a church. Known locally as "The Cultch," it's home for numerous small ensembles, including Vancouver New Music, Touchstone Theatre, and the Green Thumb Theatre. If the city has a center for innovative and contemporary dance, theater, and music, this is it. Since it opened as a performance space in 1973, its raison d'être has been to give viewers a unique experience. (East Vancouver)

12

NIGHTLIFE

This is the city that gave the world rock singer Bryan Adams. Expect a legacy of pop culture in this town, where music of all kinds permeates the city's consciousness. You name it and we've got it in spades—blues, jazz, rock, country and western, and more. The lines that could easily be drawn between bars, pubs, nightclubs, and lounges just a generation ago no longer apply. Today the neighborhood pub may also have a terrific rhythm-and-blues band or be a jazz hot spot. And nightclubs may offer dancing to rock, fusion, or 1940s music, or they may even offer film or live theater with your drinks. Vancouver has a myriad of cafés and drinking establishments that often double as meeting places for the lonely, the active, and the conversational. And because Vancouver has the largest gay and lesbian population west of Toronto, the downtown area has several gay clubs.

There are no entertainment rules. A word of advice, however: Always call before you go to find out about cover charges or show prices (if any) and—the business being what it is—to make sure the establishment is still open.

MUSIC CLUBS

Country and Western

BOONE COUNTY
801 Burnette Ave.
Coquitlam
604/525-3144
The truth is that downtown Vancouver considers itself too "sophisti-

cated" for a lot of country music. You're more likely to find people dressed for the opera and theater than for a hayride. So the best country-and-western spots—like this place—are in the suburbs. But it's worth the 45-minute trip to this raucous Coquitlam bar, where the quarters are cramped and the dominant odor is that of beer. The place has raised tables and a large dance floor, and, no, you don't have to park your boots at the door. (Eastern Suburbs)

RAILWAY CLUB
579 Dunsmuir St.
Vancouver
604/681-1625
Those in the know say this club, on the second floor of an old building, is the best of its kind in town—especially for the younger set. It's a private club, so you'll have to sign in as a guest at the door. The Railway Club was set up in the 1930s as a "private social club" for workers at the Canadian Pacific Railway to get around the then-strict liquor laws for public clubs. Those antiquated laws no longer exist, of

Vancouver's Best Nightlife

As selected by the creative department of Mainframe Entertainment, the people who created the computer-generated children's television series ReBoot *and* Beast Wars.

Best Live Music

- *Starfish Room*, 1055 Homer St., 604/682-4171 (various kinds)
- *The Yale Hotel*, 1300 Granville St., 604/681-9253 (blues)
- *Capone's*, 1141 Hamilton St., 604/684-7900 (jazz)
- *Chameleon Urban Lounge*, 810 W. Georgia St., 604/669-0806 (jazz)
- *Railway Club*, 579 Dunsmuir St., 604/681-1625 (rock, but not heavy)

Best Nightclub Dancing

- *Club Sonar*, 66 Water St., 604/683-6695
- *Luv-a-Fair*, 1275 Seymour St. , 604/685-3288
- *Celebrities Nightclub*, 1022 Davie St., 604/689-3180
- *Odyssey*, 1251 Howe St., 604/689-5256
- *Club Aviva*, 98 Brigantine St, Coquitlam, 604/526-4464

Best Swing Dancing

- *BaBalu*, 654 Nelson St., 604/605-4343
- *Waldorf Hotel*, 1489 E. Hastings St., 604/253-7141 (on Blue Lizard Nights)
- *Vesuvius*, 1176 Granville St., 604/608-4283
- *Denman Station*, 860 Denman St., 604/669-3448 (Thursday nights)

course, and you have to look hard to find railway workers anymore, but the private social club concept has stayed on. As an alternative to signing in as a guest, you can pay $10 for an annual membership that gives you a key to the front door and many discounts. The place is somewhat narrow, and a large, square bar cuts the room in half. Try to arrive early and get a seat in the front section. Music at the Railway Club includes country and western as well as some rock and blues; featured acts have included Los Lobos, the Tragically Hip, Blue Rodeo, the Smugglers, and Ginger among others. Sunday is movie-theme night. (Downtown)

Best Martinis
- *Delilah's*, 1789 Comox St., 604/687-3424
- *Capone's*, 1141 Hamilton St. , 604/684-7900
- *Deniro's*, 1030 Mainland St., 604/684-2777
- *Royal Towers Lounge*, 140 Sixth St., New Westminster, 604/528-7358

Best Outdoor Dining Patios
- *Bridges*, 1696 Duranleau St., 604/687-4400
- *The Beach House*, 150 25th St., Dundarave Pier, 604/922-1414
- *The Creek at Granville Island Hotel*, 1253 Johnston St., 604/683-7373
- *Cardero's*, 1583 Coal Harbour Quay, 604/669-7666
- *Salmon House on the Hill*, 2229 Folkstone Way, 604/926-3212

Best Cigar Lounges
- *BaBalu*, 654 Nelson St., 604/605-4343
- *Chameleon Urban Lounge*, 810 W. Georgia St., 604/669-0806

Best Shops to Buy Recorded Music
- *Zulu*, 1869 W. Fourth Ave., 604/738-3232
- *A&B Sound*, 556 Seymour St., 604/687-5837
- *Charlie's Music City*, 819 Granville St., 604/688-2500
- *Magic Flute*, 2203 W. Fourth Ave., 604/736-2727

Best Video Shops
- *Videomatica*, 1859 W. Fourth Ave., 604/734-5752
- *Virgin Megastore*, 788 Burrard St., 604/669-2289

Jazz

BLUE NOTE JAZZ BISTRO
2340 W. Fourth Ave.
Vancouver
604/733-0330
This is probably the best place in town for dining to the sounds of live mainstream jazz. The food and music are so good, in fact, that it's impossible to determine whether the Blue Note is a bistro with jazz or a jazz club that has a terrific bistro. If you're single, you just might be coupled to death here—the stylish late 20s– and early 30s–couples crowd is overwhelming. It's a bit like a New York–style supper club, but there's no connection between this place, which opened in 1993, and its New York namesake. (Point Grey)

CARNEGIE'S
1619 W. Broadway
Vancouver
604/733-4141
This place has undergone a series of changes since it opened in 1989. In 1996 club owners decided to throw out the live jazz and substitute prerecorded jazz. In June 1999, however, Carnegie's returned to its live jazz roots in the hopes of regaining its position as one of Vancouver's trendiest jazz clubs. Located on the edge of Kitsilano, the club has managed to keep many of its original patrons while attracting a "singles" crowd. It's somewhat quiet during

the week but begins to heat up for the weekend as soon as the happy-hour crowd rolls in on Friday afternoon. The décor has undergone some changes, too, but has maintained its Mediterranean character. Some tables were removed from the main room to create a bigger dance floor, but the ornate bar's still there. (Uptown)

CHAMELEON URBAN LOUNGE
Hotel Georgia
810 W. Georgia St.
Vancouver
604/669-0806
Buried in the basement of the recently renovated Hotel Georgia, the Chameleon Urban Lounge is a popular hangout for the mature, urban crowd. High-ceilinged and plush, yet at the same time dark and narrow, the lounge is known for its live jazz and funk. Patrons, when they're not swaying to the music on the tiny dance floor, like to kick back on the lounge's antique red-velvet couches. Some original art does its part to warm things up above the black-marble floor. Lines are inevitable on weekends. (Downtown)

HOT JAZZ SOCIETY
2120 Main St.
Vancouver
604/873-4131
You might feel like you've entered a time machine when you step inside this place. The club prides itself on

TOP 10 BEST CLUBS FOR MUSIC AND MEETING PEOPLE

by Tom Harrison, veteran pop/rock music critic for *The Province* newspaper and one of Canada's leading pop-culture writers

1. **Commodore Ballroom**, (870 Granville St., 604/683-9413). The club, under new ownership, reopened in December 1999, after being closed for several months for renovations. With a capacity of 1,100, this is a hot spot for touring and local acts.

2. **Railway Club**, (579 Dunsmuir St., 604/681-1625). Live music nightly, theme nights occasionally, Saturday afternoon rockabilly/roots jam. Small, intimate. 176 seats.

3. **Starfish Room**, 1055 Homer St., 604/682-4171). Emerging recording acts, popular local acts most nights. 350 capacity.

4. **The Yale Hotel**, 1300 Granville St., 604/681-9253). Blues seven nights a week; "imported" and local blues showcases on Sunday and a "super session" on Monday. 350 capacity.

5. **The Piccadilly Pub**, 620 Pender St., 604/669-1556). Theme nights and local acts, mostly of the funky/rootsy variety. In the Piccadilly Hotel. Intimate size (seats 125).

6. **Richard's on Richards**, 1036 Richards St., 604/687-6794). Varies from urban/disco dance music to touring pop/rock/folk and other types of recording acts. 450 capacity.

7. **Chameleon**, (801 W. Georgia St., 604/669-0806). Also known as the Chameleon Urban Lounge. DJs most nights, urban lounge setting, occasional live sets from local funk, Latin, or acid-jazz inspired bands. Small room in the basement of the Hotel Georgia. About 150 capacity.

8. **Vesuvius**, (1176 Granville St., 604/608-4283). Live music most nights, with an emphasis on swing and roots bands, plus theme nights. 350 capacity.

9. **The Brickyard**, (315 Carrall St., 604/685-3922). Live bands Wednesday through Saturday. Emphasis on local alternative/modern rock. 151 capacity.

10. **Purple Onion Jazz Caberet**, (15 Water St., 604/602-9442). Two rooms, one primarily for DJs and occasional live bands, and the other for jazz, lounge acts, or singer-songwriters.

featuring the popular tunes (oh, what music!) of the 1930s and the Second World War. It's classic stuff, with New Orleans–style jazz and swing on Friday nights and big-band sounds on occasional Saturdays. The place has a large dance floor for anyone who wants to relive the big-band era. It's a private club, but guests are permitted for $10. (East Vancouver)

PURPLE ONION JAZZ CABARET
15 Water St.
Vancouver
604/602-9442
This Gastown cabaret and lounge makes up for any décor limitations with a mix of jazz, cool blues, salsa and Latin rhythms, and funk. The Purple Onion is a Vancouver hot spot, so expect to wait in line an hour or so on Fridays. There is a dress code (no shorts, jeans, or T-shirts). (Downtown)

Rhythm and Blues

FAIRVIEW PUB
898 Broadway
Vancouver
604/872-1262
While it may be located in the Ramada Inn, don't expect just a hotel crowd in this pub. In fact, it draws R&B fans from over the city, seven nights a week. And with a recent $250,000 renovation it has reinforced its position as the primary showcase for the city's best rhythm-and-blues musicians. The forest green décor accents the dark cherry walls. The crowd age ranges from 25 to 50. The house musician, Chicago-born bass guitarist Jack Lavin, has been performing since 1969. He was a founding member of the Powder Blues and has performed with Chuck Berry, John Lee Hooker, Bo Diddley, Robert

Cray, and Jimmy Page. Catch him on the weekend. Other locals can be heard during the week. (Uptown)

THE YALE HOTEL
1300 Granville St.
Vancouver
604/681-9253
If Vancouver has a home for rhythm and blues, this is it. The building has been around for more than 100 years, and some of the players seem as though they may have been there at the original opening. The musicians are old pros and they're good—really good. A wonderful (and harmless) sense of seediness permeates the place. This section of Granville isn't the nicest, but the musical rewards make a trip to the Yale Hotel worthwhile. (Downtown)

PUBS AND BARS

BABALU
Hotel Dakota
654 Nelson St.
Vancouver
604/605-4343
This place attracts the martini-and cigar-lounge crowd. Located in the newly renovated Hotel Dakota, it's one of two entertainment lounges on the property—the other being Fred's Tavern, a casual drinking place. Babalu is a playful theme lounge with a luxurious Cuban motif—a palette of warm rusts and greens, Spanish-style artwork, distressed plaster walls, and furnishings the owners obviously had fun choosing. The lounge has a cool, sophisticated edge, but it's never stuffy. There's live big-band/swing on weeknights and DJ-spun lounge music on Saturdays. The light dinner and tapas menus keep the hungry subdued. (Downtown)

Bridges pub, p. 226

 Staff at Bridges

BACCHUS LOUNGE
Wedgewood Hotel
845 Hornby St.
Vancouver
604/689-9321

Following its daily stint as a favorite lunchtime restaurant (see Chapter 4, Where to Eat), the Bacchus Lounge reverts to what it does best: act as a gathering place for the neighborhood's genteel workforce. Most of the patrons at this place spend their days at the Law Courts complex across the street. Soft jazz is the entertainment of choice, smooth as a lawyer's summation. A pianist provides the cocktail-hour entertainment, followed by the soft tunes of a gentle duo or trio. (Downtown)

BACKSTAGE LOUNGE
Arts Club Theater
1585 Johnston St.
Vancouver
604/687-1354

This is one of Vancouver's best little secrets. The Backstage Lounge, located on Granville Island's water-front, is one of the most comfortable pubs in the city. Because it shares space with the Arts Club Theatre, it's a popular gathering place for the theater set. Originally designed as a place where theater patrons could relax during intermissions, it's so popular today that patrons are lucky if they can even squeeze in. The live weekend entertainment is usually a blues band. (Uptown)

BARCLAY LOUNGE
1348 Robson St.
Vancouver
604/688-8850

The Barclay Lounge is a cabaret-style lounge hosting singers whose repertoires include everything from the songs of Billie Holiday to the favorite weepies of the past three decades. The intimate and sophisticated atmosphere makes this a perfect place to take someone special. It's definitely a high-end way to spend an evening. As with everything else on Robson, there's plenty of weeknight activity here and often long lines on weekends. It's attached to O'Doul's Restaurant. (Downtown)

BAR-NONE
1222 Hamilton St.
Vancouver
604/689-7000

Calling this place a nightclub is a bit misleading. Located in trendy Yaletown, it's a favorite meeting place for the well-dressed and stylish under-40s crowd—all of whom seem to have flat stomachs and/or long legs. If you like to stand around like sardines in a row—with recorded acid-jazz and top 40s in the background—you'll enjoy this place. In a neat departure from other Vancouver clubs, this one has a long row of backgammon boards and checkerboards to augment the pool tables. (Downtown)

BIG BAM BOO
1236 W. Broadway
Vancouver
604/733-2220

Most of the people at this trendy dance spot are single, young, and swish. How trendy is it? If you get hungry dancing or become exhausted with your pickup lines, you can refuel at the sushi bar near the entrance. Downstairs has dancing to '80s pop and the current top-40s hits, or you can play pool or snack at the sushi bar upstairs. Wednesday is ladies' night—if male strippers sound appealing, come on in. Live music on Fridays. (Uptown)

BRIDGES
1696 Duranleau St.
Vancouver
604/687-4400

This cozy dockside pub, located next to the Granville Island Public Market, may be the best-situated nightspot in Vancouver—it's on the south side of the building that houses a restaurant (upstairs) and a wine bar (downstairs). Bridges combines British pub style—an area for playing darts—with North American cultural sensibilities—three TVs tuned to sporting events. A nautical theme, well-padded benches, and high bar stools do much for Bridges' intimate character. (Uptown)

CLUB MILLENNIUM
595 Hornby St.
Vancouver
604/684-2000

Club Millennium recently underwent a million-dollar renovation. Now it's a Vegas-style nightclub and the place to go for martinis and cigars. This is truly a players' club, so dress to impress. A state-of-the-art air-conditioning system takes care of the cigar smoke, and you can buy personalized cigar humidors in a rack of almost 60 near the club's retail area. Nightly entertainment varies widely, from comedy to soft rock. (Downtown)

CLUB SONAR
66 Water St.
Vancouver
604/683-6695

This place was known as the Town Pump until 1997. Touring acts—including the Doughboys, the Mighty Mighty Bosstones, Junkhouse, and Electrafixion—would stop here during their sweep through Gastown. The venue hasn't changed—it's still a narrow hall with a dance floor—but the music has. Now it's a great techno club, with DJ-mixed sounds and Vancouver's funkiest 20s crowd. If you're over the age of 26, you might feel old here. (Downtown)

DV8
515 Davie St.

Vancouver
604/682-4388

DV8 is both a mainstream pub and an after-hours hangout. It's a narrow room done in black and decorated with original art and black-and-white nude photos. The sound system delivers rock, rap, and alternative music at high decibels. When the bar closes at 2 a.m., the food operation shifts into overdrive. The menu includes pastas, salmon, and burgers, as well as pizza and quesadillas cooked in a wood-fired oven. The kitchen stays open to three in the morning on weeknights, and to four on weekends, which are really busy. (Downtown)

JOE FORTES
777 Thurlow St.
Vancouver
604/669-1277

A pianist plays here nightly for the suited set that drops in after work. It's busy after five and impossible on Saturday night, but don't let that scare you away. A good portion of the crowd is waiting for a table at the restaurant, so the lounge area often clears out rather quickly. The place has a chophouse decor, something you'd expect from a restaurant in the heart of a U.S. city. You'll find Vancouver's best selection of Belgian beers and the widest array of local microbreweries. (Downtown)

JOLLY TAXPAYER
828 W. Hastings St.
Vancouver
604/681-3574

This is a popular place for the downtown business and stockbroker types who pay half their salaries to taxes. Noisy and frantic at lunch, it attracts those looking to unwind after a day on the job. Much like a British pub, the Jolly Taxpayer is always packed

and noisy, has a wide selection of beers and ales, and often serves as an excellent solution to the day's problems. (Downtown)

LUV-A-FAIR
1275 Seymour St.
Vancouver
604/685-3288

This place is "high" everything: high tech, high energy, high decibel, and highly alternative. Not surprisingly, Luv-a-Fair attracts a very young crowd. They come for the DJ-spun alternative rock, the cheap drinks, and the industrial-style atmosphere. Located in a former warehouse, this is one of the more popular nightclubs in Vancouver, so expect a long line. Come to dance, not to listen. (Downtown)

MARBLE ARCH
518 Richards St.
Vancouver
604/681-5435

Take it off—all off. The Marble Arch is Vancouver's downtown strip bar. American tourists are usually surprised—and delighted—when they discover that local law allows female dancers to bare all. The 280 seats are usually full during lunchtime and again after working hours and through closing time. A relatively safe spot, the only danger is in the potential for whiplash as you try to keep tabs on all three stages. Triple-stage mania, as it's known locally, can be brutal. If you get tired of the strippers, the place also has TVs, video games, and pool tables. (Downtown)

MONTEREY LOUNGE AND GRILL
Pacific Palisades Hotel
1277 Robson St.
Vancouver
604/684-1277

After-Hours Eating

- **Bread Garden**, *812 Bute St., 604/688-3213—A great 24-hour place to get an early breakfast, a late snack, or a full late-night dinner. (Downtown)*
- **Doll and Penny's Café**, *1167 Davie St., 604/685-3417—This place has really comfortable booths and terrific burgers. It closes at four in the morning weekdays and at two on Sunday, but it's open 24 hours on Friday and Saturday. (Downtown)*
- **Hamburger Mary's**, *1202 Davie St., 604/687-1293—There's probably no better place Downtown to get a burger. Open 'til four in the morning. (Downtown)*
- **Vineyard Restaurant**, *2296 W. Fourth Ave., 604/733-2420—The surprisingly complete late-night menu—which includes some traditional Greek dishes—is available 24 hours a day. (Point Grey)*

Sit by the window or, in warm weather, at one of the street-side tables and watch the strange, the mainstream, and the idiosyncratic parade by on Robson Street. Light jazz, tastefully presented, will keep you company. This is one of Robson Street's most civilized watering holes, quite different from the Barclay Lounge across the street because it isn't trendy or especially sophisticated. It's just a pleasant place to unwind and escape Robson's frantic pace. (Downtown)

NO. 5 ORANGE
203 Main St.
Vancouver
604/687-3483
This anchor of the easternmost section of Gastown won international notoriety when it posted, on its marquee, a statement that said it was

refusing entry to X Files star David Duchovny after he complained about Vancouver's rain on an American television talk show. The clientele at this strip bar can be as rough as the neighborhood. (Downtown)

THE PALLADIUM
1250 Richards St. (alleyway entrance)
Vancouver
604/688-2648
Once called Graceland, The Palladium (the name changed with new ownership) is a European-style dance club. Located in the heart of the nightclub district, it still attracts enthusiastic crowds. The noise level at this place is sometimes overwhelming, but the young crowd likes it. The Palladium's weekly lineup of music includes DJ-spun tunes on Monday, disco on Tuesday, and Latino on

Wednesday. Weekends are strictly for live rock. The music is cutting edge—anything over two months old might as well be classic rock. (Downtown)

RICHARD'S ON RICHARDS
1036 Richards St.
Vancouver
604/687-6794

This was once Vancouver's primary club for hormone-overloaded youth. Those days are gone, however, and Richard's on Richards is now one of the downtown core's hipper, more established music places. Expect live and recorded music (performers have included Prince, De La Soul, Branford Marsalis, Maceo Parker, the Philosopher Kings, and the Wailers), laser lighting, valet parking, and unsurpassed hospitality. The atmosphere is surprisingly intimate for such a high-tech place. The dress code disallows T-shirts and running shoes. It's really popular on weekends, so expect lines. (Downtown)

ROXY
932 Granville St.
Vancouver
604/684-7699

Roxy is a popular gathering place for the classic-rock crowd. Entertainment is provided by live bands and a staff of Tom Cruise–wan-na-be bartenders. This fun, casual club attracts mainly university students who come to unwind after a torturous day in

class. The partying and dancing to live rock 'n' roll goes on all night long, seven nights a week. Doors open at seven, but get there early because lines begin to form by nine on weekdays and seven on weekends. (Downtown)

SHARK CLUB BAR AND GRILL
Sandman Hotel
180 W. Georgia St.
Vancouver
604/687-4275

The Shark Club, one of the city's top singles bars, is located in the Sandman Hotel, across the street from the Queen Elizabeth Theatre complex. A sports bar and nightclub, it includes a plethora of sports memorabilia, 30 big-screen TVs, and a long oak bar offering 22 different kinds of beer. Each night at exactly eight o'clock a DJ cranks up the music and the crowd heads for the dance floor. It's a great place to make new friends. The Italian dinner menu is better than you'd expect. (Downtown)

STAMP'S LANDING
610 Stamp's Landing
Vancouver
604/879-0821

Adjacent to Monk McQueen's (see Chapter 4, Where to Eat), Stamp's is a favorite among boaters who moor their vessels in False Creek. It's a small, friendly, British pub–style place that's busy almost all the time. Expect a jovial crowd, especially on week-

While both of Vancouver's major daily newspapers, the *Vancouver Sun* and the *Province*, produce weekend listings, locals consider the weekly *Georgia Straight* the city's major source for entertainment information. The paper is distributed free throughout the city.

ends, as boaters chained to their desks during the week escape to the pleasures of the sea and the bar. About a dozen brews are on tap, and the pub menu includes shepherd's pie, bangers and mash, and other artery cloggers. (Uptown)

STARFISH ROOM
1055 Homer St.
Vancouver
604/682-4171
Other places may get more publicity and notoriety, but young people in the know invariably pick this club as one of the top three or four in town. If there's a problem here, it's the lack of space—be careful on the small dance floor. The intimate underground atmosphere appeals to the 20s crowd. Music is both live and recorded and includes the newest hits as well as some "golden oldies." (Downtown)

STONE TEMPLE CABARET
1082 Granville St.
Vancouver
604/488-1333
This popular nightspot was known as The Underground before new owners changed the name in 1997. Not a lot else has changed, however: both the décor and the clientele have remained the same—rough-edged. It's a cruiser bar with a huge dance floor and all of the usual bright lights and deafening bass sounds that make conversation a bit awkward. The DJ-spun tunes span virtually every musical form—except maybe classical. (Downtown)

WETT BAR
1320 Richards St.
Vancouver
604/662-7077
This is a popular gathering place for the rapidly aging Gen-X set. The big

attraction here is the technology. The back wall is a computer-controlled hydroponics garden with a running brook, banana trees, and a live volcano. High-tech lighting flashes an image of the Milky Way on the ceiling. Add to that one of the finest video screens you're ever likely to see in a nightclub and a healthy splattering of special effects. Different bars serve different drinks: while one pours shooters and the hard stuff, another serves wine and champagne. (Downtown)

GAY CLUBS

CELEBRITIES NIGHTCLUB
1022 Davie St.
Vancouver
604/689-3180
Celebrities may be the most popular gay bar in Vancouver, but gays aren't the only ones that come here. Straight people, too, find the place appealing. Why? The music and the dancing are electrifying. Celebrities' talented DJs are masters of spin, and they hold nothing back as they crank out the latest and biggest hits. The dance floor is spacious and the music is extremely loud. Because the club is on one of the West End's busiest streets, there's plenty of traffic both inside and out. Strippers strut their stuff on Tuesdays, and Wednesday is female-impersonation night, so expect a steady parade of drag queens. (Downtown)

DENMAN STATION
860 Denman St.
Vancouver
604/669-3448
The entrance to this place is easy to find. For one, it's right next door to True Confections, one of the best

places in the city to get dessert. Second, it's marked by a symbol in the shape of a London Underground sign. Inside you can expect really high-energy music. There are a variety of special nights, such as male strippers on Monday, go-go dancers on Friday and Saturday, and live drag on Saturday. (Downtown)

HERITAGE HOUSE HOTEL
455 Abbott St.
Vancouver
604/685-7777
This hotel, located on the edge of Chinatown, has three gay bars, each with a different character. Charlie's Lounge, on the main floor, is quiet and high-end. Chuck's Pub, on the other hand, is more of a sports bar and features a pool table, TVs, and a dartboard. The third establishment, Lotus Cabaret, is one of only a few downtown country-and-western lounges and has a "women only" night on Fridays. (Downtown)

HOMER'S
1249 Howe St.
Vancouver
604/689-2444
This casual pub with a mostly gay clientele is definitely not a cruisers establishment. Rather, it caters to a billiards crowd, and you'll find a mix of serious pool dudes and others who couldn't sink a beach ball. Regulars claim the menu—which includes burgers, fries, and other finger food, as well as gourmet pizza and salads—is the most varied in the city. (Downtown)

ODYSSEY
1251 Howe St.
Vancouver
604/689-5256
Odyssey and Homer's have the same owners and are next door to each other, but Odyssey has a far different style than its neighbor. While Homer's is a place for serious pool players, Odyssey hosts a variety of live entertainment on the weekends and a CD-spinning DJ during the week. The entertainment includes male go-go dancers and live drag. After you work up a sweat on the dance floor, you can walk outside into the back garden to cool off. (Downtown)

COMEDY CLUBS

LAFFLINES COMEDY CLUB
26 Fourth St.
New Westminster
604/525-2262
This is the place to go if you're into local humor. Unlike some of the Lower Mainland's other major comedy clubs, Lafflines uses strictly local talent. Most are names you've never heard—Kevin Fox, Doug Funk—but the comedy style in this club, which opened in 1991, is well known throughout the region for its hard-edged, biting humor. The jokes are funnier, though, if you're up to date on Vancouver politics, weather, and events and are familiar with the idiosyncrasies of the locals. Friday and Saturday evenings are best. $10 admission. (Eastern Suburbs)

VANCOUVER THEATRESPORTS LEAGUE
Stanley Theatre
2780 Granville St.
Vancouver
604/738-7013
Cool out. Loosen up. Chill, baby. There's a lot of belly laughter from material that's sometimes raunchy, definitely insulting, and always innovative. This is no-holds-barred comedy, where ignoring the politically

correct about anything—politics, religion, race, family—is the standard this longtime comedy institution has always held dear. So don't go if you're particularly sensitive about these topics. The comics work as an ensemble, using themes shouted to them by the audience for their routines. They then compete with one another and a referee decides who is the funniest. It's best to go feeling loose. Wednesday and Thursday, $7.50 all ages; Friday and Saturday, $14.50 adults, $10.50 students and seniors. (Uptown)

YUK YUKS
750 Pacific Blvd.
Vancouver
604/687-5233
Think you're funny? Well, Wednesday is amateur night. Come on in, walk up to the open mike, and put your ego on the line. It's the intellectual equivalent of "So You Think You Can Box." Only instead of your face, it's your ego that gets whacked. Yuk Yuks seats just over 200, so the sight lines are perfect, and the comedy is exceptional. It's a fun place that's busy on weekends. Located on the old Expo '86 Plaza of Nations site, along False Creek. Cover charge is $5 on Wednesday and Thursday and $10 on Friday and Saturday. (Downtown)

GAMBLING

Casinos in Vancouver may not be up to Las Vegas or Monte Carlo standards, but visitors are always surprised at the amount of gambling taking place throughout the Lower Mainland. There are no slot machines (the provincial government wants them; the city council says "No!"), and the clubs close at two in the morning. Casinos turn most of

their profits over to a variety of charities.

GATEWAY CASINO
611 Main St., Third Floor
Vancouver
604/688-9412
The Chinese gamble in a way that North American gamblers may not be familiar with. This is the place to find out how it's done. Located in the heart of Chinatown, The Gateway has interesting games like Pai Gow poker—a complicated form of poker that involves two hands of cards—and Sic Bo—an ancient Chinese dice game. There may be times that you think you need a Mandarin or Cantonese phrase book, but if you simply let yourself absorb the atmosphere you'll find the going to be easy. As is true with most of Vancouver's gambling establishments, the majority of money collected here goes to charities. Maximum bets are $500. (Downtown)

GREAT CANADIAN CASINO
1133 W. Hastings St.
Vancouver
604/682-8415
Located Downtown in the Renaissance Hotel, the Great Canadian Casino offers both traditional Western games and Asian games. Most of the clientele comes from the string of hotels in the downtown area, and as a result, the setting is decidedly upscale. A strange mix of sophisticated travelers and the curious, it's nonetheless always exciting. Men probably won't feel comfortable without a jacket. The company that runs this place also has casinos uptown (709 W. Broadway, 604/872-5543), in Richmond (8440 Bridgeport St., 604/273-1895), and in Surrey (13538 73rd Ave., 604/543-8388). Though the surroundings change from place to

Garden Terrace, p. 234

place, the games are basically the same. (Downtown)

ROYAL DIAMOND CASINO
750 Pacific Blvd.
Vancouver
604/685-2340

The Royal Diamond is located in the same Plaza of Nations area as Yuk Yuks—a convenient place to grab a laugh after you lose your cash. This is a relaxing place with a younger crowd than you'll find at other city casinos. The atmosphere is stylish and comfortable, with a $500 limit on card games. Pai Gow is one of the more popular poker games. After you've finished blowing all your money, enjoy a walk along the False Creek waterfront. Free parking. (Downtown)

POOL HALLS

AUTOMOTIVE
1095 Homer St.
Vancouver
604/682-0040

Oh, how things have changed in this former bastion of male hormonal overload. It used to be a place for greasy hair, leather, tattoos, and raunchy jokes. These days, if the jokes are off-color, they're told in a whisper. Today Automotive is bright and cheery, and the air is fresh. It's a combination lounge and pool hall—you'll find the pool tables in the main section of the building, beyond the entry to the lounge. If you're waiting for a table, choose a seat in a room that looks like it's straight out of the 1960s or try to get a seat in an Austin Mini—yes, an actual car—that has probably the most competed-for seats in any of Vancouver's bars. The crowd at this trendy place is definitely hip. (Downtown)

SOHO CAFE
1144 Homer St.
Vancouver
604/688-1180

The trendsetter among the city's many upscale pool-hall cafés and lounges, The Soho is still a favorite among the well-dressed youngsters who think they're slumming when they drink a local brew rather than wine. The place has a great feel to it, with redbrick walls and wood décor. Locals claim the food here is better than at any other pool hall. Pool tables are in the basement. (Downtown)

QUIET PLACES

CASCADE'S LOUNGE
Pan Pacific Hotel
300-999 Canada Pl.
Vancouver
604/682-5511

Arrive here in the late twilight and look out over the water to the dark-edged mountains outlined by the orange sky. If you look hard enough you might see a bald eagle soaring toward Squamish. Think about it: Is there a place in the world as gorgeous? The lounge is an open design and features piano music. The oak tables are set alongside or near one of the glass walls of the Pan Pacific's lobby area, a perfect place from which to watch the cruise ships and absorb the view of Stanley Park and the downtown waterfront. Just take it all in. (Downtown)

GALLERY
Hyatt Regency Vancouver
655 Burrard St.
Vancouver
604/683-1234

If you're looking for intimate atmosphere, you can't do better than this place. Soft music, comfy chairs, warm colors, and soundless TVs make this a perfect downtown getaway. The Gallery is in the lobby area of the Hyatt. Patrons are, naturally, traveling businesspeople, tourists, and local businesspeople looking to escape the workplace. The staff is remarkably attentive. (Downtown)

GARDEN TERRACE
Four Seasons Hotel
791 W. Georgia St.
Vancouver
604/689-9333

The Garden Terrace is located in a high atrium next to the lobby area of the Four Seasons Hotel. An award-winning garden surrounds the terrace's 120 seats, each of which is placed carefully to instill a high degree of privacy. Piano music and luxuriously soft chairs round out the elegant setting. You'll find a delightful selection of finger food on the surprisingly diverse menu. (Downtown)

GERARD LOUNGE
Sutton Place Hotel
845 Burrard St.
Vancouver
604/682-5511

You can describe the Gerard Lounge's atmosphere with a single word: money. The lounge is a hangout for the many filmmakers and movie-industry workers who retire to the lounge after a day of filming. It's something like an Old Boy's Club, a place where trophy heads of animals that have been shot around the world hang on the walls. Even so, the Gerard Lounge is a remarkably soothing place, with its dark, mahogany tones, upholstered leather chairs, and slate-top tables. The lounge itself seats only about 50, but you'll find 24 additional seats in the passageway between the bar and the Fleuri restaurant. A pianist provides soft background music, which you can hear in the passageway as well as the bar. (Downtown)

On a good-weather day or evening, take a picnic down to one of the beaches or to one of the many rocky points in Stanley Park or on Point Grey, open a bottle of wine, and just enjoy the views.

Downtown Vancouver, along Granville Street between West Georgia and Smithe Streets, is where you'll find the major movie houses, most of which have six or more theaters within their complex.

MOVIE HOUSES OF NOTE

The major movie houses are Downtown, though every shopping center has its own collection. As in most cities, multiple screens are the latest trend, so expect theaters to have five, six, or more films to choose from.

FIFTH AVENUE CINEMAS
2110 Burrard St.
Vancouver
604/734-7469
Just north of Fourth Avenue, across the Burrard Street Bridge, the six-theater Fifth Avenue Cinemas complex shows a variety of flicks originally shown at the International Vancouver Film Festival, as well as other quality independent productions. It's also one of the few movie houses in the city that regularly screens Canadian productions on a first-run basis. (Point Grey)

PACIFIC CINEMATIQUE
1131 Howe St.
Vancouver
604/688-8202
When the Vancouver Film Festival is over, this is where you'll find the unusual and unique—the films shown here aren't shown anywhere else in the city. This movie house is in the same building as the independent filmmakers cooperative, Cineworks. If you want to get behind the screened works, the Pacific Cinematique has a film reference library that features thousands of film-related books, periodicals, and catalogs, as well as a fine collection of international films. (Downtown)

VANCOUVER INTERNATIONAL FILM FESTIVAL
Vancouver
604/685-0260
This is the biggest film event in the city, with 400 or so screenings of about 300 films from 50 countries at seven theaters over 17 days in October. The third-largest film festival in North America, it has everything from avant-garde to mainstream to experimental drama and documentary. Many of the films refuse categorization as they break traditional boundaries. (various venues)

13

DAY TRIPS FROM VANCOUVER

Don't even try to resist the urge you feel to get into your car and drive to the mountains, or to board a ferry for a trip into Howe Sound or across the Strait of Juan de Fuca. Out-of-town exploration is part of the Vancouver experience, so plan for a day or two on the road, just as you would if you were visiting Paris, San Francisco, or New York.

Because Vancouver is hemmed in by mountains to the north, the sea to the west, agricultural reserve land to the east, and the U.S. border to the south, travel usually necessitates climbing through the mountains, crossing the border, going to sea, or driving across miles of farmland. Leaving the city may take a little time and require some advance planning, but most excursions are worth the effort.

DAY TRIP: Bowen Island

Distance from Vancouver: 20-minute ferry ride

The short ferry trip from West Vancouver's Horseshoe Bay—with views of the North Shore mountains, Point Grey, **Point Atkinson Lighthouse**, and **Howe Sound**—takes you to Bowen Island and a world of casual living. The island is visible from virtually any waterfront point in the city. Just look west—it's the first Mountain-humped (760-meter **Mount Gardner**) landmass you can see at the entrance to Howe Sound.

Bowen Island is a popular nearby getaway for Vancouverites (and they don't usually share this information with tourists) who want to escape the noise of the city. One of the best things about the trip is that a car is unnecessary. As a foot passenger on a small BC Ferry ship, you'll walk off the dock at **Snug Cove** and find yourself in the heart of the island's commercial district on Government Street. There you'll be greeted by scores of sailboats docked at the marina, **Doc Morgan's Inn and Restaurant** with its flower-laden porch, a couple of charming pubs, a bookstore, craft shops, bakeries, and the restored **Union Steamship Company Store**, now the island's library and post office.

Three roads branch out from Snug Cove. Try driving or cycling to **Killarney Lake**, where in the summer you'll find the water is warm enough for a swim. Or hike to the top of **Mount Gardner** for one of the best views in the area. With only 3,000 people living on the 14-by-6 kilometer island, it's easy to isolate yourself, whether you travel on foot, with a bicycle, or by car.

At one time Bowen Island was home to the Squamish Indians. But after the Europeans moved in, it quickly became a popular getaway for the well-to-do. In 1928 the now-defunct Union Steamship Company, which provided transportation across Howe Sound, built 100 cabins and a large hotel to accommodate the influx of vacationers. Today the hotel is gone, and much of the site has been turned into the **Crippen Regional Park**, a 600-acre area featuring beaches, walking and cycling trails, and a large picnic area.

Dining on the island is excellent. If you happen to arrive on a private yacht, **Bushwacker Pizza** (604/947-2782) will deliver to your boat—or anywhere else for that matter. So take along your cell phone. Order a takeout meal from **Dunfield's Deli** (604/947-2782) or sample the island's best lunch at the **Snug Coffee House** (604/947-0402). Try dinner at **Doc Morgan's Inn and Restaurant** (604/947-0808), but don't get so caught up in dessert that you miss the last ferry at 9:45 p.m. If you're planning a trip to the island between April and September and are in the mood for something completely different, sign up for Harbour Air's **Fly & Dine at Doc's** (604/688-1277) package, a bargain at $130 per person with dinner. A limousine will whisk you from the Vancouver waterfront terminal to the ferry; then, after your meal, a seaplane will scoop you up from the marina dock for a gorgeous sunset flight along Point Grey, over Stanley Park, and back to the city.

Getting There from Vancouver: Take Highway 99 north over the Lion's Gate Bridge to Horseshoe Bay, and either park your car in the lot (to travel as a foot passenger) or get into the Bowen Island car lineup. Try taking Marine Drive through West Vancouver to Horseshoe Bay. It's a gorgeous trip that follows the waterfront of English Bay. You can also take the blue Horseshoe Bay bus from downtown Vancouver at Georgia and Granville Streets. It will drop you off at the terminal.

DAY TRIP: Hell's Gate

Distance from Vancouver: 250 kilometers or about 2 1/2 hours by car

VANCOUVER REGION

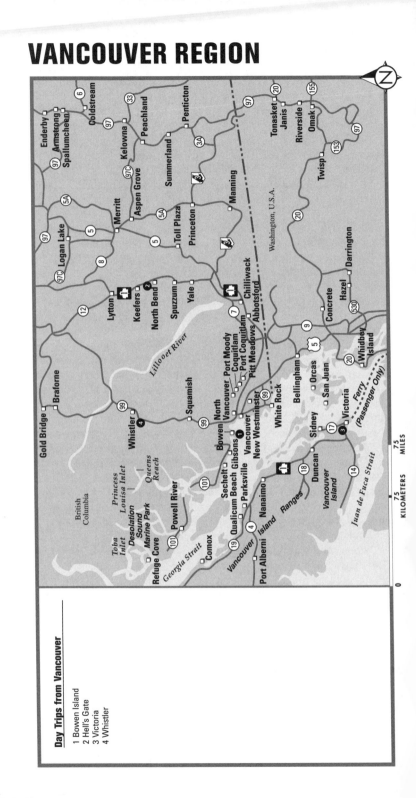

Day Trips from Vancouver

1 Bowen Island
2 Hell's Gate
3 Victoria
4 Whistler

K.D. Wong/Blackbird Design

Hell's Gate in Fraser Canyon

Hell's Gate, located deep within the scenic **Fraser Canyon**, is considered by many to represent nature in its grandest form. Two million salmon challenge the Fraser River here each year in early to mid November as they make their epic journey to their inland spawning grounds. The foaming canyon torrent, the thrashing salmon, and the grandeur of the surrounding mountains make Hell's Gate a photographer's dream.

You'll witness all the action as you descend from the highway in a 25-passenger tram. At the lower terminal, after a 152-meter flight across the canyon, you'll be faced with several choices. You can browse through the gold-panning shop, where there is a large selection of gifts and souvenirs. Or you can spend time at the informative exhibits that explain how the fishway was built and that describe the life cycle of the spawning salmon. Observation points at the terminal offer exhilarating views of the fierce river. At the river's peak flow more than 200 million gallons of water leap and surge through the 33.5-meter gorge every minute.

If during your visit you develop an appetite for fish, try the freshly grilled salmon steaks and salmon chowder at the **Salmon House Restaurant** (604/867-9277). When you're through, head over to the **Fudge Factory** to sample from the more than 30 flavors of homemade fudge.

Getting There from Vancouver: Hell's Gate is located in the scenic Fraser Canyon on Trans-Canada Highway 1, just 52 kilometers north of Hope and 48 kilometers south of Lytton. The trip from Vancouver takes about two and a half hours.

DAY TRIP: Victoria

Distance from Vancouver: 69 kilometers by car plus about 2 hours by ferry

If you have only one day to explore beyond Vancouver, Victoria is the place to go. Vancouverites refer to the spectacular ferry trip to British Columbia's capital as "going overseas."

Victoria's main attractions are within a few blocks of the downtown core. In the summer horse-drawn carriages or double-decker buses (the city is more British than Great Britain) shuttle visitors around town.

Almost every tour begins and ends either in front of the Legislative Buildings or, in many cases, at the **Empress Hotel** (250/384-8111), where the buses are located.

The Empress is a symbol both of the city and of Canada's links with the Canadian Pacific Railway. Originally opened in 1908, the hotel is one of many great chateaus built by the Canadian Pacific Railway as it moved west across the country. Other hotels with the same lineage include the Chateau Frontenac in Quebec City, Chateau Laurier in Ottawa, Chateau Lake Louise, and the Banff Springs Hotel. The high, beamed ceiling and wood floors of the Empress lobby lend a historic and traditional atmosphere. Try the hotel's exotic **Bengal Lounge** for a light lunch, or, if you're around at three, satiate your appetite with a high-tea meal of honeyed crumpets, scones with cream and jam, and finger sandwiches.

Completed in 1897, the ornate Legislative Buildings (actually a single building consisting of several seamlessly connected parts) dominates the inner harbor. On one side of the building is a statue of Sir James Douglas; on the other is one of Sir Matthew Baille Begbie, the man in charge of law and order during the gold-rush era. Atop the dome is a gilded statue of Captain George Vancouver, the first European to discover Vancouver Island. In front is a statue of Queen Victoria. At night the building is outlined by 3,000 lights. Tours of the Legislative Buildings are offered several times each day, but hours change seasonally. (Call 250/387-3046 for information.)

The **Royal British Columbia Museum** (675 Belleville St., 250/387-3701) is a Disneyland of science and humanities, a place where both adults and children can wander for hours. The museum takes visitors in stages from the twentieth century back in time 12,000 years. Exhibits are arranged so that you can follow the ring of time through the industrial era to the early days of fur trading and exploration. Then you're thrust forward from early examples of human habitation in British Columbia to the effects of modern history on aboriginal cultures.

The harbor area in front of The Empress and the Legislative Buildings is one of the busiest places in the city. You can park the car and take a leisurely walk around Victoria's waterfront. The walkway along the shore and below the Empress Hotel affords wonderful views of downtown across the Inner Harbour. The James Bay waterfront beyond the Parliament Buildings winds past the rustic, bustling commercial docks of Fisherman's Wharf. A walkway below Government Street takes you dockside for an inner-harbor stroll to the **Royal London Wax Museum** (470 Belleville St., 250/388-4461). You can meander among 300 wax figures of royalty, writers, leaders, and legends—including England's longest reigning monarch (Queen Elizabeth II). Open year-round, this venerable Victoria attraction (in business for four decades) is located in what was once the CPR Steamship Terminal, on the waterfront, below the Legislative Buildings. Tour guides provide well-researched insights.

The oldest part of Victoria is near **Centennial Square** between

Government and Douglas Streets, and Pandora and Fisgard Streets. The buildings in this area date from the late 1800s. **Victoria City Hall**, originally constructed in 1878, has high, arched windows and a clock tower.

One block northwest is **Chinatown**, the oldest and arguably the smallest Chinese district in Canada. While it doesn't have the excitement and big-city pace of Vancouver's Chinatown, it does have a number of quaint shops and traditional restaurants. **Market Square** is a collection of funky shops in a complex where, in 1887, some 23 factories produced 90,000 pounds of opium a year for what was then a legal business. Be sure to walk **Fan Tan Alley**, Canada's narrowest "street."

South of Chinatown and north of The Empress—virtually between the two—lies **Bastion Square**, with its gas lamps, restaurants, cobblestone streets, and small shops. At the **Maritime Museum** (28 Bastion Square, 250/385-4222) you'll find dugout canoes, model ships, Royal Navy charts, photographs, uniforms, and bells chronicling Victoria's seafaring history. The building was the city's original courthouse. A little used 90-year-old open-cage lift, believed to be the oldest in North America, ascends to the third floor.

It's easy to shop in Victoria because virtually everything is centralized. Begin at The Empress and walk north along **Government Street**. In quick succession you'll come across George Straith (woolens), British Woolens (women's), Sasquach Trading Company (Cowitchan sweaters), E. A. Morris Tobacconist (unusual pipe-tobacco blends), Munro's Books (best selection of Victoriana in the city), Campbell's British Shop (British imports), Roger's Chocolates and English Sweet Shop (the world's finest chocolates), and the Gallery of the Arctic (quality Inuit art). At last count, Victoria had more than 60 antiques shops specializing in coins, stamps, estate jewelry, rare books, crystal, china, furniture, paintings, and other works of art. If you turn right at

Rainbow over the Empress Hotel in Victoria

© John Elk

Fort Street and walk four blocks you'll come to **Antique Row** between Blanshard and Cook Streets. The Connoisseurs Shop and David Robinson, Ltd., offer a wide selection of eighteenth-century pieces.

More than 5,000 varieties of flowers draw visitors 20 kilometers north of Victoria to **Butchart Gardens** (Benevenuto Ave., 250/652-4422). Once a limestone quarry, it was transformed in 1904 when a Canadian cement pioneer named Robert Butchart began building bridges and walkways and planting shrubs and flowers on the 25-acre site.

Getting There from Vancouver: The most convenient way to Victoria is via round-trip bus tours through the Maverick or Pacific Coach lines. The tours depart from many downtown hotels. Other companies (including Greyhound) also offer regular service—via the ferries—to and from Victoria. Take Highway 99 south to Highway 17, then go west to the ferry terminals. For quicker access, take a Helijet (604/273-1414) or a Harbour Air (604/688-0212) floatplane. Both airplane terminals are along the Vancouver waterfront.

DAY TRIP: Whistler

Distance from Vancouver: 121 kilometers or 2 hours by car

High in the coastal mountains north of Vancouver, this one-time ugly duckling has become quite the place. Twenty years ago the only inhabitants were a few cross-country skiers and tourists who came down the road from the Whistler Mountain gondolas to watch the huge black bears rummaging through restaurant leftovers in what was once a garbage dump.

Today Whistler/Blackcomb is a world-class ski destination that is consistently named as the best overall North American resort by virtually every ski magazine. The village sits at the base of two magnificent mountains—6,282-foot Blackcomb and 7,118-foot Whistler. The roundhouse at the 6,420-foot level of Whistler Mountain, home to **Pika's** (250/905-2367), a casual deli/cafe, is one of the most spectacular restaurant sites anywhere. Be sure you take a ride up one of the two mountains—up Blackcomb Mountain from the Upper Village next to the **Chateau Whistler** (4599 Chateau Blvd., 604/938-8000) or up Whistler Mountain from the main village, behind the **Pan Pacific Hotel** (4320 Sundial Crescent, 604/905-2999). Once you reach the summit of either peak, you'll have a magnificent view of the surrounding mountains and valley.

Despite its well-deserved fame as a top ski area, Whistler is more than a winter wonderland. Wintertime downhill and cross-country areas become mountain biking and hiking areas in the summer months. There's even July schussing on backcountry glaciers and peaks. If you want to spend your day doing something adventurous, contact **Whistler Outdoor Experience Company** (604/932-3389) or **The Escape Route** (604/932-3338).

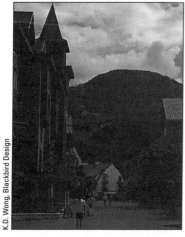

K.D. Wong, Blackbird Design

Whistler, well known as a top ski area

They'll help you plan hiking, paragliding, and whitewater-rafting trips. If golf is more your style, try any of Whistler's three superb championship golf courses: **Whistler Golf Course** (604/932-4544), designed by Arnold Palmer; the Robert Trent Jones–designed **Chateau Whistler Golf Course** (604/938-2092); and Jack Nicklaus' **Nicklaus North Golf Course** (604/938-9898). All are expensive, charging between $85 and $125 a round.

While the hills have always been there, and skiing and other modes of outdoor recreation have been favorite Whistler pastimes for almost 20 years, it's the village that has brought the region recognition as a world-class resort. Actually, there are really three villages connected by footpaths and roads. **Whistler Village** and **Village North** are side by side, connected by a walker's overpass above the main access road. The **Upper Village** is also known as Blackcomb Village and is home to the area's most prominent architectural symbol, the Chateau Whistler Resort.

As you approach Whistler, you'll pass the Whistler Creek area. Don't be fooled—this is not the resort. Actually, it was the original Whistler village, but has since been overwhelmed by the prime village area two minutes down the road. If you're interested in staying overnight, there are 10,000 beds available in a variety of accommodations—bed-and-breakfasts, hotels, resorts, and condos. (Call Central Reservations, 604/664-5625 or 800/944-7853.)

On a day-trip, you won't be able to experience even a small percentage of what the region has to offer. But Whistler is a wonderful walking village, full of lounges, restaurants, nightclubs, bars, and excellent shops. When it's time to eat, try a casual lunch in the main village at **Araxi Restaurant** (604/932-4540), or have dinner at **Arthur's** (604/905-2999), a Continental-style restaurant in the Pan Pacific Hotel offering a friendly atmosphere and superb cuisine.

Getting There from Vancouver: Take Highway 99 (the Sea to Sky Highway) by crossing the Lion's Gate Bridge to the North Shore. From there, follow the signs to Whistler. The road is spectacular, running along Howe Sound to Squamish and into the mountains. It's about a two-hour drive. You'll pass the Robert Muirs–designed Furry Creek golf club, a public facility built on the side of a mountain; the BC Mining Museum at Britannia Beach; and, just before you reach Squamish, the 650-meter granite face of the Stawamus Chief. Stop and look up the face of the mountain to see climbers hanging by their fingertips. For more information contact the Whistler Resort Association, Whistler Village, Whistler, BC Canada, V0N 1B0, 604/664-5625.

EMERGENCY PHONE NUMBERS

Police/Ambulance/Fire, 911
Battered Women's Support Services
604/687-1867
Crisis Intervention and Suicide Prevention Centre
604/872-3311
Forest Fire Reporting
800/663-5555
Poison Control Centre
604/682-5050 or 604/682-2344
Rape Crisis Centre
604/255-6344

HOSPITALS AND EMERGENCY MEDICAL CENTERS

BC Cancer Clinic
600 W. 10th Ave.
Vancouver
604/877-6000
Burnaby Hospital
3935 Kincaid St.
Burnaby
604/434-4211
Holy Family Hospital
7801 Argyl St.
Vancouver
604/321-6886
Lions Gate Hospital
231 E. 15th Ave.
North Vancouver
604/988-3131
Mount St. Joseph Hospital
3080 Prince Edward St.
Vancouver
604/874-1141
Richmond Hospital
7000 Westminster Hwy.
Richmond
604/278-9711

Royal Columbian Hospital
330 E. Columbia St.
New Westminster
604/520-4253
St. Paul's Hospital
1081 Burrard St.
Vancouver
604/682-2344
St. Vincent's Hospital
749 W. 33rd Ave.
Vancouver
604/876-7171
Surrey Memorial Hospital
13750 96th Ave.
Surrey
604/581-2211
UBC Hospital
2211 Westbrook Mall
Vancouver
604/822-7121
Vancouver General Hospital
855 W. 12th Ave.
Vancouver
604/875-4111
Women's Hospital and Health Centre
4500 Oak St.
Vancouver
604/875-2424

OTHER IMPORTANT NUMBERS

411 Seniors Centre
604/684-8171
AIDS/STD Information Line
604/872-1238
Alcohol and Drug Tryline
800/663-1441
Alzheimer Society
604/681-6530
BC AIDS Line
604/872-6652

BC Paraplegic Association
604/324-3611
Canadian Cancer Society
604/872-4400
Canadian Mental Health Association
604/872-4902
Canadian National Institute for the
Blind
604/431-2121
Child Find
604/251-3463
Gambling Help Line
888/795-6111
Gay and Lesbian Centre
604/684-6869
Help Line for Children
Dial "0" and ask for Zenith 1234
Meals on Wheels
604/732-7638
Neighborhood Houses Association
of Vancouver
604/875-9111
Telephone Directory Assistance
(local)
411
Time
Dial "0" and ask for the time
Western Institute for the Deaf and
Hard of Hearing
604/736-7391 (voice); 604/736-2527
(TTD)

AIRLINES (MAJOR)

Air Canada
604/688-5515
Air France
800/667-2747
Air New Zealand
800/663-5494
Air Transat
800/470-1011
Alaska Airlines
800/252-7522
American Airlines
800/433-7300

America West
800/235-9292
British Airways
800/247-9297
Canada 3000 Airlines
604/609-3000
Canadian Airlines
604/279-6611
Cathay Pacific
604/899-8520
Delta Airlines
800/221-1212
El Al Israel Airlines
800/361-6174
Frontier Airlines
800/432-1359
Horizon Air
800/547-9308
Japan Airlines
800/525-3663
Korean Air
800/438-5000
Lufthansa German Airlines
800/563-5954
Malaysia Airlines
800/552-9264
Mexicana
800/531-7923
Northwest Airlines/KLM
800/225-2525
Philippine Airlines
800/435-9725
Qantas
800/227-4500
SAS
800/221-2350
Singapore Airlines
604/689-1223
Southwest Airlines
800/435-9792
Thai Airways International
800/668-8103
United Airlines
800/241-6522
Westjet Airlines
800/538-5696

AIRLINES (REGIONAL)

Air BC
604/685-5158
Baxter Aviation
800/661-5599
Canadian Regional Airlines
604/279-6611
Harbour Air Seaplanes
800/665-0212
Helijet Airways
604/273-1414
KD Air
604/899-8508
North Vancouver Air
800/228-6608
Pacific Coastal Airlines
800/663-2872
Pacific Spirit Airlines
800/665-2359
Seair Seaplanes
604/273-8900
Shuswap Air
800/663-4074
Thetis Air
888/284-3847
West Coast Air
604/606-6888

CANADIAN CONSULATES IN THE UNITED STATES

Atlanta
404/532-2000
Boston
617/262-3760
Buffalo
716/858-9500
Chicago
312/616-1860
Dallas
214/922-9806
Detroit
313/567-2340
Los Angeles
213/346-2700
Miami
305/579-1600
Minneapolis
612/332-7486
New York City
212/596-1600
San Juan
787/790-2205
Seattle
206/443-1777
Washington, DC
202/682-1740

FOREIGN CONSULATES

Austria
604/683-5808
Belgium
604/684-6838
Brazil
604/687-4589
Britain
604/683-4421
Chile
604/681-9162
China
604/736-3910
Columbia
604/685-6435
Costa Rica
604/681-2152
Denmark
604/684-5171
Ecuador
604/420-7767
Finland
604/688-4483
France
604/681-2301
Germany
604/684-8377
Greece
604/681-1381
Guatemala
604/688-5209
Honduras
604/685-7711

India
604/662-8811
Indonesia
604/682-8855
Ireland
604/683-9233
Italy
604/684-7288
Japan
604/684-5868
Korea
604/683-1820
Liberia
604/684-5988
Malaysia
604/685-9550
Malta
604/739-3200
Mexico
604/684-3547
Monaco
604/682-4633
Netherlands
604/684-6448
New Zealand
604/684-7388
Norway
604/683-7977
Philippines
604/685-7645
Poland
604/688-3530
Portugal
604/688-6514
Senegal
604/267-1417
Singapore
604/669-5115
Slovak Republic
604/682-0991
Spain
604/299-7760
Sweden
604/683-5838
Switzerland
604/684-2231
Taiwan
604/689-4111

Thailand
604/687-1143
United States
604/685-4311
Uruguay
604/681-1377

INFORMATION SERVICES FOR THE NON—ENGLISH SPEAKING

All Languages (MOSAIC)
604/254-9626
Chinese (SUCCESS)
604/684-1628
Multicultural Helpline
604/572-4060

MULTICULTURAL RESOURCES

Affiliation of Multicultural and Service Agencies of BC
604/298-5949
Louis Riel Metis Council
604/581-2522
Vancouver Aboriginal Friendship Centre Society
604/251-4844

RECORDED INFORMATION

British Columbia Ferries
888/223-3779
Road Conditions
604/299-9000
Vancouver Cultural Alliance/Arts Hotline
604/681-3535
Weather
604/664-9010

VISITOR INFORMATION

Tourism Association of Southwestern British Columbia
604/688-3677
Tourism British Columbia
604/660-3767
Tourism Vancouver
604/682-2222

CITY TOURS
AAA Horse & Carriage
604/681-5115
Aqua Bus Ferries
604/689-5858
Baxter Aviation
604/683-6525
Burrard Water Taxi
604/293-1160
Captain Billy's Magical Tours
604/687-2220
Early Motion Tours
604/687-5088
Gray Line of Vancouver
604/879-3363
Harbour Air
604/688-1277
Harbour Ferries
604/687-9558
Hike BC
604/540-2944
Lotus Land Tours
604/684-4922
Pacific Coach Lines
604/662-7575
Paddlewheel River Adventures
604/525-4465
Starline Tours
604/274-9287 or 522-3506
Transit Information (including Seabus, Sky Train)
604/521-0400
Urban Adventure Vancouver Cycle Tours
604/831-0367
Vancouver Helicopters
604/270-1484
Vancouver Trolley Company

604/451-5581
Velo-City Cycle Tours
604/924-0288
West Coast City and Nature Sightseeing
604/451-1600

POST OFFICES

Post offices are located at a variety of commercial outlets. Look for the Canada Post sign displayed in windows.

Canada Post
Main Post Office
349 West Georgia Street
604/662-5722

CAR RENTAL

Alamo
800/327-9633
Avis
800/879-2847
Budget
800/268-8900
Dollar
800/800-4000
Enterprise
800/736-8222
Hertz
800/263-0600
National/Tilden
800/227-7368
Thrifty
800/367-2277

DISABLED ACCESS INFORMATION

BC Coalition of People with Disabilities
604/875-0188
BC Lions Society for Children with Disabilities
604/873-1865

BC Paraplegic Association
604/324-3611
Kinsmen Rehabilitation Foundation
604/736-8841
Parking Permits for People with Disabilities
604/718-7744
Public Transit for Disabled Persons
604/521-0400 or 604/875-6381
Vancouver Resource Centre for the Physically Disabled
604/731-1020

BABYSITTING/CHILDCARE

Baby Sitter Next Door
604/261-8482
Drake Medox Doula Services
604/682-2801
Information Daycare
604/739-4143
Kidscenes Inc.
604/688-8309
Moppet Minders Child and Home Care Services
604/942-8167
Philcan Domestic Personnel
604/873-1272
Wee Watch Vancouver
604/323-9630

NEWSPAPERS

Daily

Globe & Mail (National)
604/685-0308
National Post
604/605-2748
Province
604/605-2478
Vancouver Sun
604/605-2478

Weekly (Entertainment)

Georgia Straight
604/730-7000

Neighborhood Papers

Burnaby Now
604/444-3451
Coquitlam Now
604/942-4192
New Westminster News Leader
604/438-6397
North Shore News
604/980-0511
Richmond News
604/270-8031
Richmond Review
604/606-8700
Vancouver Courier
604/738-1411
Vancouver Echo
604/437-7030
West End Times
604/682-1424
Westender
604/606-8677
World Journal
604/876-1338

MAGAZINES

BC Report
604/682-8202
BC Woman
604/540-8448
Common Ground
604/733-2215
Vancouver Magazine
604/877-7732
Western Living
604/877-7732
Westworld
604/299-7311

BOOKSTORES

Blackberry Books, Ltd.
1663 Duranleau St.
604/685-6188

Black Sheep Books
2742 Fouth St.
604/732-5087

Booktique
2960 Granville St.
604/736-3727

Chapters
788 Robson St.
604/682-4066

Chapters
2505 Granville St.
604/731-7822

Cody Books Ltd.
Champlain Mall
3200 E. Fifth Ave.
604/437-5553

Duthie Books
919 Robson St.
604/684-4496

Granville Book Co.
850 Granville St.
604/687-2213

Hager Books Ltd.
2176 41st Ave.
604/263-9412

People's Co-Op Bookstore
1391 Commercial Dr.
604/253-6442

RADIO STATIONS

AM 1040, adult talk

CBU (CBC) AM 690, news/current affairs
CBUF (CBC) FM 97.7, French
CBU-FM (CBC) FM 105.7, classical
CFMI FM 101.1, classic rock
CFOX FM 99.3, current rock
CFUN AM 1410, talk
CHKG FM 96.1, ethnic & Chinese music
CHMB AM 1320, Chinese
CISL AM 650, oldies
CJJR FM 93.7, country
CJVB AM 1470, news/talk
CKBD AM 600, adult favorites/nostalgia
CKKS FM 96.9, adult contemporary
CKLG AM 730, hot adult contemporary
CKNW AM 980, news/information/talk
CKWX AM 1130, news
CKZZ FM 95.4, contemporary hits
KISM FM 92.9, adult classic rock
QMFM FM 103.5, nostalgia/oldies
STAR-FM FM 104.9, adult contemporary

TELEVISION STATIONS

Vancouver is almost 100-percent cable saturated, with access to 66 Canadian and U.S. channels from a variety of cities. Depending on where you're staying, television channel settings can vary. Weekly listings can be found in the Friday editions of the Vancouver Sun *and the* Province *or in* TV Guide *(Canada) or the locally published* TV Week.

CBUT, CBC
CBUFT, CBC (French)
BCTV, CTV
CKVU, Global
VTV, BBS

INDEX

Accommodations
  Downtown, 33-47; East Vancouver, 50; Eastern Suburbs, 53-54; North Shore, 50-53; Point Grey, 48-49; Southern Suburbs, 54-57; Uptown; 47
After Hours Eating, 228
Amateur Sports, 186-187
Animals and the Great Outdoors, 135-138
Art Museums, 117-121
Arts Club Theatres, 204
Audience-Friendly Theaters, 215

Ballet British Columbia, 212
Bard On The Beach, 204
Bars and Pubs, 224-231
BC Golf Museum, 127
BC Lions, 184-185
BC Museum of Mining, 127-128, 138
BC Place Stadium, 183, 214
BC Sports Hall of Fame, 128, 144
Beaches, 150-151, 189
Belcarra Regional Park, 147
Blood Alley Square, 93
Bonkers Indoor Playgrounds, 144
Brackendale, 147
Britannia Heritage Shipyard, 114-115
Buddhist Temple, 115
Burnaby Village Museum, 121, 138

Canadian Craft Museum, 117-118,
Canadian Football League Rules, 184
Canadian Museum of Flight and Transportation, 121-122
Canadian Pacific Railway Roundhouse, 95, 144-145
Canada Place Complex, 93
Canadian Broadcasting Corporation, 93
Canadian Pacific Railway, 95
Capilano Suspension Bridge, 109
Capilano Canyon Regional Park and Hatchery, 147-148
Carr, Emily, 118
Central Park, 148
Chan Centre For The Performing Arts, 214
Children's Clothing, 143
Children's Farmyard Petting Zoo and Miniature Railway, 135-136
Chinese Cultural Centre, 94-95
Chinese Cultural Society, 206
Chocolate Shops, 175
Christ Church Cathedral, 96

City of Vancouver Archives, 122
City Tours
  Downtown, 93-105; East Vancouver, Eastern Suburbs, 113; North Shore, 109-113; Point Grey, 107-109; Southern Suburbs, 114-116; Uptown, 105-107
Classical Music, 206-212
Cleveland Dam and Fish Hatchery, 136
CN Theatre, 142
Coastal Jazz and Blues Society, 206-207
Comedy Clubs, 231-232
Concert Venues, 214-218

Dancing On The Edge Festival, 212-213
Dance Performance, 212-214
Day Trips, 237-245
  Bowen Island, 237-239; Hell's Gate, 239-240; Victoria, 240-243; Whistler, 243-245
Deighton, Gassy Jack, 113
Dr. Sun Yat-Sen Garden, 148

Early Music Vancouver, 206
East Pender Street, 96
English Bay Beach, 148-149
Emily Carr School of Art and Design, 119
Expo 86, 94

Factory Outlets, 180-181
Fantasy Garden World, 115-116
Film Production, 205
Ford Centre For The Performing Arts, 214-215
Fort Langley National Historic Park, 113
Friends of Chamber Music, 207-208

Galleries, 128-134
Gambling, 232-233
Gateway Theatre, 215-216
Gay Clubs, 230-231
General Motors Place, 216
Geology Museum, 122
Getting Around
  Air Travel, 28-30
  Biking, 28
  Bus Service, 31
  Driving, 26-27
  Public Transportation, 25-26
  Train Service, 30-31
Gordon Southam Observatory, 122

Granville Mall, 96, 99
Granville Island, 105
Granville Island Brewery, 105-106
Granville Island Public Market, 106-107
Granville Island Sports Fishing
  Museum and Model Ships Museum,
  128
Greater Vancouver Zoological Centre,
  136
Greenpeace, 152
Green Thumb Theatre, 142
Group of Seven, 123
Grouse Mountain, 109-110
Gulf of Georgia Cannery, 116, 123-124

Harbour Centre Tower, 99
Hastings Jill Store Museum, 124
Hong Kong Bank Building, 101
Hotel Europe, 101
Hudson's Bay Company (The Bay), 160

Jewelry Stores, 169
Johnson, Pauline, 97

Karen Jaimieson Dance, 213
Kids Adventure Playground, 136-137
Kids, Museums, 138-142
Kids, Shops, 143-144
Kids, Things to Do, 135-145
Kids, Theaters, 142-143
Kitsilano Beach, 149-150
Kokoro Dance, 213-214

Library Square, 101
Lighthouse Park, 110, 150
Lonsdale Quay Market, 110-112
Lynn Canyon Park and Ecological
  Centre, 151

Malkin Bowl, 216
Maple Leaf Square, 101-102
Maplewood Children's Farm, 137
Markets, 173-174
Marine Building, 127
Mount Seymour Provincial Park, 151-
  152
Movie Houses, 236
Museum of Anthropology, 119, 139
Music Club, 219-225
Music In The Morning, 208

Nightclubs, Best Lists, 220-222
Nitobe Memorial Gardens, 153

Orpheum Theatre, 216, 217

Pacific National Exhibition Grounds,
  109
Pacific Space Centre 124-125, 139
Pacific Spirit Regional Park, 153-154
Park and Tilford Gardens, 154
Parks, Gardens 147-156
PGA, Air Canada Championship, 185
Phoenix Chamber Choir, 208-209
Public Art, 129

Queen Elizabeth Park and Bloedel
  Floral Conservatory, 154
Queen Elizabeth Theatre and
  Playhouse, 216-217

Reifel, George C., Migratory Bird
  Sanctuary, 149
Restaurants
  By Cuisine, 59-60; Character
  Restaurants, 60; Downtown, 60-73;
  East Vancouver, 83-87; Eastern
  Suburbs, 89; North Shore, 87-89;
  Point Grey, 77-83; South Suburbs, 89-
  91; Uptown, 73-77; View Restaurants,
  82
Richmond Go-Kart Track, 145
Richmond Nature Park, 137
Robson Square, 102-103
Roedde House Preservation Society,
  125
Royal Hudson Steam Train, 112
Russian Submarine, 139-140

Sam Kee Building, 103-104
Science World, 125, 140-141
Seabus, 145
Seafood, 176
Sea Village, 107
Seymour Demonstration Forest, 113
Schools, 22-23
Science and History Museums, 121-
  126
Shopping Malls, 176-180
Shops, 157-181
  Chinatown, 162-164; Downtown, 158-
  162; Granville Island, 171-172;
  Kitsilano, 165-168; Point Grey, 164-
  165; Uptown, 168-170
Significant Buildings in Vancouver, 98-
  99
Sport BC, 188
Sports, 182-202
  Baseball, 183-184; Basketball, 184;
  Bicycling, 189-190; Fishing, 189;
  Football, 184-185; Golf Courses, 189-
  194; Skiing, 196-197; Swimming, 197-

198; Tennis, 198-200;
Running/Walking, 199-200; Tickets,
189.
Stanley Park, 102-103, 155
Stanley Theatre, 218
Steam Clock, 104

Theater, 203-206
Theater Tickets, 207
Theatre Under The Stars, 204
Triumpf, 107-108

UBC Botanical Gardens, 155
University of British Columbia, 108-109
Uzume Taiko, 209

Vancouver Aquarium, 104, 137-138
Vancouver Art Gallery, 104-105, 119-
120, 141
Vancouver Bach Choir, 209
Vancouver Canadians, 183
Vancouver Cantata Singers, 209
Vancouver Canucks, 185
Vancouver, Captain George, 10
Vancouver Chamber Choir, 209
Vancouver East Cultural Centre, 218
Vancouver 86ers, 188-189
Vancouver Fringe Festival, 203-204
Vancouver Grizzlies, 184
Vancouver Holocaust Education
Centre, 125-126
Vancouver International Airport, 29
Vancouver International Children's

Festival, 142-143, 204
Vancouver Literature, 213
Vancouver Maritime Museum, 126,
141-142
Vancouver Museum, 126, 142
Vancouver New Music Society, 209-
210
Vancouver Opera, 210-211
Vancouver Playhouse Theatre
Company, 204-205
Vancouver Police Centennial Museum,
128
Vancouver Recital Society, 211
Vancouver Symphony Orchestra, 211-
212
Vancouver Theatresports League, 205
VanDusen Botanical Garden, 155-156
Vanier Park, 132

Waterfront Station, 105
Welcome
Cruising to Alaska, 4
Currency, 20
Economy/Business, 19-22
History, 7
Holidays, 18
Housing, 22
Languages Spoken in Vancouver, 12
People of Vancouver , 11
Spelling differences, 3
Time Line, 8-9
Weather, 12-15
Zoo, 135-136

Guidebooks that really *guide*

City•Smart™ Guidebooks

Pick one for your favorite city: *Albuquerque, Anchorage, Austin, Calgary, Charlotte, Chicago, Cincinnati, Cleveland, Denver, Indianapolis, Kansas City, Memphis, Milwaukee, Minneapolis/St. Paul, Nashville, Pittsburgh, Portland, Richmond, Salt Lake City, San Antonio, San Francisco, St. Louis, Tampa/St. Petersburg, Tucson.* US $12.95 to $15.95

Retirement & Relocation Guidebooks

The World's Top Retirement Havens, Live Well in Honduras, Live Well in Ireland, Live Well in Mexico. US $15.95 to $16.95

Travel•Smart® Guidebooks

Trip planners with select recommendations to *Alaska, American Southwest, Arizona, Carolinas, Colorado, Deep South, Eastern Canada, Florida, Florida Gulf Coast, Hawaii, Illinois/Indiana, Kentucky/Tennessee, Maryland/Delaware, Michigan, Minnesota/Wisconsin, Montana/Wyoming/Idaho, New England, New Mexico, New York State, Northern California, Ohio, Pacific Northwest, Pennsylvania/New Jersey, South Florida and the Keys, Southern California, Texas, Utah, Virginias, Western Canada.* US $14.95 to $17.95

Rick Steves' Guides

See *Europe Through the Back Door* and take along guides to France, Belgium & the Netherlands; Germany, Austria & Switzerland; Great Britain & Ireland; Italy; Scandinavia; Spain & Portugal; London; Paris; or Best of Europe. US $12.95 to $21.95

Adventures in Nature

Plan your next adventure in *Alaska, Belize, Caribbean, Costa Rica, Guatemala, Hawaii, Honduras, Mexico.* US $17.95 to $18.95

Into the Heart of Jerusalem

A traveler's guide to visits, celebrations, and sojourns. US $17.95

The People's Guide to Mexico

This is so much more than a guidebook—it's a trip to Mexico in and of itself, complete with the flavor of the country and its sights, sounds, and people. US $22.95

JOHN MUIR PUBLICATIONS
A DIVISION OF AVALON TRAVEL PUBLISHING
5855 Beaudry Street, Emeryville, CA 94608

Please check our web site at www.travelmatters.com for current prices and editions, or visit your local bookseller.

ABOUT THE AUTHOR

Ray Chatelin lives in Vancouver, British Columbia with his photographer-wife, Toshi and combines travel writing with arts and television journalism. He is the author of, or major contributor to, ten travel books, and has written for major magazines and newspapers in the USA and Canada. He has won major awards for travel journalism, screenwriting, and music criticism.

JOHN MUIR PUBLICATIONS
and its City•Smart Guidebook authors
are dedicated to building community
awareness within City•Smart cities.
We are proud to work with Literacy BC
as we publish this guide to Vancouver.

Literacy BC was founded in 1990 and provides a strong
leadership role for literacy in B.C. As the provincial "one
stop" Literacy Resource Centre, with a province wide toll-free
Helpline and Resource Centre. They provide information, referral,
and consultation to adult learners, literacy programs, workforce
and family literacy initiatives and the general public.

More than 40% of working people in British Columbia have a hard
time with the every day demands of reading, writing, and using
numbers. Be involved. . .literacy is everybody's business.

For more information, please contact:
Literacy BC
601-510 West Hastings Street
Toll free in BC 800/663-1293
Fax: 604-684-8250
www.nald.ca/lbc/htm